This Can Happen

CHAIRMAN
Rabbi Moshe Kotlarsky

PRINCIPAL BENEFACTOR
Mr. George Rohr

EXECUTIVE DIRECTOR
Rabbi Efraim Mintz

—

CURRICULUM DEVELOPMENT
Rabbi Baruch Shalom Davidson
Rabbi Mordechai Dinerman
Rabbi Ahrele Loschak
Rabbi Naftali Silberberg
Rabbi Ari Sollish
Rabbi Yanki Tauber

INSTRUCTOR ADVISORY BOARD
Rabbi Yishaya Benjaminson
Rabbi Dovid Flinkenstein
Rabbi Meir Hecht
Rabbi Meir Moscowitz
Rabbi Yochanan Posner

FLAGSHIP DIRECTOR
Rabbi Shmuly Karp

CURRICULUM COORDINATOR
Mrs. Rivki Mockin

FLAGSHIP ADMINISTRATOR
Mrs. Naomi Heber

Cover Art: *Bais Hamikdash*, acrylic on canvas, 1994, nachshonart.com

Printed in the United States of America
© Copyrighted and Published 2021
by The Rohr Jewish Learning Institute
832 Eastern Parkway, Brooklyn, NY 11213

718-221-6900
WWW.MYJLI.COM

This Can ~~Never~~ Happen

A credible case for feeling good about the future

STUDENT TEXTBOOK

The Rohr Jewish Learning Institute
gratefully acknowledges the pioneering
and ongoing support of

George and Pamela Rohr

Since its inception, the Rohr JLI has been
a beneficiary of the vision, generosity, care,
and concern of the Rohr family.

In the merit of the tens of thousands of hours
of Torah study by JLI students worldwide,
may they be blessed with health, *Yiddishe
nachas* from all their loved ones, and
extraordinary success in all their endeavors.

Citation Types

SCRIPTURE

The icon for Scripture is based on the images of a scroll and a spiral. The scroll is a literal reference; the spiral symbolizes Scripture's role as the singular source from which all subsequent Torah knowledge emanates.

TALMUD AND MIDRASH

The Talmud and Midrash are fundamental links in the chain of the Torah's oral tradition.

SAGES

Many generations of Jewish sages devoted their lives to expounding on and elucidating the texts of Scripture and the Talmud. The quill symbolizes the product of their toil.

MYSTICS

The mystics explore the inner, esoteric aspect of the Torah. The icon for mystical texts is based on the "*sefirot* tree" commonly present in kabbalistic charts.

LAWS AND CUSTOMS

Ultimately, the teachings emerging from Scripture, the Talmud, and the writings of the later sages find expression in Torah law—known as halachah, "the way"—and the customs adopted by the various Jewish communities through the generations.

PERSPECTIVES

Personal perspectives expressed in essays, diaries, and other works make up a significant part of the total Jewish experience.

STORIES

Sometimes, the best way to illustrate an idea is by painting a picture through a story or a parable. Indeed, stories and parables, with their emphasis on the telling and listening experience, occupy an important place in Jewish teaching.

Contents

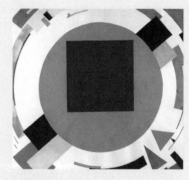

Foreword

"ADDING IN STUDY OF THE TORAH ON THE TOPICS OF MASHIACH AND THE REDEMPTION IS THE STRAIGHT PATH TO ACCOMPLISH THE ACTUAL REVELATION AND COMING OF MASHIACH AND THE REDEMPTION."

—THE REBBE

For thousands of years, our nation awaited, desperately yearned, and incessantly prayed for the Redemption. In recent generations, many of the leading Jewish figures have informed us that the Redemption is imminent. Prominent in our times was the Lubavitcher Rebbe, who on numerous occasions publicly insisted that our generation is the last of exile and the first of the Redemption. He encouraged everyone to open their eyes to this reality and prepare themselves for this event. In October of 1991, when asked by a CNN correspondent about his message for the world about Mashiach, the Rebbe responded: "Mashiach is ready to come now: it is only on our part to do something additional in the realm of goodness and kindness."

There is a lot to discover about this apparently already-dawning future. The questions posed by the Jews of today are numerous and often intense, whereas the answers lie buried in an incredible accumulation of misinformation.

What is the Redemption all about? Is it at all realistic to believe that this will happen anytime soon? Why do we need it? How central is this belief to Judaism? Who is the Mashiach personality who will usher in this Redemption?

To deliver satisfactory answers to queries of this nature, and to provide the empowering insights that are needed now more than ever, the Rohr Jewish Learning Institute (JLI) has produced this new, highly informative, and transformative course, *This Can Happen*. It plumbs the depths of Jewish scholarship and tradition from throughout the ages to bring refreshing and, most likely, surprising perspectives on this issue, which has remained so mysterious to many until now.

It is our fervent hope that the study of this topic by tens of thousands of students around the globe will create a shift in awareness of this all-important topic. Most importantly, we hope that it spurs heightened anticipation for the Redemption, spawning a flood of positive deeds and acts of kindness—fueled by the clarity of this course and performed for the purpose of pressing home the final peg of positivity that is needed to procure the Redemption in actuality—immediately.

HERALD FROM THE ROOF
Yehoshua Wiseman, oil on canvas, Israel

START WITH THE SCIENCE

In a society marked by chaos and discord, it's hard to believe our world is actually better than it's ever been. Let's dive into the data of what's wrong—and what's right—with the world.

I. BELIEF IN A MUCH BETTER TOMORROW

We Jews have many beliefs. We believe that G-d* created the world in six days and rested on the seventh. We believe that the Land of Israel is the most sacred parcel of land on earth. While these beliefs—and many others—are important components of the Jewish doctrine, these do not constitute *principal* Jewish beliefs. Some eight centuries ago, Maimonides, one of the most venerated Jewish philosophers of all time, distilled the most fundamental Jewish beliefs into thirteen principles. Interestingly, he devoted two of them to the belief in the ultimate Redemption that will be ushered in by the Mashiach (Messiah) and the subsequent Resurrection of the Dead. The belief in the future Redemption occupies what seems to be a disproportionate amount of space in the very core of the traditional Jewish belief system.

In this chapter, we will turn to the remarkable descriptions of the messianic era provided by the prophets of old.

---

* Throughout this book, "G-d" and "L-rd" are written with a hyphen instead of an "o" (both in our own translations and when quoting others). This is one way we accord reverence to the sacred divine name. This also reminds us that, even as we seek G-d, He transcends any human effort to describe His reality.

The Twelfth Principle

TEXT 1

Siddur, "The Thirteen Principles"

אֲנִי מַאֲמִין בֶּאֱמוּנָה שְׁלֵמָה בְּבִיאַת הַמָּשִׁיחַ.

וְאַף עַל פִּי שֶׁיִּתְמַהְמֵהַּ, עִם כָּל זֶה אֲחַכֶּה לוֹ בְּכָל יוֹם שֶׁיָּבוֹא.

I believe with perfect faith in the
coming of the Mashiach.

Although he may tarry, I await his arrival every day.

SIDDUR

The siddur is the Jewish
prayer book. It was
originally developed by the
sages of the Great Assembly
in the 4th century BCE,
and later reconstructed
by Rabban Gamliel after
the destruction of the
Second Temple. Various
authorities continued to
add prayers, from then
until contemporary times.
It includes praise of G-d,
requests for personal and
national needs, selections
of the Bible, and much else.
Various Jewish communities
have slightly different
versions of the siddur.

EXERCISE 1.1

**What attracted you to this course? Are there
any specific Redemption-related topics that
you are most interested in clarifying?**

TEXT 2

An Era of Abundance

Maimonides, *Mishneh Torah,* Laws of Kings 12:5

RABBI MOSHE BEN MAIMON (MAIMONIDES, RAMBAM) 1135–1204

וּבְאוֹתוֹ הַזְמַן לֹא יִהְיֶה שָׁם לֹא רָעָב וְלֹא מִלְחָמָה.
וְלֹא קִנְאָה וְתַחֲרוּת. שֶׁהַטּוֹבָה תִּהְיֶה מֻשְׁפַּעַת הַרְבֵּה.
וְכָל הַמַּעֲדַנִּים מְצוּיִין כֶּעָפָר.

In that era, there will be no famine or war, no envy or competition. For goodness will be in abundance, and all delights will be as commonplace as dust.

Halachist, philosopher, author, and physician. Maimonides was born in Córdoba, Spain. After the conquest of Córdoba by the Almohads, he fled Spain and eventually settled in Cairo, Egypt. There, he became the leader of the Jewish community and served as court physician to the vizier of Egypt. He is most noted for authoring the *Mishneh Torah*, an encyclopedic arrangement of Jewish law; and for his philosophical work, *Guide for the Perplexed*. His rulings on Jewish law are integral to the formation of halachic consensus.

THE PEACEABLE KINGDOM (DETAIL)
1845, Edward Hicks, American, 1780–1849, oil on canvas, Yale University Art Gallery

TEXT 3

Eradication of Poverty

Zechariah 14:21

וְלֹא יִהְיֶה כְנַעֲנִי עוֹד בְּבֵית ה' צְבָאוֹת בַּיּוֹם הַהוּא.

On that day, there will no longer be an impoverished person in the house of G-d.

ZECHARIAH

Biblical book. The book of Zechariah contains the prophecies delivered by Zechariah in the 4th century BCE to the exiles that had returned to the Land of Israel. Zechariah's prophecies comfort and encourage the people, exhort them to improve their religious observance, and foretell the future Redemption.

TEXT 4

Plentiful Food

Isaiah 30:23

וְנָתַן מְטַר זַרְעֲךָ אֲשֶׁר תִּזְרַע אֶת הָאֲדָמָה, וְלֶחֶם תְּבוּאַת הָאֲדָמָה, וְהָיָה דָשֵׁן וְשָׁמֵן.

G-d will give rain for your seed with which you shall sow the soil. [He will give you plentiful] bread, the yield of the land. And the land will be rich and abundant.

ISAIAH

Biblical book. The book of Isaiah contains the prophecies of Isaiah, who lived in the 6–7th centuries BCE. Isaiah's prophecies contain stern rebukes for the personal failings of the contemporary people of Judea and the corruption of its government. The bulk of the prophecies, however, are stirring consolations and poetic visions of the future Redemption.

TEXT 5

Disabilities Will Vanish

Isaiah 35:5–6

אָז תִּפָּקַחְנָה עֵינֵי עִוְרִים, וְאָזְנֵי חֵרְשִׁים תִּפָּתַחְנָה.

אָז יְדַלֵּג כָּאַיָּל פִּסֵּחַ, וְתָרֹן לְשׁוֹן אִלֵּם.

At that time, the eyes of the blind will be opened,
and the ears of the deaf will be unstopped.

At that time, the lame shall skip like a deer,
and the tongue of the mute shall sing.

TEXT 6

Cessation of Hostilities

Isaiah 2:4

לֹא יִשָּׂא גוֹי אֶל גּוֹי חֶרֶב, וְלֹא יִלְמְדוּ עוֹד מִלְחָמָה.

Nation shall not lift sword against nation,
nor shall anyone train for war anymore.

TEXT 7

Disarmament

Isaiah 2:4

וְכִתְּתוּ חַרְבוֹתָם לְאִתִּים, וַחֲנִיתוֹתֵיהֶם לְמַזְמֵרוֹת.

Nations shall beat their swords into plow
blades and their spears into pruning tools.

TEXT 8

Elimination of Crime

Isaiah 60:18

לֹא יִשָּׁמַע עוֹד חָמָס בְּאַרְצֵךְ, שֹׁד וָשֶׁבֶר בִּגְבוּלָיִךְ.

No longer will violence be heard in your land,
nor robbery or devastation within your borders.

THE PEACE NEGOTIATIONS
BETWEEN JULIUS
CIVILIS AND THE ROMAN
GENERAL CERIALIS
Otto van Veen,
1600–1613, oil on panel,
Rijksmuseum, Amsterdam

II. BACK TO THE PRESENT

How outlandish and far-fetched are the prophecies we just read? To answer this question, we will contrast the idyllic description of the messianic era with the times we are living in today. Let us attempt to evaluate the general current state of our world and the wider trends in several key quality-of-life areas.

EXERCISE 1.2

How would you rate the state of our world today compared to its state fifty years ago—have conditions generally improved or deteriorated?

(a) Greatly improved

(b) Somewhat improved

(c) More or less the same

(d) Somewhat deteriorated

(e) Greatly deteriorated

Are you optimistic or pessimistic about the future?

(a) Very optimistic

(b) Somewhat optimistic

(c) Somewhat pessimistic

(d) Very pessimistic

FIGURE 1.1

A Nostalgic View

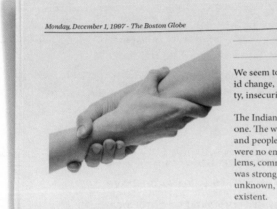

Monday, December 1, 1997 - The Boston Globe

Letters to the Editor

Changing Era

We seem to be in an era of rapid change, increasing instability, insecurity, and danger. . . .

The Indian life was a difficult one. The winters were harsh, and people died. But there were no employment problems, community harmony was strong, substance abuse unknown, crime nearly non-existent.

What warfare there was between tribes, was largely ritualistic and seldom resulted in indiscriminate or wholesale slaughter. While there were hard times, life was, for the most part, stable and predictable. The seasons passed in their turn and with them came, with few exceptions, a means of providing food, warmth and shelter.

FIGURE 1.2

Perceptions of the State of Global Affairs

Chris Jackson, "Global Perceptions of Development Progress: 'Perils of Perceptions' Research," published by Ipsos MORI, September 18, 2017

Survey Question: "In the last 20 years, has the proportion of the world population living in extreme poverty decreased, increased, or remained the same?"

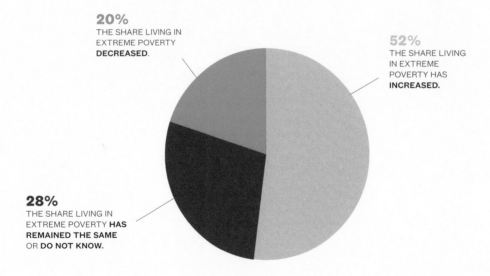

20%
THE SHARE LIVING IN EXTREME POVERTY **DECREASED**.

52%
THE SHARE LIVING IN EXTREME POVERTY HAS **INCREASED**.

28%
THE SHARE LIVING IN EXTREME POVERTY **HAS REMAINED THE SAME** OR **DO NOT KNOW**.

FIGURE 1.3

Perceptions of Crime Rates

news.gallup.com/poll/1603/crime.aspx

Survey Question: "Is there more crime in the U.S. than there was a year ago, or less?"

	MORE	LESS	SAME	NO OPINION
2020	78	14	6	3
2019	64	24	9	3
2018	60	25	8	7
2017	68	19	9	5
2016	70	20	6	4
2015	70	18	8	4
2014	63	21	9	7
2013	64	19	9	7
2011	68	17	8	8
2010	66	17	8	9
2009	74	15	6	5
2008	67	15	9	9
2007	71	14	8	6
2006	68	16	8	8
2005	67	21	9	3
2004	53	28	14	5
2003	60	25	11	4
2002	62	21	11	6
2001	41	43	10	6
2000	47	41	7	5
1998	52	35	8	5
1997	64	25	6	5
1996	71	15	8	6
1993	87	4	5	4
1992	89	3	4	4
1990	84	3	7	6
1989	84	5	5	6

FIGURE 1.4

Expectations for the Future
YouGov 2015 Survey

Survey Question: "All things considered, do you think the world is getting better, worse, or neither getting better nor worse?"

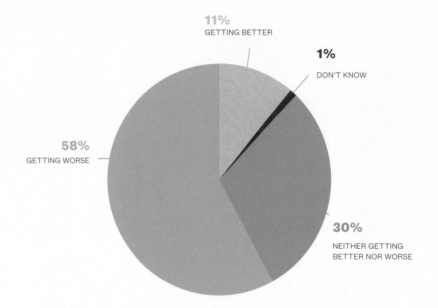

11% GETTING BETTER

1% DON'T KNOW

58% GETTING WORSE

30% NEITHER GETTING BETTER NOR WORSE

III. THE FACTS

Unlike the popular pessimism, the Torah sees civilization as marching toward a radically *better* destiny. The prophesied Redemption will not be a sudden transition from complete darkness to light. Rather, as we approach the era of Redemption, we will notice changes in the world that are in line with the messianic prophecies.

In this section, we will examine the data and see how, hiding in plain sight, many of the messianic prophecies are beginning to materialize.

THE REDEMPTION
Yehoshua Wiseman, Israel

TEXT 9

A Foretaste of Redemption

The Rebbe, Rabbi Menachem Mendel Schneerson,
Torat Menachem 5725:1 (41), pp. 41–42

כָּל הָעִנְיָנִים דְּלֶעָתִיד לָבוֹא מַתְחִילִים עוֹד לִפְנֵי בִּיאַת
הַמָּשִׁיחַ. וְעַל דֶּרֶךְ הָעִנְיָן דְּ"טוֹעֲמֶיהָ חַיִּים זָכוּ", שֶׁבְּעֶרֶב שַׁבָּת
טוֹעֲמִים מִמַּאַכְלֵי הַשַּׁבָּת, וּכְמוֹ כֵן בָּאֶלֶף הַשִּׁשִׁי, (עוֹד לִפְנֵי
בִּיאַת הַמָּשִׁיחַ) טוֹעֲמִים כְּבָר מֵהַגִּלּוּיִים דִּימוֹת הַמָּשִׁיחַ.

וְלֹא רַק בְּנוֹגֵעַ לְעִנְיָנִים רוּחָנִיִּים . . . אֶלָּא כְּמוֹ הַדִּין
דְּ"טוֹעֲמֶיהָ" בְּנוֹגֵעַ לְעֶרֶב שַׁבָּת כִּפְשׁוּטוֹ, שֶׁצָּרִיךְ לִטְעוֹם
מֵהַדָּגִים . . . הֲרֵי עוֹד קוֹדֶם בִּיאַת הַמָּשִׁיחַ תִּהְיֶה לִבְנֵי יִשְׂרָאֵל
רִבּוּי הַשְׁפָּעָה בְּגַשְׁמִיּוּת, וְיוּכְלוּ לַעֲבוֹד ה' מִתּוֹךְ הָרְחָבָה.

All of the experiences of the future Redemption
begin even before Mashiach's arrival. Just as Jewish
law encourages us to sample the Shabbat foods in
the hours before the onset of Shabbat, similarly,
in the sixth millennium—even before the onset
of the Redemption—we can already sample the
experiences that will fully materialize in the future.

In addition to receiving a foretaste of the *spiritual*
delights we will experience then, the instruction
to taste from the Shabbat foods means, quite
simply, to taste the fish! The same is true of the
era preceding the Redemption—we will then have
physical blessings in abundance, and we will be
able to serve G-d out of material prosperity.

RABBI MENACHEM
MENDEL SCHNEERSON
1902-1994

The towering
Jewish leader of
the 20th century, known
as "the Lubavitcher
Rebbe," or simply as "the
Rebbe." Born in southern
Ukraine, the Rebbe
escaped Nazi-occupied
Europe, arriving in
the U.S. in June 1941.
The Rebbe inspired
and guided the revival
of traditional Judaism
after the European
devastation, impacting
virtually every Jewish
community the world
over. The Rebbe often
emphasized that the
performance of just
one additional good
deed could usher in
the era of Mashiach.
The Rebbe's scholarly
talks and writings have
been printed in more
than 200 volumes.

FIGURE 1.5

World Population Living in Extreme Poverty, 1820–2015

OurWorldInData.org

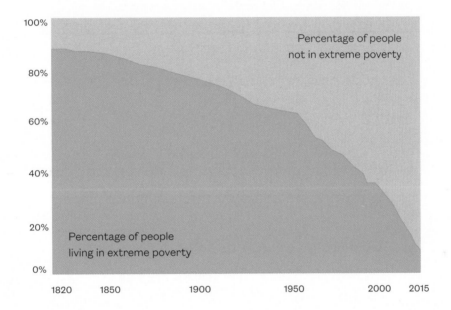

Percentage of people not in extreme poverty

Percentage of people living in extreme poverty

"Mashiach: It's Already in the News!" In this fascinating lecture, **Rabbi Ari Shishler** reshapes our imaginings of the Redemption prophecies: *myjli.com/canhappen*

FIGURE 1.6

World Population Living in Extreme Poverty, 1981–2017

World Bank, Development Research Group

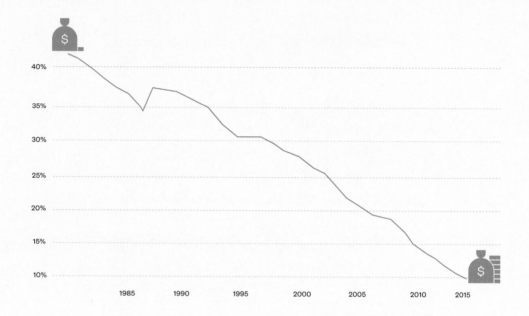

TEXT 10

A Daily Upbeat Headline

Nicholas Kristof, "This Has Been the Best Year Ever,"
The New York Times, December 28, 2019

If you're depressed by the state of the world, let me toss out an idea: In the long arc of human history, 2019 has been the best year ever. . . .

As recently as 1981, 42 percent of the planet's population endured "extreme poverty," defined by the United Nations as living on less than about $2 a day. That portion has plunged to less than 10 percent of the world's population now.

Every day for a decade, newspapers could have carried the headline "Another 170,000 Moved Out of Extreme Poverty Yesterday." Or if one uses a higher threshold, the headline could have been: "The Number of People Living on More Than $10 a Day Increased by 245,000 Yesterday."

Mrs. Fruma Schapiro
explores the question
of "Mashiach:
Fantasy or Reality?":
myjli.com/canhappen

TEXT 11

A Most Underappreciated Development

Bill Gates and Melinda Gates, "We Were Making Headway on Global Poverty. What's About to Change?"
The New York Times, September 22, 2018

This huge drop in the number of people living on less than $1.90 per day is among the most underappreciated and most important developments of our generation.

REMEMBRANCE
1914, Marc Chagall, gouache, ink, and graphite on paper, Solomon R. Guggenheim Museum, N.Y.

BILL GATES
1955–

William Henry Gates. Entrepreneur, investor, philanthropist. Gates is best known as the principal founder of Microsoft Corporation. In 2014, he stepped down as chairman of Microsoft and now pursues a number of philanthropic endeavors through the Bill & Melinda Gates Foundation. The foundation primarily focuses on fighting disease and poverty in developing countries.

MELINDA GATES
1964–

Philanthropist. Gates co-founded the Bill & Melinda Gates Foundation, the world's largest private charitable organization, with her husband. She is the author of *The New York Times* bestseller, *The Moment of Lift: How Empowering Women Changes the World*.

FIGURE 1.7

Global Annual Rate of People Dying Due to Famine (per 100,000)

OurWorldinData.org

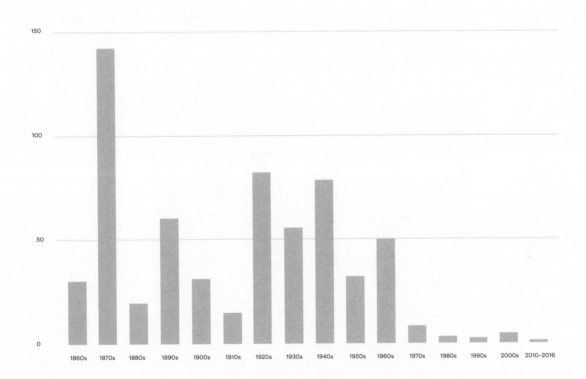

TEXT 12

Too Many Products?

"What to Do When There Are Too Many Product Choices on the Store Shelves?" *Consumer Reports*, January 2014

A new survey by the Consumer Reports National Research Center confirms that option overload can be a hindrance as well as a help. Almost 80 percent of the 2,818 subscribers surveyed said they'd found an especially wide range of choices in the previous month, and 36 percent of those said they were overwhelmed by the information they had to process to make a buying decision. . . .

Between 1975 and 2008, the number of products in the average supermarket swelled from an average of 8,948 to almost 47,000, according to the Food Marketing Institute, a trade group. (In the past few years, that number has fallen slightly, in part because of a growth spurt among smaller stores.)

"Consumers have always had choices, but today options have exploded beyond all reason," says Barry Schwartz, author of *The Paradox of Choice* (HarperCollins, 2003) and a psychology professor at Swarthmore College.

FIGURE 1.8

Global Life Expectancy, 1800–2015

OurWorldinData.org

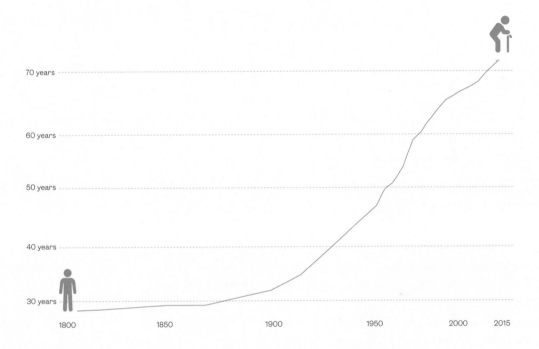

In "On the Bright Side,"
Rabbi Mendel Rubenfeld
challenges his listeners to
look around themselves
and see how news events
point toward Mashiach's
imminent arrival:
myjli.com/canhappen

FIGURE 1.9

Progress in Disease Eradication, Prevention, and Control

ERADICATED	REDUCED	MANAGEABLE
SMALLPOX	MALARIA	DIABETES
POLIO	MEASLES	AIDS
RABIES	TUBERCULOSIS	
SYPHILLIS	HEPATITIS A	
TETANUS	HEPATITIS B	
	MUMPS	

TEXT 13

A Question of When, Not If

Peter Jaret, "An End to Blindness? New Technologies Could Save the Eyesight of Millions," *AARP Bulletin*, 2015

If you had seen Lisa Kulik and her husband strolling the grounds of the University of Southern California's Eye Institute last summer, you would have thought nothing of it. But for Kulik, that simple walk around the campus was "a miracle." Blind for more than two decades from an inherited eye disease called retinitis pigmentosa, Kulik was seeing again—clearly enough to make out the sidewalk and the grassy edge—thanks to a sophisticated microchip implanted in one of her eyes.

The device, called the Argus II, is just one of a growing number of bold new approaches to treating blindness, offering hope to the millions of mostly older Americans in danger of losing their sight from macular degeneration, glaucoma, diabetic retinopathy and other eye diseases. In fact, progress in ophthalmology is so rapid that some researchers have already begun to envision an end to many forms of vision loss. "We still have a lot to learn," admits Stephen Rose, chief research officer for the Foundation Fighting Blindness. "But it's not a question of if we'll end blindness. It's really just a question of when."

FIGURE 1.10   Speaking of Muteness

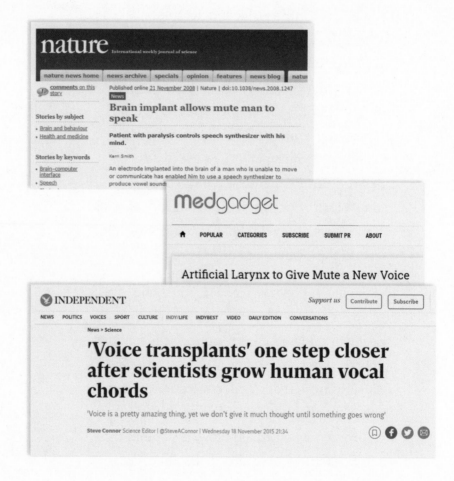

FIGURE 1.11

State-Based Battle-Related Deaths Globally (per 100,000), 1946–2016

OurWorldinData.org

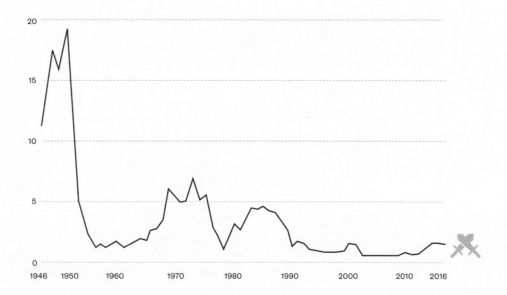

TEXT 14

Peace Is in Fashion

Joshua S. Goldstein and Steven Pinker, "War Really Is
Going Out of Style," *The New York Times*, December 17, 2011

Armed conflict hasn't vanished, and today anyone
with a mobile phone can broadcast the bloodshed.
But our impressions of the prevalence of war,
stoked by these images, can be misleading. . . .

For centuries, wars reallocated huge territories,
as empires were agglomerated or dismantled
and states wiped off the map. But since shortly
after World War II, virtually no borders have
changed by force, and no member of the United
Nations has disappeared through conquest. . . .

Perhaps the deepest cause of the waning of war is
a growing repugnance toward institutionalized
violence. Brutal customs that were commonplace for
millennia have been largely abolished: cannibalism,
human sacrifice, heretic-burning, chattel slavery,
punitive mutilation, sadistic executions. Could
war really be going the way of slave auctions?

JOSHUA S. GOLDSTEIN
1952–

Political scientist and
author. Joshua Goldstein
received his doctorate
in political science from
MIT, and was a professor
of international relations
at American University.
He is currently a research
scholar in political
science at the University
of Massachusetts,
Amherst. Goldstein is the
author of a number of
books and articles about
international relations,
war, and climate change.

STEVEN PINKER
1954–

Psychologist and author.
Born in Montreal,
Steven Pinker received
his doctorate in
experimental psychology
from Harvard University,
where he now serves as a
professor of psychology.
Pinker's academic
specializations are in the
fields of mental imagery
and the psychology of
language, and he has
published extensively
on these topics.

FIGURE 1.12

Estimated Global Nuclear Warhead Inventories, 1945–2020

Kristenson/Korda/Norris, Federation of American Scientists 2020

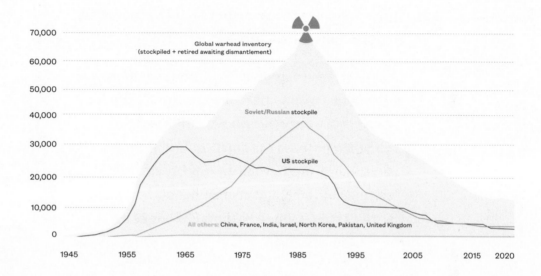

TEXT 15

Soldiers Combating . . . Pollution

Samuel Osborne, "China Reassigns 60,000 Soldiers to Plant Trees in Bid to Fight Pollution," *The Independent*, February 13, 2018

China has reportedly reassigned over 60,000 soldiers to plant trees in a bid to combat pollution by increasing the country's forest coverage.

A large regiment from the People's Liberation Army, along with some of the nation's armed police force, have been withdrawn from their posts on the northern border to work on non-military tasks inland. . . .

It comes as part of China's plan to plant at least 84,000 square kilometres (32,400 square miles) of trees by the end of the year, which is roughly equivalent to the size of Ireland.

FIGURE 1.13

Homicide Rates across Western Europe (per 100,000), 1300–2016

OurWorldinData.org

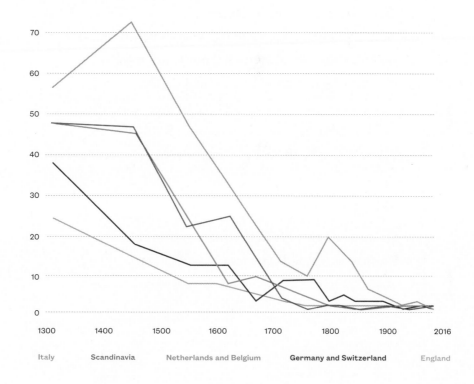

Italy   Scandinavia   Netherlands and Belgium   **Germany and Switzerland**   England

Feelings vs. Facts

Maggie Koerth and Amelia Thomson-DeVeaux, "Many Americans Are Convinced Crime Is Rising in the U.S. They're Wrong," FiveThirtyEight.com, August 3, 2020

In 2019, according to a survey conducted by Gallup, about 64 percent of Americans believed that there was more crime in the U.S. than there was a year ago. It's a belief we've consistently held for decades now, but as you can see in the chart below, we've been, just as consistently, very wrong.

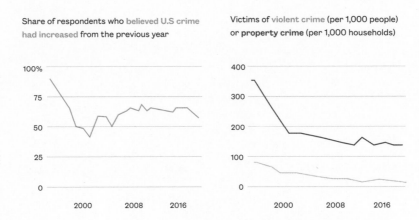

Share of respondents who believed U.S crime had increased from the previous year

Victims of violent crime (per 1,000 people) or property crime (per 1,000 households)

Crime rates do fluctuate from year to year. In 2020, for example, murder has been up but other crimes are in decline so that the crime rate, overall, is down. And the trend line for violent crime over the last 30 years has been down, not up. The Bureau of Justice Statistics found that the rate of violent crimes per

1,000 Americans age 12 and older plummeted from 80 in 1993 to just 23 in 2018. The country has gotten much, much safer, but, somehow, Americans don't seem to feel that on a knee-jerk, emotional level.

"The biggest challenge really, and we're seeing this as a society across the board right now, is that even though our organizations, our businesses, our government entities are becoming more data driven, we as human beings are not," said Meghan Hollis, a research scholar at the Ronin Institute for Independent Scholarship.

KEY POINTS

1   Belief in the Redemption is central to the Jewish belief
     system. The Redemption consists of both physical
     and spiritual dimensions. In terms of the physical side,
     ancient biblical prophecies describe a fabulous era in
     which there will be an abundance of food and material
     goodness, poverty will be eradicated, disabilities will
     vanish, war and crime will cease, and weaponry will
     be repurposed for peaceful and productive goals.

2   The Redemption will not be a sudden transition from
     darkness to light. Rather, as we approach the era
     of Redemption, there will be steady improvements
     of our condition that in many ways reflect the
     promised experiences of the future Redemption.

3   Today, as we rapidly approach the time of Redemption,
     we witness a host of sweeping positive societal
     changes. Contrary to popular perception, the present
     is in many ways the best time ever to be alive.

4   The global population suffering from extreme poverty
     has drastically declined, food is more readily available
     and there are far fewer incidences of famine, the average
     human life span has nearly tripled, child mortality

rates have drastically decreased, many diseases have been eradicated or significantly reduced, remarkable strides have been made in ending or greatly reducing many disabilities, violent crime is down, the number of wars and war-related deaths has drastically declined, and the vast majority of nuclear missiles have been decommissioned and, instead, governments are devoting military resources for humanitarian purposes.

5 Despite the occasional setback, we are currently in a state of exponential positive growth. We can expect positive change to become even more rapid and exciting in the coming years. It will continue to accelerate until we reach the pinnacle, with the arrival of the Redemption.

ADDITIONAL READINGS

Where Is Our World Heading?

By Rabbi Mendel Kalmenson

RABBI MENDEL KALMENSON
Author, lecturer, and
noted expert on Chasidic
thought. Rabbi Kalmenson
serves as the rabbi of Beit
Baruch and directs Chabad
of Belgravia in Central
London. He is the author of
the popular titles *Positivity
Bias* and *A Time to Heal*.

The Rebbe once said to a Gerer Chasid named Rabbi Neiman, "The world says that I am crazy about Moshiach—and they are absolutely right!"[1]

Indeed, if there is one thing that the Rebbe and Chabad in general are known for, it is their fervent belief in the imminent arrival of Moshiach. This teleological driving force was at the root of everything the Rebbe said and did. But what does this actually mean, and what does it have to do with the Rebbe's Positivity Bias?

Without getting too deep into the finer points of Jewish philosophy and prophecy, Moshiach is the main developing character, both perpetually absent and potentially present at all times, throughout our story of Creation and Redemption. His inevitable arrival will signal the ultimate redemption and goal of history, when the world will be made right and truth will be as clear as day for all to see.

The Rebbe's belief in Moshiach as the culmination of the Divine/human drama gave him and all those he inspired more than a hope, but rather a vivid faith in the ultimately positive outcome to all of the world's bitter exiles and alienations.

A foundational aspect of this is that we all have our work cut out for us in order for it to occur; we are charged with spiritually preparing ourselves and the world for redemption. From this perspective, history has been a millenia-long crash-course on bringing Moshiach into our midst from out of the hovering realms of pure poetic potential.

It is this very combination of belief in G-d's ultimate goodness and in our own personal power to positively impact the world that forms the basis of the Rebbe's Positivity Bias.

The Rebbe believed that we are living in Messianic times. From when he was a small child, the Rebbe dreamed of that imminent great day, and despite the immensely challenging times he lived through, he never stopped nursing that dream. In a letter[2] addressed to Yitzchak Ben-Zvi, the second president of Israel, the Rebbe wrote:

> From the time when I was a child attending cheder, and even earlier than that, there began to take form in my mind a vision of the future redemption—the redemption of Israel from its last exile, redemption such as would explain the suffering, the decrees, and the massacres of exile....

In many ways, this dream is what made the Rebbe unique among other towering Jewish figures of our time. Most leaders see their life and impact in terms of their specific generation, but the Rebbe viewed his role through the wider lens of history in its entirety. He saw his generation as a whole, while at the same time also as a small but critical part of a much larger super-structure and meta-process.

Therefore, wherever you look in the Rebbe's teachings, there it is: the dream of Moshiach. Sometimes implicit, but more often explicit, in almost every one of his talks and letters, the Rebbe reveals the aspiration that is closest to his heart: A burning desire to see our imperfect world enter into an era of peace and wholeness, devoid of war and suffering, replete with revealed goodness and the pursuit of G-dly knowledge.

Indeed, the Rebbe most clearly articulated the contours of this dream on the very night he assumed the mantle of Chabad-Lubavitch leadership, 10 Shevat, 5711 (1951), in his discourse entitled Bati L'gani.

In this, his first public teaching as Rebbe, he cites centuries of Midrashic history, revealing this world's ultimate importance to G-d as His "garden" and most-desired "abode," as well as its simultaneous spiritual vacancy—"the Shechinah (the Divine Presence) is in exile"[3] —waiting to be welcomed back home. And this is where we come in. As G-d's entrusted "gardeners," it is our job to maintain and cultivate the world for G-d's eternal residence.

In the words of the Rebbe on the very night he assumed that name, after thousands of years of baby steps and quantum leaps, going all the way back to Adam and Eve in the Garden of Eden, "it is up to us to complete the job and usher in the final redemption."

There it is: The Rebbe's world-redeeming dream. Nothing less than bringing humanity across the finish line of history and ushering in the Messianic era.

But how?

Not to Change Reality, But to Open Our Eyes

One of the axiomatic teachings regarding Moshiach that the Rebbe would often share is that Moshiach will not come to change reality; rather, he will expose reality for what it truly is.

In support of this idea, he would often say that the Hebrew word for exile has the same letters as the Hebrew word for redemption except for the addition of the letter alef. Alef is the very first letter in the Hebrew alphabet.

Numerically, alef equals one and therefore represents the Divine Oneness inherent within all of reality.

Paradoxically, the word elef, spelled the same as alef, means one thousand, implying multiplicity. Furthermore, the letter alef is essentially silent, having no sound of its own—merely giving breath to vowels and voice to movement.

Alef, therefore, represents the silent presence of ultimate unity concealed beneath the surface of the striving and suffering world of multiplicity, just waiting to be revealed. Moshiach will empower us all to hear and see the silent and invisible alef in exile, thereby transforming it into redemption, once and for all.

In this seemingly simple word-play, the Rebbe is pointing out a powerful paradigm shift in our understanding of Moshiach.

Moshiach does not mean the articulation of a totally different word or world. The letters or infrastructure of our lives and the universe will fundamentally stay the same, except that the alef will be revealed, quietly smiling at us out of the tumult of our experiences, revealing the garden of oneness within.[4]

Signs of the Times

The Rebbe was once asked: If you could choose any era in history in which to live, which would it be?

"This one," he answered immediately.[5]

Throughout his myriad spiritual teachings, his inspiring personal interactions, and his bold public outreach projects, the Rebbe spiritually developed and actively expressed the idea that we are "the last generation of exile and the first of Redemption."[6]

We are thus living on the transitional cusp of an unfathomable evolution of consciousness—a spiritual revolution. This is both an unbelievable privilege and an awesome responsibility, as our individual and collective lives are literally and metaphorically laying the final stones for the bridge between exile and redemption.

Based on this eschatological understanding of where we are in the process of history, the Rebbe saw the signs of Moshiach's imminent arrival everywhere—from world events to social trends, and advances in technology and medicine. From his inaugural address, and on thousands of occasions thereafter, the Rebbe declared it his mission to empower others to see the world through a similar lens, to understand and appreciate the nature of the miraculous and meaningful times we are living through, to get a glimpse of the hidden alef within the world and events swirling around us.

Traditionally, the vast multitude of Biblical prophecies relating to the redemption have been viewed through a supernatural lens, and were thus considered as being irreconcilably removed from our daily reality and experience. They were understood as miraculous "aberrations," and therefore as clear signs of Divine intervention.

Today, however, according to the Rebbe, many of the prophesied "miracles" pertaining to the Messianic era have begun to come into existence at varying degrees of actualization. As such, the fulfillment of the words of the prophets no longer requires a wild imagination or blind leap of faith to behold. According to the Rebbe, it is more a matter of "opening our eyes" to see beneath the surface of "natural" events and advances, in order to recognize the Hand of the Creator at work in history.

For instance:

The Rebbe saw in the rise of feminism the beginning stages of Jeremiah's prophecy: For the L-rd has created something new on the earth, a woman shall rise above a man.[7]

In many countries and cultures the world over there has continued to be a general shift in the direction of including and advancing women's voices, issues, and rights. Today, women are increasingly gaining political power and make up more than a fifth of members of national parliaments, and counting.[8]

Similarly, as we have explored, the Rebbe saw in the emergent counterculture of the 1960s, many examples of prophesied socio-generational shifts and conflicts that would occur leading up to the arrival of Moshiach; for example, the words of Isaiah that the youth will be insolent and rebellious towards their elders.[9]

Rather than interpreting those words apocalyptically, the Rebbe chose to focus on the potential positive outcomes of such radical expressions of youth, and thereby sought to validate them and strengthen their good points.

The Rebbe, along with various other Chasidic leaders, including his father-in-law, the Previous Rebbe, felt what they considered to be the beginnings of the "birth pangs"[10] of Moshiach in the various cataclysmic events of the 20th century, particularly World War II.

In related fashion, the Rebbe saw[11] the Six-Day War, and the corresponding mass spiritual awakening and immigration of impassioned Jews moving to Israel, as a symbolic nod to Isaiah's prophecy that It will come to pass on that day that the great shofar will sound. . . .[12] The prophecy goes on to describe the in-gathering of Jews "lost" and "dispersed" in exile, as they return to Jerusalem in the final redemption.

With the appearance of various communication technologies over the course of the 20th century—from the phone to radio to television to the beginnings of the internet—the Rebbe saw the potential, not for more discord and confusion, but for more communication and connection. Additionally, with the introduction of the World Wide Web, by making all information accessible to the furthest reaches of the globe, the groundwork has been laid for the world to be filled with the word of G-d,[13] literally!

This redemptive view of the world is the ultimate expression of the Rebbe's Positivity Bias. Wars, revolutions, uprisings, rapid shifts in consciousness—as unsettling as these things may be to our lives in the moment and to the established order of the day—are ultimately leading us towards a more perfect union, a higher system of truth and harmony. This was the unyielding faith of the Rebbe.

The Time is now! The world is ready for more light! Are we?

Can we keep our composure and direction amid what appears to be the madness of a new world being born? Can we hold on to the promise of goodness and G-dliness revealed? Can we see through the brokenness and not lose hope? This takes work and faith. The work of developing and maintaining a positive outlook to keep moving toward the light. We need faith that the sparks really are there, waiting to be acknowledged and uplifted.

Indeed, despite what the pessimists will have us believe, we are actually living in unprecedented good times. Rather than regressing, which is what it often feels like, our world is progressing, and at breakneck speed. But it often takes the cultivation of a positive and expansive outlook to see the resplendent forest through the smoldering trees.

In January 2018, *Time Magazine* welcomed Bill Gates as its first guest editor in its 94-year history. Gates designed the edition around a mindset that he had endorsed for years: optimism. He then invited the world's greatest minds and experts on world progress to share their findings. In an interview he gave explaining why he decided to edit an issue of *Time*, he explained:[14]

"Reading the news today doesn't exactly leave you feeling optimistic. But many of the awful events we read about have happened in the context of a bigger, positive trend. On the whole, the world is getting much better."

This is not some naively optimistic view; it's backed by data.

According to Swedish economic historian Johan Norberg, who wrote an important book on the topic called "Progress":

"If someone had told you in 1990 that over the next 25 years world hunger would decline by 40%, child mortality would halve, and extreme poverty would fall by three quarters, you'd have told them they were a naive fool.

"But the fools were right. This is truly what has happened."[15]

And not just that:

For most of human history worldwide, life expectancy was around thirty years. Today, in most developed parts of the world, it is over eighty. By 2030, it will reach over ninety years in certain parts of the world.

In the 1990s there were more than 60,000 nuclear arms around the world, but by 2018, that number had fallen to approximately 10,000 nuclear arms.[16]

Two hundred years ago, 90% of the world lived in extreme poverty; today that number is 10%.

Indeed, according to the prominent Israeli public intellectual Yuval Harari, more people die today from eating too much than from eating too little.

Through too many medical advances to count, today the "lame are dancing" with the aid of prosthetics, the "blind can see," as 80% of visual impairment has already been cured,[17] and through stem cell research scientists are well on their way to curing deafness,[18] bringing to life the Messianic

prophecies of Isaiah:[19] Then will the eyes of the blind be opened and the ears of the deaf unstopped. Then will the lame leap like a deer. . . .

As pointed out by the Rebbe in one of his talks,[20] even the UN, despite its many intrigues and imperfections, channeled this Messianic energy of the time when it decided to prominently display the prophetic words of Isaiah in the entrance hall, expressing an intention to work towards the redemptive cause of lasting international peace: "And then they will beat their swords into ploughshares, and nations will learn war no more."[21]

The list goes on. And each new "miracle" reveals the fulfillment on some level of yet another prophetic vision related to the dawning of the Messianic age of Redemption according to our prophets of old.

Gates concludes his interview: "This issue of *Time* [is] a crash course in why and how the world is improving. I hope you'll be inspired to make it even better."

Passing the Baton

On a cold Tuesday night in February, 1992, just two years before passing away at the age of 92, the Rebbe could be seen standing at the front of Chabad Headquarters at 770 Eastern Parkway for hours and hours on end. Personally greeting the thousands who had lined up, the Rebbe handed each person a freshly printed copy of what would be the very last discourse he edited and distributed before his passing.

Opening with the verse (Exodus 27:20) *Ve'atah Tetzaveh*—And you will connect/command—this discourse has come to be considered the Rebbe's last ethical will and testament.

Along with his first public discourse, Bati L'gani, it provides a kind of bookend to the more than forty years of his transformational teachings.

In it, among many other things, the Rebbe acknowledges[22] and articulates certain unique historical and spiritual aspects of Jewish experience in the current day and age. The Rebbe cites the well-known rabbinic metaphor comparing the Jew to an olive, because his inner oil and light are only revealed when he is crushed. The Rebbe then states that historically speaking, the Jewish People were most "productive" and pious when they were "crushed" through harsh decrees, oppressions, and massacres.

These externally-imposed conditions activated a super-rational dimension of the soul, which allowed our ancestors to stubbornly and miraculously hold fast to their Jewish traditions and faith in the face of death, disgrace, and ostracization.

But we are all familiar with the saying, "It is easier to fight for one's principles than to live up to them." According to the Rebbe, this is precisely the existential situation in which contemporary Jews find themselves. For now, with the disappearance of the vast majority of daily, systematic threats to the Jewish ways of life, the modern Jew is faced with an even bigger challenge: To find the inspiration within to be willing to live as a Jew, and not just to be willing to die as one.

Additionally, following the European Enlightenment, the general societal trend in the Western World has been a decrease in organized expressions of religiosity and a corresponding increased slide towards secular humanism. While outwardly this may appear to many as a sign of spiritual degeneration, the Rebbe recognized it for the opportunity that it was. For this is but another way in which the Jew of today is free of many of the external pressures to engage and express his commitment to Jewish faith and identity that prevailed in the past. The modern Jew, according to the Rebbe, is increasingly left to his or her own devices to connect with their Jewish community, heritage, and tradition.

The Rebbe saw Jewish history through the lens of a human life. Like a baby, whose first steps and development require constant hands-on attention and reassuring affection, the Jewish People in their national infancy during Biblical times required overt miracles and revealed G-dliness to help them learn to walk out of Egypt. This spiritual caretaking continued as Israel grew up through Divine revelations, and under the wing of priests and prophets, judges and kings. But as time passed, the Jewish People continued to mature spiritually, and along with this maturation the revealed presence and providence of G-d diminished correspondingly. This journey has created the conditions for us to grow into our own faith and develop a connection with G-d and a spiritual worldview that comes from within, without external pressure or even revelation. This has given us the exceptional opportunity to manifest the ultimate, deepest, and highest level of faith.

"For so long as a Jew's compliance with the Will of G-d is externally motivated—however commendable such

motivation is in itself—it is not yet quite complete," said the Rebbe in 1991.

Indeed, it is clear from many public talks and pronouncements during this period, that the Rebbe was very consciously preparing his followers and future admirers for his departure. Through it all, one radical message consistently rings loud and clear: We all must become self-starters. We cannot rely on "help" from without, not even through faith-awakening hardship, let alone external positive support, constant guidance, and new teachings. We must find that eternal light within our own souls and ignite it, not once, but over and over again, through good deeds, the cultivation of a positive and providential perspective, and passionate expressions of holiness and faith.

"What else can I do so that all Jewish People should agitate, truthfully cry out, and effectively bring Moshiach in actuality. . . . We are still in exile. . . . and more importantly, in an internal exile with regards to serving G-d," cried out the Rebbe in the spring of 1991. "The only thing I can do is give it over to you: Do all you can . . . to actually bring our righteous Moshiach, immediately and directly. . . . I have done my part, from now on you must do all that you can."[23]

Perhaps, in statements such as these, the Rebbe was alluding to the fact that the time had come, and we were now ready, for each of us to become a tzaddik and reveal the Rebbe within.

In the winter of 1992, around the same time as the publication of V'atah Tetzaveh, Gabriel Erem, the CEO and publisher of *Lifestyles Magazine*, approached the Rebbe as he distributed dollars. "On the occasion of your 90th birthday," Erem told the Rebbe, "we are publishing a special issue . . . What is your message to the world?"

"Ninety," the Rebbe replied, "is the value of the Hebrew letter tzaddik. The meaning of the word 'tzaddik,' is 'a truly righteous person,' [the highest spiritual attribution]. And that is a direct indication that it is in the power of every Jew to become a real tzaddik, a righteous person, and indeed they should do so for many years, 'until 120' (for the rest of their life)."[24]

This message, the Rebbe added, applies equally to non-Jews as well.

Traditionally, the word tzaddik has been applied exclusively to saintly leaders of exceptional spiritual stature, but in this instance, and increasingly towards the end of his life, the Rebbe applied it to everyone.

It is no longer enough for an elite caste of holy leaders to tend to G-d's garden. We must, each and every one of us, accept G-d's invitation to play our role in the final phase of the meta-historical drama of world redemption.

This democratization of Divine responsibility is precisely the paradigmatic shift the Rebbe sought to inspire and strengthen within each individual, the Jewish People, and humanity as a whole.

From the redemptive dream of a precocious child to a daring vision of cosmic renewal, the stories and teachings explored throughout the course of this book all in some sense culminate in the Rebbe's clarion call to action:

Our generation is uniquely positioned to calibrate the conditions for monumental shift. The future is up to each one of us. Become the tzaddik you already are. The world is G-d's garden; we are each its humble gardeners. Care for it and beautify it in the way that only you can.

We are no longer waiting for Moshiach, Moshiach is waiting for us!

A new day is approaching; let's awaken the dawn.

ENDNOTES

[1] *Sippurim Meichadar HaRabbi*, p. 76.
[2] Dated 11 Nissan 5716, the Rebbe's 54th birthday. *Igrot Kodesh*, vol. 12, p. 414.
[3] *Mechilta* of R. Yishmael, Bo 14.
[4] See *Sefer Hasichot* 5751, vol. 2, p. 520 ff.
[5] As told by R. Tzvi Telsner.
[6] *Sefer Hasichot* 5751, vol. 2, p. 595.
[7] Jeremiah 31:22.
[8] www.time.com/magazine/us/5087338/january-15th-2018-vol-191-no-1-u-s/
[9] 3:5.
[10] Isaiah 27:16.
[11] See *Torat Menachem—Sefer Hamaamarim* 5728, p. 10.
[12] Isaiah 27:13.
[13] Habakkuk 2:14.
[14] time.com/magazine/us/5087338/january-15th-2018-vol-191-no-1-u-s.
[15] www.theguardian.com/global-development-professionals-network/2017/feb/14/despite-many-obstacles-the-world-is-getting-better
[16] ourworldindata.org/nuclear-weapons
[17] www.medicalnewstoday.com/articles/291090.php
[18] www.sciencedaily.com/releases/2010/05/100513123720.htm
[19] 35:5-6.
[20] A free translation of this talk was published in *Sichos in English*, vol. 51 (Brooklyn, N.Y.: SIE). See "Swords into Plowshares: Disarmament as in Isaiah," 5752 (1992).
[21] 2:4.
[22] For an English translation of the discourse see *Nurturing Faith* (Brooklyn, N.Y.: Kehot, 2005).
[23] A free translation of this talk was published in *Sichos in English*, vol. 48 (Brooklyn, N.Y.: SIE). See "Helping to Bring Mashiach," 5751 (1991).
[24] Eli Rubin, "Everyone a Tzaddik: Miracles, Transmission and Ascent," www.Chabad.org/2619824.

The World Is Actually Becoming a Better Place—And This Is the Data to Prove It (Excerpt)

By Julius Probst

Swedish academic Hans Rosling has identified a worrying trend: not only do many people across advanced economies have no idea that the world is becoming a much better place, but they actually even think the opposite. This is no wonder when the news focuses on reporting catastrophes, terrorist attacks, wars and famines.

Who wants to hear about the fact that every day some 200,000 people around the world are lifted above the US$2-a-day poverty line? Or that more than 300,000 people a day get access to electricity and clean water for the first time every day? These stories of people in low-income countries simply doesn't make for exciting news coverage. But, as Rosling pointed out in his book *Factfulness*, it's important to put all the bad news in perspective.

While it is true that globalization has put some downward pressure on middle-class wages in advanced economies in recent decades, it has also helped lift hundreds of millions of people above the global poverty line—a development that has mostly occurred in South-East Asia.

The recent rise of populism that has swept across Western countries, with Trump, Brexit, and the election of populists in Hungary and Italy, among various other factors, is thus of great concern if we care about global welfare. Globalization is the only way forward to ensure that economic prosperity is shared among all countries and not only a select few advanced economies.

While some people glorify the past, one of the big facts of economic history is that until quite recently a significant part of the world population has lived under quite miserable conditions—and this has been true throughout most of human history. The following seven charts show how the world has become a much better place compared to just a few decades ago.

1. Life expectancy continues to rise

Even during the Industrial Revolution, average life expectancy across European countries did not exceed around 35 years. This does not imply that most people died in their late 30s or even 40s, since it was mostly very high levels of child mortality rates that pulled down the average. Women dying in childbirth was obviously a big problem too. So were some common diseases such as smallpox and the plague, for example, which now have been completely eradicated in high-income countries.

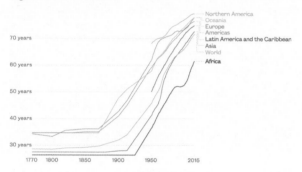

2. Child mortality continues to fall

More than a century ago, child mortality rates were still exceeding 10 per cent—even in high-income countries such as the US and the UK. But thanks to modern medicine, and better public safety in general, this number has been reduced to almost zero in rich countries.

Plus, developing economies like India and Brazil now have much lower child mortality rates today than advanced economies had at similar income levels about one century ago.

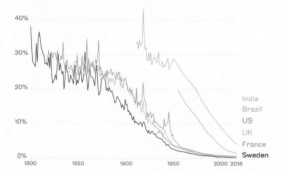

[...]

4. GDP growth has accelerated in developed countries

Technological leaders, the US and Western Europe, have been growing at about 2 per cent per year, on average, for the past 150 years. This means that real income levels roughly double every 36 years.

While there were many long-lasting ups and downs, like the Great Depression or the recent Great Recession, the constancy of the long-run growth rate is actually quite miraculous. Low-income countries, including China and India, have been growing at a significantly faster pace in recent decades and are quickly catching up to the west. A 10 per cent growth rate over a prolonged period means that income levels double roughly every seven years. It is obviously good news if prosperity is more shared across the globe.

[...]

6. More people are living in democracies

Throughout most of human history people lived under oppressive non-democratic regimes. As of today, about half of the human population is living in a democracy. Out of those still living in autocracies, 90 per cent are in China. While the country has recently moved in the other direction, there is reason to believe that continued economic development might eventually lead to democratization (according to modernization theory).

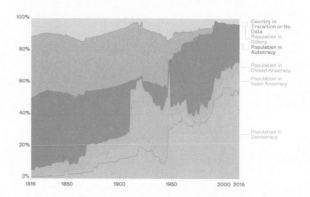

7. Conflicts are on the decline

Throughout history, the world has been riven by conflict. In fact, at least two of the world's largest powers have been at war with each other more than 50 per cent of the time since about 1500.

While the early 20th century was especially brutal with two world wars in rapid succession, the postwar period has been very peaceful. For the first time ever, there has been no war or conflict in Western Europe in about three generations, and international organizations including the EU and the UN have led to a more stable world.

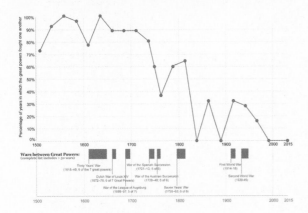

ENDNOTES

[1] Riley (2005), Clio Infra (2015), and UN Population Division (2019)

[2] Gapminder (2017) & UN IGME (2018)

[3] Gapminder (2017)

[4] Maddison Project Database (2018)

[5] Gapminder

[6] World Population by Political Regime they live in (OWID (2016))

[7] Steven Pinker (2011) - The Better Angels of Our Nature: Why Violence Has Declined. Based on data from Levyt, J.S., & Thompson, W.R. (2011) - The Arc of War

© Julius Probst/*The Independent* (London: January 4, 2019)

2

WHO NEEDS A REDEMPTION?

Though it will solve every speck of ill in the world, the idea of Redemption is not a response to strife. Rather, it's an independent and foundational tenet of Jewish belief. Where does it fit within the bigger story of Creation?

I. THE PLACE OF MASHIACH IN JUDAISM

The Jewish concept of Redemption is not just about world peace, universal prosperity, and curing disease. There are also the prophecies describing the rebuilding of the Holy Temple in Jerusalem, the return of the Jewish people to their homeland, and that all of humankind will recognize G-d and serve Him. This explains the prominent place the belief in the Redemption has in Jewish belief and practice.

TEXT 1

The Restoration of the House of David

Maimonides, *Mishneh Torah*, Laws of Kings 11:1, 4 and 12:5

**RABBI MOSHE
BEN MAIMON
(MAIMONIDES, RAMBAM)
1135–1204**

Halachist,
philosopher,
author, and physician.
Maimonides was born
in Córdoba, Spain. After
the conquest of Córdoba
by the Almohads, he fled
Spain and eventually
settled in Cairo, Egypt.
There, he became the
leader of the Jewish
community and served
as court physician to
the vizier of Egypt.
He is most noted for
authoring the *Mishneh
Torah*, an encyclopedic
arrangement of
Jewish law; and for his
philosophical work,
Guide for the Perplexed.
His rulings on Jewish
law are integral to
the formation of
halachic consensus.

הַמֶּלֶךְ הַמָּשִׁיחַ עָתִיד לַעֲמֹד וּלְהַחֲזִיר מַלְכוּת דָּוִד לְיָשְׁנָהּ
לַמֶּמְשָׁלָה הָרִאשׁוֹנָה. וּבוֹנֶה הַמִּקְדָּשׁ וּמְקַבֵּץ נִדְחֵי
יִשְׂרָאֵל. וְחוֹזְרִין כָּל הַמִּשְׁפָּטִים בְּיָמָיו כְּשֶׁהָיוּ מִקֹּדֶם . . .

וְאִם יַעֲמֹד מֶלֶךְ מִבֵּית דָּוִד הוֹגֶה בַּתּוֹרָה וְעוֹסֵק בְּמִצְוֹת
כְּדָוִד אָבִיו. כְּפִי תּוֹרָה שֶׁבִּכְתָב וְשֶׁבְּעַל פֶּה. וְיָכֹף כָּל יִשְׂרָאֵל
לֵילֵךְ בָּהּ וּלְחַזֵּק בִּדְקָהּ. וְיִלְחֵם מִלְחֲמוֹת ה'. הֲרֵי זֶה בְּחֶזְקַת
שֶׁהוּא מָשִׁיחַ. (אִם עָשָׂה וְהִצְלִיחַ וּבָנָה מִקְדָּשׁ בִּמְקוֹמוֹ
וְקִבֵּץ נִדְחֵי יִשְׂרָאֵל הֲרֵי זֶה מָשִׁיחַ בְּוַדַּאי. וִיתַקֵּן אֶת הָעוֹלָם
כֻּלּוֹ לַעֲבֹד אֶת ה' בְּיַחַד שֶׁנֶּאֱמַר כִּי אָז אֶהְפֹּךְ אֶל עַמִּים
שָׂפָה בְרוּרָה לִקְרֹא כֻלָּם בְּשֵׁם ה' לְעָבְדוֹ שְׁכֶם אֶחָד) . . .

וּבְאוֹתוֹ הַזְּמַן לֹא יִהְיֶה שָׁם לֹא רָעָב וְלֹא מִלְחָמָה. וְלֹא
קִנְאָה וְתַחֲרוּת. שֶׁהַטּוֹבָה תִּהְיֶה מֻשְׁפַּעַת הַרְבֵּה. וְכָל
הַמַּעֲדַנִּים מְצוּיִין כֶּעָפָר. וְלֹא יִהְיֶה עֵסֶק כָּל הָעוֹלָם
אֶלָּא לָדַעַת אֶת ה' בִּלְבַד . . . שֶׁנֶּאֱמַר (יְשַׁעְיָהוּ יא, ט)
"כִּי מָלְאָה הָאָרֶץ דֵּעָה אֶת ה' כַּמַּיִם לַיָּם מְכַסִּים".

The king Mashiach is destined to arise and
restore the sovereignty of the House of David
to its former rule. He will build the Temple
and gather the dispersed of Israel. In his days,
all the Torah's laws will be reinstated. . . .

When there arises a king from the House of David who studies Torah and fulfills the *mitzvot* like his ancestor David, in accordance with both the Written Torah and the Oral Torah; and he will influence all of Israel to walk in its ways and repair its breaches; and he will fight the battles of G-d, he is presumed to be Mashiach. If he does this and is successful, and he builds the Temple in its place and gathers the dispersed of Israel, then he is definitely Mashiach. He will then improve the entire world to serve G-d together, as it is written, "Then I will transform the nations to a pure language, that they will all call upon the name of G-d and serve Him with one purpose" (ZEPHANIAH 3:9). . . .

In that era, there will be no famine or war, no envy or competition. For goodness will be in abundance, and all delights will be as commonplace as dust. The sole occupation of the world will be only to know G-d. . . . As it is written, "The earth will be filled with the knowledge of G-d as waters cover the sea" (ISAIAH 11:9).

TEXT 2

Entreat and Repeat

Siddur, the Amidah

SIDDUR

The siddur is the Jewish prayer book. It was originally developed by the sages of the Great Assembly in the 4th century BCE, and later reconstructed by Rabban Gamliel after the destruction of the Second Temple. Various authorities continued to add prayers, from then until contemporary times. It includes praise of G-d, requests for personal and national needs, selections from the Bible, and much else. Various Jewish communities have slightly different versions of the siddur.

Second Blessing

אַתָּה גִבּוֹר לְעוֹלָם אֲדֹנָ-י, מְחַיֶּה מֵתִים אַתָּה, רַב לְהוֹשִׁיעַ.

מוֹרִיד הַטָּל. מְכַלְכֵּל חַיִּים בְּחֶסֶד, מְחַיֶּה מֵתִים בְּרַחֲמִים רַבִּים, סוֹמֵךְ נוֹפְלִים, וְרוֹפֵא חוֹלִים, וּמַתִּיר אֲסוּרִים, וּמְקַיֵּם אֱמוּנָתוֹ לִישֵׁנֵי עָפָר. מִי כָמוֹךָ בַּעַל גְּבוּרוֹת וּמִי דוֹמֶה לָּךְ, מֶלֶךְ מֵמִית וּמְחַיֶּה וּמַצְמִיחַ יְשׁוּעָה: וְנֶאֱמָן אַתָּה לְהַחֲיוֹת מֵתִים. בָּרוּךְ אַתָּה ה', מְחַיֶּה הַמֵּתִים.

You are mighty forever, my L-rd; You resurrect the dead; You are powerful to save.

He causes the dew to descend. He sustains the living with lovingkindness, resurrects the dead with great mercy, supports the falling, heals the sick, releases the bound, and fulfills His trust to those who sleep in the dust. Who is like You, mighty One! And who can be compared to You, King, who brings death and restores life, and causes deliverance to spring forth! You are trustworthy to revive the dead. Blessed are You L-rd, who revives the dead.

Seventh Blessing

רְאֵה נָא בְעָנְיֵנוּ וְרִיבָה רִיבֵנוּ, וּגְאָלֵנוּ מְהֵרָה לְמַעַן שְׁמֶךָ, כִּי אֵ-ל גּוֹאֵל חָזָק אָתָּה. בָּרוּךְ אַתָּה ה', גּוֹאֵל יִשְׂרָאֵל.

O behold our affliction and wage our battle; redeem us speedily for the sake of Your Name, for You G-d are the mighty Redeemer. Blessed are You L-rd, Redeemer of Israel.

Tenth Blessing

תְּקַע בְּשׁוֹפָר גָּדוֹל לְחֵרוּתֵנוּ, וְשָׂא נֵס לְקַבֵּץ גָּלֻיּוֹתֵינוּ, וְקַבְּצֵנוּ יַחַד מֵאַרְבַּע כַּנְפוֹת הָאָרֶץ לְאַרְצֵנוּ. בָּרוּךְ אַתָּה ה', מְקַבֵּץ נִדְחֵי עַמּוֹ יִשְׂרָאֵל.

Sound the great shofar for our freedom, raise a banner to gather our exiles, and bring us together from the four corners of the earth into our land. Blessed are You L-rd, who gathers the dispersed of His people Israel.

What will it be like to live in a spiritual utopia? **Rabbi Meir Levinger** explores the topic in "Mashiach: A Spiritual Revolution": *myjli.com/canhappen*

Eleventh Blessing

הָשִׁיבָה שׁוֹפְטֵינוּ כְּבָרִאשׁוֹנָה וְיוֹעֲצֵינוּ כְּבַתְּחִלָּה, וְהָסֵר מִמֶּנּוּ
יָגוֹן וַאֲנָחָה, וּמְלוֹךְ עָלֵינוּ אַתָּה ה' לְבַדְּךָ בְּחֶסֶד וּבְרַחֲמִים,
בְּצֶדֶק וּבְמִשְׁפָּט. בָּרוּךְ אַתָּה ה', מֶלֶךְ אוֹהֵב צְדָקָה וּמִשְׁפָּט.

Restore our judges as in former times, and our
counselors as of yore; remove from us sorrow
and sighing; and reign over us, You alone, O
L-rd, with kindness and compassion, with
righteousness and justice. Blessed are You L-rd,
King who loves righteousness and justice.

Fourteenth Blessing

וְלִירוּשָׁלַיִם עִירְךָ בְּרַחֲמִים תָּשׁוּב, וְתִשְׁכּוֹן בְּתוֹכָהּ כַּאֲשֶׁר
דִּבַּרְתָּ, וְכִסֵּא דָוִד עַבְדְּךָ מְהֵרָה בְּתוֹכָהּ תָּכִין, וּבְנֵה אוֹתָהּ
בְּקָרוֹב בְּיָמֵינוּ בִּנְיַן עוֹלָם. בָּרוּךְ אַתָּה ה', בּוֹנֵה יְרוּשָׁלָיִם.

Return in mercy to Jerusalem Your city, and dwell
therein as You have promised; speedily establish
therein the throne of David Your servant, and
rebuild it, soon in our days, as an everlasting edifice.
Blessed are You L-rd, who rebuilds Jerusalem.

Fifteenth Blessing

אֶת צֶמַח דָּוִד עַבְדְּךָ מְהֵרָה תַצְמִיחַ, וְקַרְנוֹ תָּרוּם בִּישׁוּעָתֶךָ, כִּי לִישׁוּעָתְךָ קִוִּינוּ כָּל הַיּוֹם. בָּרוּךְ אַתָּה ה', מַצְמִיחַ קֶרֶן יְשׁוּעָה.

Speedily cause the scion of David Your servant to flourish, and increase his power by Your salvation, for we hope for Your salvation all day. Blessed are You L-rd, who causes the power of salvation to flourish.

Seventeenth Blessing

רְצֵה ה' אֱלֹקֵינוּ בְּעַמְּךָ יִשְׂרָאֵל וְלִתְפִלָּתָם שְׁעֵה, וְהָשֵׁב הָעֲבוֹדָה לִדְבִיר בֵּיתֶךָ, וְאִשֵּׁי יִשְׂרָאֵל וּתְפִלָּתָם בְּאַהֲבָה תְקַבֵּל בְּרָצוֹן, וּתְהִי לְרָצוֹן תָּמִיד עֲבוֹדַת יִשְׂרָאֵל עַמֶּךָ. וְתֶחֱזֶינָה עֵינֵינוּ בְּשׁוּבְךָ לְצִיּוֹן בְּרַחֲמִים. בָּרוּךְ אַתָּה ה', הַמַּחֲזִיר שְׁכִינָתוֹ לְצִיּוֹן.

Look with favor, L-rd our G-d, on Your people Israel, and pay heed to their prayer; restore the service to Your Sanctuary, and accept with love and favor Israel's fire-offerings and prayer; and may the service of Your people Israel always find favor. May our eyes behold Your return to Zion in mercy. Blessed are You L-rd, who restores His Divine Presence to Zion.

FIGURE 2.1

Observances Related to the Redemption (partial list)

DAILY PRAYERS

Seven of the nineteen blessings of the Amidah are prayers for Mashiach and the future Redemption.

Numerous other requests for Mashiach appear in the course of our prayers.

MEALTIMES

The ritual "washing of the hands" before eating bread is because of the laws of ritual purity relating to the Holy Temple; at each meal, we anticipate that these laws may take immediate effect.

Special preference is given to the fruits of the "seven kinds" with which the Holy Land is blessed (listed in Deuteronomy 8:8).

The chapter of Psalms recited at the end of the meal—Psalm 137 ("By the rivers of Babylon . . .") on weekdays, and Psalm 126 ("A song of Ascents. When G-d will return the exiles of Zion . . .") on Shabbat and special days—speak of our yearning for Redemption.

Grace after Meals includes prayers for the rebuilding of Jerusalem.

THE JEWISH CALENDAR

Three weeks of the Jewish year, from 17 Tamuz to 9 Av, are dedicated to mourning the destruction of the Holy Temple and praying for the Redemption.

The future Redemption is a dominant theme of the Passover *seder* (items on the *seder* plate, Elijah's cup, etc.) and of the eighth day of Passover.

WEDDINGS

One of the "seven blessings" recited under the wedding canopy and throughout the week of celebration that follows a wedding is centered on the prophecy of Isaiah (33:10–11), "It shall yet be heard . . . in the cities of Judah and in the streets of Jerusalem . . . the voice of happiness and the voice of joy, the voice of a bridegroom and the voice of a bride."

Many have the custom of breaking a glass at the conclusion of the wedding ceremony as a remembrance of the destruction of the Holy Temple.

DEATH AND MOURNING

Many of the prayers and observances associated with a funeral and burial affirm our belief in the future Resurrection of the Dead.

The traditional words of consolation said to a mourner are, "May G-d console you amongst the other mourners of Zion and Jerusalem."

FIGURE 2.2

Maimonides's Thirteen "Foundations" of Jewish Faith

1 There is a G-d Who is perfect in every way, and is not dependent on any other existence for anything. All other existences were created by G-d and are utterly dependent upon Him for their existence.

2 G-d is absolutely one. There are no composite parts or aspects within His being.

3 G-d is not physical, nor does He possess any physical properties.

4 G-d is timeless and eternal.

5 It is imperative to worship G-d, obey His commandments, and not worship any other power or entity.

6 G-d communicates to humanity through prophecy.

7 Moses's prophecy was true, and he is the chief of all the prophets.

8 The Torah is of divine origin.

9 G-d is not physical, nor does He possess any physical properties.

10 G-d knows and concerns Himself with everything that a person does.

11 G-d rewards those who do good and punishes those who do evil.

12 **The belief in and anticipation of the coming of Mashiach.**

13 **The belief in the future Resurrection of the Dead.**

QUESTION

Why is the belief in and yearning for Mashiach so central to Jewish life? What makes the belief in Mashiach so fundamental to Judaism?

POGROM (DETAIL)
(Jewish refugees after a pogrom in Russia) c. 1915, artist unknown, oil on cardboard, Judaica Collection Max Berger, Vienna

II. A SOLUTION TO A NOT-YET-EXISTENT PROBLEM

Is the Jewish belief in Redemption a response to our nation's millennia-long displacement and persecution? The evidence indicates otherwise.

TEXT 3

The Redemption Promise

Deuteronomy 30:3–5, 8

וְשָׁב ה' אֱלֹקֶיךָ אֶת שְׁבוּתְךָ וְרִחֲמֶךָ, וְשָׁב וְקִבֶּצְךָ מִכָּל
הָעַמִּים אֲשֶׁר הֱפִיצְךָ ה' אֱלֹקֶיךָ שָׁמָּה. אִם יִהְיֶה נִדַּחֲךָ
בִּקְצֵה הַשָּׁמָיִם, מִשָּׁם יְקַבֶּצְךָ ה' אֱלֹקֶיךָ וּמִשָּׁם יִקָּחֶךָ.

וֶהֱבִיאֲךָ ה' אֱלֹקֶיךָ אֶל הָאָרֶץ אֲשֶׁר יָרְשׁוּ אֲבֹתֶיךָ
וִירִשְׁתָּהּ, וְהֵיטִבְךָ וְהִרְבְּךָ מֵאֲבֹתֶיךָ... וְאַתָּה תָשׁוּב
וְשָׁמַעְתָּ בְּקוֹל ה' וְעָשִׂיתָ אֶת כָּל מִצְוֹתָיו.

G-d will return your exiles, and He will have mercy upon you. He will return and gather you from all the nations amongst whom G-d has scattered you. If your outcasts will be at the ends of the heavens, from there G-d will gather you, from there He will take you.

G-d will bring you into the land your ancestors possessed, and you will possess it; and He will do you good and multiply you, more than your ancestors. . . . And you will return and listen to the voice of G-d, and fulfill all His commandments.

So Mashiach comes . . . then what? Listen in on a conversation between **Rabbi Manis Friedman** and **Dr. Michael Chighel**: *myjli.com/canhappen*

TEXT 4A

The Hovering Spirit

Genesis 1:1–2

בְּרֵאשִׁית בָּרָא אֱלֹקִים, אֵת הַשָּׁמַיִם וְאֵת הָאָרֶץ.
וְהָאָרֶץ הָיְתָה תֹהוּ וָבֹהוּ וְחֹשֶׁךְ עַל פְּנֵי תְהוֹם,
וְרוּחַ אֱלֹקִים מְרַחֶפֶת עַל פְּנֵי הַמָּיִם.

In the beginning, G-d created the heavens and the earth. And the earth was chaotic and desolate, and darkness was on the face of the watery depths; and the spirit of G-d hovered upon the waters.

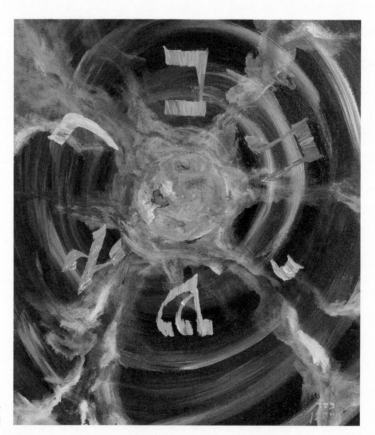

BEREISHIT
Yehoshua Wiseman, Israel

TEXT 4B

Foretelling the End at the Beginning

Rabbeinu Bechaye, Genesis 1:1–2

RABBI BACHYA BEN ASHER IBN HALAWA (RABBEINU BECHAYE) C. 1255–1340

Biblical commentator. Rabbeinu Bechaye lived in Spain and was a disciple of Rabbi Shlomo ben Aderet, known as Rashba. He is best known for his multifaceted commentary on the Torah, which interprets the text on literal, Midrashic, philosophical, and kabbalistic levels. Rabbeinu Bechaye also wrote *Kad Hakemach*, a work on philosophy and ethics.

"וְרוּחַ אֱלֹקים", זֶה רוּחוֹ שֶׁל מָשִׁיחַ.

וּבֵאוּר הַמִּדְרָשׁ הַזֶּה, כִּי ה' יִתְבָּרֵךְ בְּפַרְשָׁה זוֹ "מַגִּיד מֵרֵאשִׁית אַחֲרִית". וְהַכָּתוּב כִּוֵּן לִרְמוֹז סוֹף הַזְּמַן בִּתְחִלַּת הַזְּמַן. לְהוֹרוֹת כִּי תַכְלִית כַּוָּנַת הַבְּרִיאָה הִיא לִימוֹת הַמָּשִׁיחַ. וְזֶהוּ תְּחִלַּת הַמַּחֲשָׁבָה סוֹף הַמַּעֲשֶׂה.

"The spirit of G-d [hovered upon the waters]—this is the soul of Mashiach" (MIDRASH, *BEREISHIT RABAH* 2:4).

The meaning of this Midrash is: In this passage, G-d is "foretelling the end at the beginning" (ISAIAH 46:10). The Torah's intention is to indicate the end of time at the very beginning of time, to teach us that the ultimate purpose of G-d's Creation of the world is the days of Mashiach. Thus, the original thought is actualized in the conclusion of the work.

FIGURE 2.3

Recap

THE CONCEPT OF REDEMPTION:

 is central to Jewish prayer and practice,

 is a central pillar of the Jewish faith,

 predates Exile—it is not a response to our nation's displacement or our historic suffering and persecution, and

 predates the Creation of the world!

III. WHY DID G-D MAKE A WORLD?

To understand why the Redemption is so central to Judaism, we need to wade deep into the ocean of ontology and explore matters that are at the mysterious core of everything. Let's take the plunge!

Here are some questions to start:

Why did G-d create this world?

The mystics speak of numerous other spiritual "worlds" that comprise the "Creation System." Why were *they* created?

What is the definition of a *world*?

How are the other worlds different from ours and from each other?

TEXT 5

The Primordial Desire

Rabbi Shne'ur Zalman of Liadi, *Tanya*, chapter 36

RABBI SHNE'UR ZALMAN OF LIADI (ALTER REBBE) 1745–1812

Chasidic rebbe, halachic authority, and founder of the Chabad movement. The Alter Rebbe was born in Liozna, Belarus, and was among the principal students of the Magid of Mezeritch. His numerous works include the *Tanya*, an early classic containing the fundamentals of Chabad Chasidism; and *Shulchan Aruch HaRav,* an expanded and reworked code of Jewish law.

וְהִנֵּה מוּדַעַת זֹאת מַאֲמַר רַזַ"ל שֶׁתַּכְלִית
בְּרִיאַת עוֹלָם הַזֶּה הוּא שֶׁנִּתְאַוֶּה הַקָּדוֹשׁ בָּרוּךְ
הוּא לִהְיוֹת לוֹ דִירָה בַּתַּחְתּוֹנִים . . .

וְנוֹדַע שֶׁיְּמוֹת הַמָּשִׁיחַ וּבִפְרָט כְּשֶׁיִּחְיוּ הַמֵּתִים הֵם תַּכְלִית
וּשְׁלֵימוּת בְּרִיאַת עוֹלָם הַזֶּה שֶׁלְּכָךְ נִבְרָא מִתְּחִילָתוֹ.

As is known, the sages have said that the purpose of the creation of this world is that "G-d desired that He should have a home in the lowly world." . . .

It is [also] known that the days of Mashiach, and especially the time of the Resurrection of the Dead, are the fulfillment and culmination of the creation of this world, and the purpose for which it was originally created.

Mrs. Shimona Tzukernik
on how to "Actualize the
Potential within Existence":
myjli.com/canhappen

TEXT 6

The Purpose of It All

Rabbi Shne'ur Zalman of Liadi, *Tanya*, chapter 33

וְזֶה כָּל הָאָדָם וְתַכְלִית בְּרִיאָתוֹ וּבְרִיאַת כָּל הָעוֹלָמוֹת
עֶלְיוֹנִים וְתַחְתּוֹנִים לִהְיוֹת לוֹ דִירָה זוֹ בַּתַּחְתּוֹנִים.

This is what the human being is all about;
this is the purpose of the human being's
creation, and of the creation of all the worlds,
both the lofty and the lowly: that G-d should
have this home in the lowly world.

THE MISHKAN
2015, Baruch Nachshon,
acrylic on canvas, Hebron,
The artist's archive,
nachshonart.com

Defining the Term "Lowest"

Rabbi Shne'ur Zalman of Liadi, *Tanya*, chapter 36

וְהִנֵּה לֹא שַׁיָּיךְ לְפָנָיו יִתְבָּרֵךְ בְּחִינַת מַעְלָה וּמַטָּה
כִּי הוּא יִתְבָּרֵךְ מְמַלֵּא כָּל עָלְמִין בְּשָׁוֶה.

אֶלָּא בִּיאוּר הָעִנְיָן כִּי קוֹדֶם שֶׁנִּבְרָא הָעוֹלָם הָיָה הוּא לְבַדּוֹ
יִתְבָּרֵךְ יָחִיד וּמְיוּחָד וּמְמַלֵּא כָּל הַמָּקוֹם הַזֶּה שֶׁבָּרָא בּוֹ הָעוֹלָם.
וְגַם עַתָּה כֵּן הוּא לְפָנָיו יִתְבָּרֵךְ רַק שֶׁהַשִּׁנּוּי הוּא אֶל הַמְקַבְּלִים
חַיּוּתוֹ וְאוֹרוֹ יִתְבָּרֵךְ שֶׁמְּקַבְּלִים עַל יְדֵי לְבוּשִׁים רַבִּים הַמְכַסִּים
וּמַסְתִּירִים אוֹרוֹ יִתְבָּרֵךְ כְּדִכְתִיב כִּי לֹא יִרְאַנִי הָאָדָם וָחָי". . .

וְזֶהוּ עִנְיַן הִשְׁתַּלְשְׁלוּת הָעוֹלָמוֹת וִירִידָתָם מִמַּדְרֵגָה לְמַדְרֵגָה
עַל יְדֵי רִיבּוּי הַלְּבוּשִׁים הַמַסְתִּירִים הָאוֹר וְהַחַיּוּת שֶׁמְּמֶנּוּ
יִתְבָּרֵךְ עַד שֶׁנִּבְרָא עוֹלָם הַזֶּה הַגַּשְׁמִי וְהַחוּמְרִי מַמָּשׁ וְהוּא
הַתַּחְתּוֹן בַּמַּדְרֵגָה שֶׁאֵין תַּחְתּוֹן לְמַטָּה מִמֶּנּוּ בְּעִנְיַן הֶסְתֵּר
אוֹרוֹ יִתְבָּרֵךְ וְחֹשֶׁךְ כָּפוּל וּמְכוּפָּל עַד שֶׁהוּא מָלֵא קְלִיפּוֹת
וְסִטְרָא אַחֲרָא שֶׁהֵן נֶגֶד ה' מַמָּשׁ לוֹמַר אֲנִי וְאַפְסִי עוֹד.

וְהִנֵּה תַּכְלִית הִשְׁתַּלְשְׁלוּת הָעוֹלָמוֹת וִירִידָתָם מִמַּדְרֵגָה
לְמַדְרֵגָה אֵינוֹ בִּשְׁבִיל עוֹלָמוֹת הָעֶלְיוֹנִים הוֹאִיל וְלָהֶם יְרִידָה
מֵאוֹר פָּנָיו יִתְבָּרֵךְ אֶלָּא הַתַּכְלִית הוּא עוֹלָם הַזֶּה הַתַּחְתּוֹן.

שֶׁכָּךְ עָלָה בִּרְצוֹנוֹ יִתְבָּרֵךְ לִהְיוֹת נַחַת רוּחַ לְפָנָיו יִתְבָּרֵךְ
כַּד אִתְכַּפְיָא סִטְרָא אַחֲרָא וְאִתְהַפֵּךְ חֲשׁוֹכָא לִנְהוֹרָא
שֶׁיָּאִיר אוֹר ה' אֵין סוֹף בָּרוּךְ הוּא בִּמְקוֹם הַחֹשֶׁךְ וְהַסִּטְרָא
אַחֲרָא שֶׁל כָּל עוֹלָם הַזֶּה כּוּלּוֹ בְּיֶתֶר שְׂאֵת וְיֶתֶר עָז
וְיִתְרוֹן אוֹר מִן הַחֹשֶׁךְ מֵהֶאָרָתוֹ בְּעוֹלָמוֹת עֶלְיוֹנִים.

Now, in regard to G-d, the distinctions of "higher" and "lower" do not apply, as G-d pervades all realms of existence equally. But the explanation of the matter is as follows:

Before the world was created, G-d was exclusively and singularly one, and He pervaded the entire "space" in which He created the world. Insofar as G-d is concerned, it is still the same now. The change [brought about by the divine act of Creation] relates only to those on the receiving end of the vitality and energy that G-d infuses into creation, which they receive via the many "garments" that conceal and obscure the divine radiance. As it is written, "For no human can see Me and live" (EXODUS 33:20). . . .

This is the concept of the *hishtalshelut*, the downward descent of the worlds, level after level, by means of the multitude of "garments" that conceal the energy and vitality that emanate from G-d—until this physical and materialistic world was created, which is the lowest in degree, of which there is none lower in regard to the concealment of G-d's radiance. [This is a world] of doubled and redoubled darkness, to the extent that it is full of unholiness—namely, elements that actually oppose G-d, declaring "I am, and there is nothing else besides me."

Clearly, the purpose of the *hishtalshelut* of the worlds and their descent, level after level, is not for the sake of the higher, spiritual worlds, as they constitute a descent from the radiance of the divine presence. Rather, the ultimate purpose of creation is this lowest world.

For such was G-d's desire: that He should derive satisfaction when the forces opposing G-dliness are overcome and when darkness is transformed into light. The result is that the infinite radiance of G-d is revealed within this physical world, the place of darkness and the opposing forces, with "the advantage of the light that comes from the darkness" (ECCLESIASTES 2:13)—with an even greater intensity than its revelation in the higher worlds.

FIGURE 2.4   The Four Worlds

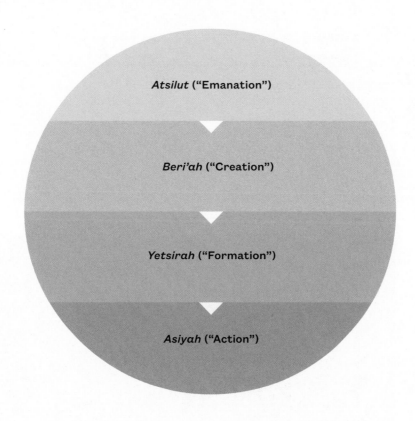

FIGURE 2.5

The Meaning of "World"

עוֹלָם   הֶעְלֵם

olam—"world"   *helem*—"concealment"

THERE IS NO OTHER BESIDES HIM (G-D)
2013, Baruch Nachshon, acrylic on canvas, Hebron, The artist's archive, nachshonart.com

TEXT 8

If the Eye Were Allowed to See . . .

Rabbi Shne'ur Zalman of Liadi, *Tanya*,
Shaar Hayichud Veha'emunah, chapter 3

וּמַה שֶּׁכָּל נִבְרָא וְנִפְעָל נִרְאֶה לָנוּ לְיֵשׁ וּמַמָּשׁוּת זֶהוּ
מֵחֲמַת שֶׁאֵין אָנוּ מַשִּׂיגִים וְרוֹאִים בְּעֵינֵי בָּשָׂר אֶת כֹּחַ
ה' וְרוּחַ פִּיו שֶׁבַּנִּבְרָא אֲבָל אִילוּ נִיתְּנָה רְשׁוּת לָעַיִן
לִרְאוֹת וּלְהַשִּׂיג אֶת הַחַיּוּת וְרוּחְנִיּוּת שֶׁבְּכָל נִבְרָא
הַשּׁוֹפֵעַ בּוֹ מִמּוֹצָא פִּי ה' וְרוּחַ פִּיו לֹא הָיָה גַּשְׁמִיּוּת
הַנִּבְרָא וְחוּמְרוֹ וּמַמָּשׁוֹ נִרְאֶה כְּלַל לְעֵינֵינוּ . . .

אִם כֵּן אֶפֶס בִּלְעָדוֹ בֶּאֱמֶת.

The fact that every creation and event appears
to us as tangible and real is only because we do
not apprehend and see with our physical eyes
the G-dly energy and divine breath within each
creation. But if the eye were allowed to see and
apprehend the vitality and spirituality being
infused into every creation by the divine utterance
. . . the physicality, materiality, and substance of
that creation would be utterly invisible to us. . . .

As such, there literally is nothing besides Him.

IV. WHAT IMPERFECT PEOPLE GIVE TO A PERFECT G-D

The ultimate objective of G-d's entire creation enterprise is to be found not in the spiritual Heavens, but in this lowly, physical world; not in asceticism and lofty spiritual pursuits, but in physical actions in the here and now. This world is ours to fix; we must reveal the divine truth here, in the least likely of places.

TEXT 9

It Is Not in Heaven

Deuteronomy 30:11, 12, 14

כִּי הַמִּצְוָה הַזֹּאת אֲשֶׁר אָנֹכִי מְצַוְּךָ הַיּוֹם, לֹא נִפְלֵאת הִוא מִמְּךָ וְלֹא רְחֹקָה הִוא. לֹא בַשָּׁמַיִם הִוא, לֵאמֹר מִי יַעֲלֶה לָּנוּ הַשָּׁמַיְמָה וְיִקָּחֶהָ לָּנוּ וְיַשְׁמִעֵנוּ אֹתָהּ וְנַעֲשֶׂנָּה . . .

כִּי קָרוֹב אֵלֶיךָ הַדָּבָר מְאֹד, בְּפִיךָ וּבִלְבָבְךָ לַעֲשֹׂתוֹ.

This mitzvah that I command you this day is not mysterious to you, nor is it far away. It is not in heaven, that you should say, "Who will go up to heaven for us and get it for us, and teach it to us so that we can do it?" . . .

Rather, the matter is very close to you, in your mouth and in your heart, to do it.

If you were perfect in every way—infinite, eternal, and utterly self-sufficient—what would there still be for you to desire?

JODENBREESTRAAT (JEW'S STREET) IN AMSTERDAM
1905, Max Liebermann, Kaiser Wilhelm Museum, Krefeld

TEXT 10

Further Assembly Required

Midrash, *Bereishit Rabah* 11:6 and Rashi, ad loc.

BEREISHIT RABAH

An early rabbinic commentary on the Book of Genesis. This Midrash bears the name of Rabbi Oshiya Rabah (Rabbi Oshiya "the Great"), whose teaching opens this work. This Midrash provides textual exegeses and stories, expounds upon the biblical narrative, and develops and illustrates moral principles. Produced by the sages of the Talmud in the Land of Israel, its use of Aramaic closely resembles that of the Jerusalem Talmud. It was first printed in Constantinople in 1512 together with 4 other Midrashic works on the other 4 books of the Pentateuch.

כָּל מַה שֶׁנִבְרָא בְּשֵׁשֶׁת יְמֵי בְּרֵאשִׁית צְרִיכִין עֲשָׂיָה, כְּגוֹן הַחַרְדָל צָרִיךְ לְמִתּוּק. הַתּוּרְמוּסִים צָרִיךְ לְמִתּוּק. הַחִטִּין צְרִיכִין לְהִטָּחֵן. אֲפִילוּ אָדָם צָרִיךְ תִּיקוּן.

רַשִׁ"י: הֲדָא הוּא דִכְתִיב, "אֲשֶׁר בָּרָא אֱלֹקִים לַעֲשׂוֹת" (בְּרֵאשִׁית ב, ג). "בָּרָא וְעָשָׂה" אֵין כְּתִיב כַּאן, אֶלָּא לוֹמַר שֶׁהַכֹּל צָרִיךְ תִּיקוּן.

Everything that was created in the six days of Creation requires further doing. The mustard seed needs to be tempered, legumes need to be softened, grain needs to be milled. Even the human being requires fixing.

Rashi: This is the meaning of what it says, "[All His work,] which G-d created to make" (GENESIS 2:3). The Torah doesn't say "created and made," [but rather, "created to make"]; this is to teach us that everything requires fixing.

TEXT 11

Uncloaking the Divine

Isaiah 30:20

ISAIAH

Biblical book. The book
of Isaiah contains the
prophecies of Isaiah,
who lived in the 6–7th
centuries BCE. Isaiah's
prophecies contain
stern rebukes for the
personal failings of the
contemporary people of
Judea and the corruption
of its government. The
bulk of the prophecies,
however, are stirring
consolations and
poetic visions of the
future Redemption.

וְלֹא יִכָּנֵף עוֹד מוֹרֶיךָ וְהָיוּ עֵינֶיךָ רֹאוֹת אֶת מוֹרֶיךָ.

No longer shall your Master be cloaked;
your eyes will see your Master.

RECEIVING THE TORAH
2000, Baruch Nachshon,
acrylic on canvas, Hebron,
The artist's archive,
nachshonart.com

KEY POINTS

1   Mashiach is more than a Jewish belief. It is one of the thirteen "foundations" of Judaism, and pervades every area of Jewish observance, Jewish history, and the Jewish consciousness. Judaism sees Mashiach and the future Redemption as the purpose for which G-d created the world, and the goal of everything we do.

2   Like everything in existence, Mashiach has both a "body" and a "soul." The body of Mashiach—its outer physical reality—is the perfect world described by the prophets: a world of universal peace and prosperity. But this is only the external expression of an internal spiritual dynamic that empowers our progress toward this perfected world.

3   The soul of Mashiach is the process by which, through our observance of the *mitzvot*, the world is brought into harmony with its Creator and comes to fully express the goodness and perfection of G-d. Chasidic teaching describes this process as the goal "to make a home for G-d in the lowly world."

4   Our physical world is the "lowliest" in the chain of worlds that constitute G-d's creation. This is not because G-d is any less present in it—the divine reality equally pervades all realms of existence—but because it is here that G-dliness is most concealed, allowing for a world

that can act contrary to the will of its Creator, and even deny G-d's existence. All the flaws and imperfections that plague our world are the product of this concealment.

5   Our task in life is to serve as G-d's "partners in creation" in developing the messianic world. As a perfect being, G-d experiences challenge and achievement through us, when we transform our lives and environment into a "home" that expresses the divine goodness and perfection, resulting in "the advantage of the light that comes from the darkness."

ADDITIONAL READINGS

Faith and Dogma in Judaism

By Rabbi J. David Bleich

RABBI DR. J. DAVID BLEICH
1936–

Expert on Jewish law, ethics, and bioethics. Rabbi Bleich serves as professor of Talmud at the Rabbi Isaac Elchanan Theological Seminary, an affiliate of Yeshiva University, as well as head of its postgraduate institute for the study of Talmudic jurisprudence and family law. A noted author, he is most famous for his 6-volume *Contemporary Halakhic Problems.*

One widespread misconception concerning Judaism is the notion that Judaism is a religion which is not rooted in dogma. The view that Judaism has no dogmas originated with Moses Mendelssohn[1] and subsequently gained wide currency. In some circles this idea has been maintained with such vigor that it has been somewhat jocularly described as itself constituting the "dogma of dogmalessness." Nevertheless, even a superficial acquaintance with the classical works of Jewish philosophy is sufficient to dispel this misconceived notion. To be sure, membership in the community of Israel is not contingent upon a formal creedal affirmation. This, however, does not imply that members of the community of Israel are free to accept or to reject specific articles of faith. Birth as a Jew carries with it unrenounceable obligations and responsibilities, intellectual as well as ritual.

While great stress is placed upon fulfillment of commandments and performance of good deeds, it is a gross error to assume that this stress is accompanied by a diminution of obligations with regard to belief. It is certainly true that lessened concern with explication of the dogmas of Judaism was evidenced during certain periods of Jewish history. This, however, was the result of an unquestioning acceptance of basic principles of faith rather than of disparagement of the role of dogma. In some epochs formulations of essential beliefs were composed by foremost thinkers as a corrective measure designed to rectify this lack of attention; in other ages endeavors designed to explicate the dogmas of Judaism constituted a reaction to creedal formulations on the part of other religions.

The importance of correct belief as a religious obligation is stressed in particular in the writings of Bahya ibn Pakuda. In the introduction to his widely acclaimed *Ḥovot ha-Levavot* (properly translated as *Duties of the Intellect* rather than *Duties of the Heart*),[2] Bahya wrote that the Torah demands of man that he acquire the knowledge requisite for fulfillment of the obligations of the intellect, just as it makes demands of him with regard to fulfillment of the obligations of the physical organs. Nevertheless, he found that his predecessors had devoted themselves in their writings to the discussion and detailed clarification of "duties of the organs" but had neglected to set forth systematically the principles pertaining to the "duties of the intellect" and their ramifications. *Ḥovot ha-Levavot* was composed to fill this lacuna.

The role of dogma as the fulcrum of Judaism was most dramatically highlighted by Maimonides. His *magnum opus*, the *Mishneh Torah*, is devoted to a codification of Jewish law. Yet the opening section of this work is entitled *Hilkhot Yesodei ha-Torah* ("Laws of the Foundations of the Torah") and includes a detailed presentation of Jewish belief together with unequivocal statements declaring acceptance of those beliefs to be binding upon all Jews. Dogma, then, does not stand apart from the normative demands of Judaism but is the *sine qua non* without which other values and practices are bereft of meaning. By incorporating this material in his *Mishneh Torah*, Maimonides demonstrated that basic philosophical beliefs are not simply matters of intellectual curiosity but constitute a branch of *Halakhah*. By placing them at the very beginning of this monumental work he demonstrated that they constitute the most fundamental area of Jewish law. In Judaism, profession of faith is certainly no less significant than overt actions. Contrary to the dictum of Moses Mendelssohn, Judaism imposes obligations not only with regard to action but with regard to religious belief as well.

Bahya demonstrates the existence and the binding nature of obligations incumbent upon the intellect, not simply on the basis of Scripture and tradition, but on the basis of reason as well. Reason dictates that the heart and mind, the choicest and most unique elements of human existence, should not be exempt from obligations imposed in the service of G-d. The manifold references in Scripture to man's duty to love G-d and, moreover, the very existence of a biblical code establishing rules of conduct for mankind implies the existence of a divine lawgiver. While in his *Sefer ha-Mitzvot* Maimonides cites the verse "I am the L-rd your G-d who has brought you out of the land of Egypt" (Exodus 20:2) as constituting the first in his list of 613 commandments, i.e., belief in the existence of a Deity, others among his predecessors failed to do so, not because they did not feel belief in G-d to be incumbent upon each Jew, but because they viewed such belief to be already assumed by, and hence outside of, a system of commandments. There can be no commandment without one who commands. As Bahya puts it, there can be no fulfillment of physical duties without assent of the mind. Accordingly, acceptance of obligatory commandments presumes antecedent acceptance of the existence and authority of G-d.

Nahmanides pursues this argument to its logical conclusion by declaring that a heretic need not anticipate reward even for meritorious deeds which he has performed. In the introduction to his commentary on the Book of Job, Nahmanides writes, "There is no merit in the actions of the evil persons who deny G-d . . . even if they comport themselves in accordance with beautiful and good traits all their days," and proceeds to query how it is possible for them to be the recipients of any form of beneficence. A noted talmudic scholar, the late Rabbi Elchanan Wasserman, although apparently unaware of Nahmanides' comments, categorizes the fulfillment of a commandment on the part of an unbeliever as *mitasek*, an unmeditated, thoughtless performance devoid of religious significance.[3] Commandments, regardless of their intrinsic rationality, are binding and significant in the theological sense only because they constitute the fulfillment of a divine command. Thus, not only the existence of G-d but also the authenticity of revelation as a historical event and the divinity of the entire corpus of Torah are inherent even in those moments of Judaism which concern themselves with action and conduct rather than belief.

To be sure, the formal promulgation of a creed of faith is unknown in Judaism. By the same token, official synods for the comprehensive codification of the laws and regulations governing ceremonial obligations or other areas of human conduct are also virtually unknown to Judaism. Within Judaism, *Halakhah* is hardly monolithic in nature. "Judges and bailiffs shall you appoint for yourselves in all your gates" (Deuteronomy 16:18), commands the Torah. Each community possesses not only the authority but also the obligation to appoint ecclesiastical authorities. In all matters of doubt or dispute their decisions are binding upon all who are subject to their authority. Only when local authorities were unable to resolve a complex question was the question referred to the Great Court sitting in Jerusalem, whose decision was binding upon all of Israel. Inevitably, divergent practices arose in different locales. With the redaction of the Mishnah, and later of the Gemara, binding decisions were promulgated with regard to any matters of

Halakhah which served to establish normative practices in areas which previously had been marked by diversity born of dispute. This, of course, did not preclude subsequent disagreement with regard to other questions which had not been expressly resolved.

Since matters of belief are inherently matters of *Halakhah*, it is not at all surprising that disagreements exist with regard to substantive matters of belief just as is the case in other areas of Jewish law. Thus, while there is unanimity among all rabbinic authorities with regard to the existence of a body of Jewish law that is binding in nature with respect to matters of faith, there is considerable disagreement of opinion with regard to precisely which beliefs are binding and which are not, as well as, in some instances regarding substantive matters of faith.

The concept of the Messiah is one example of a fundamental principle of belief concerning which, at one point in Jewish history, there existed a legitimate divergence of opinion, since resolved normatively. The Gemara, *Sanhedrin* 99a, cites the opinion of the Amora, Rav Hillel, who asserted, "There is no Messiah for Israel." Rashi modifies the literal reading of this dictum by explaining that Rav Hillel did not deny the ultimate redemption of Israel but asserted, rather, that the redemption will be the product of direct divine intervention without the intermediacy of a human agent. Nevertheless, Rav Hillel certainly denied that reestablishment of the monarchy and restoration of the Davidic dynasty are essential components of the process of redemption. Rabbi Moses Sofer quite cogently points out that were such views to be held by a contemporary Jew he would be branded a heretic.[4] Yet, the advancement of this opinion by one of the sages of the Talmud carried with it no theological odium. The explanation is quite simple. Before the authoritative formulation of the *Halakhah* with regard to this belief, Rav Hillel's opinion could be entertained. Following the resolution of the conflict in a manner which negates this theory, normative *Halakhah* demands acceptance of the belief that the redemption will be effected through the agency of a mortal messiah. As is true with regard to other aspects of Jewish law, the Torah "is not in Heaven" (Deuteronomy 30:12) and hence halakhic disputes are resolved in accordance with canons of law which are themselves part of the Oral Law.

Certainly, there remain many points regarding various articles of faith which have not been formally resolved by the sages of the Talmud. Indeed, in subsequent periods controversies did arise with regard to significant theological issues, such as, for example, the nature of providence and freedom of the will. In the absence of a definitive ruling, the question which presents itself is, would the exponent of a certain view with regard to any of these matters consider an opponent and his followers simply to be in error, or would he view them as heretics as well? The answer is itself a matter of *Halakhah* having many ramifications, and as proves to be the case, is the subject of considerable dispute.

The Mishnah which forms the opening section of the last chapter of *Sanhedrin* posits that all Jews enjoy a share in the world-to-come, but proceeds to exclude from this ultimate reward those who espouse certain heretical doctrines which are then enumerated in the text of the Mishnah. Maimonides' understanding of the underlying principle expressed in the Mishnah is that denial of a share in the world-to-come is not in the nature of punishment for failure to discharge a religious duty, but rather that profession of certain creeds is a necessary condition of immortality. The reason which prompts an individual to deny any specific article of faith is irrelevant. The person who has been misled or who, through error in the syllogistic process, reaches false conclusions, fails to affirm the basic propositions of Jewish faith and hence cannot aspire to the ultimate intellectual reward. This is entirely consistent with Maimonides' view, as will be explained below, that development of the intellect in recognition of fundamental metaphysical truths culminates in the perfection of the intellect and leads naturally to the ability of the soul to participate in the intellectual pleasures of the world-to-come. The nature of these pleasures is such that they simply cannot be apprehended by the totally undeveloped intellect. Thus, attainment of a share in the world-to-come is more in the nature of development of potential than of reward and punishment. Accordingly, the causes and motivating forces which lead either to belief or to nonbelief are irrelevant.

Simon ben Zemah Duran, who was followed in this matter, by his pupil, Joseph Albo, adopted an opposing view. Duran asserts that intellectual rejection of any doctrine of revelation constitutes heresy. Scripture must be accepted as divinely revealed and the contents of Scripture in their entirety must be acknowledged as absolute truth. Conscious denial of the veracity of any biblical statement constitutes heresy. Nevertheless, for Duran, one who is ignorant or fails to interpret the details of a revealed doctrine correctly may be an unwitting transgressor, but is not to be considered a heretic. For example, it is possible to interpret the biblical narrative concerning the creation of the universe in a manner which assumes the existence of a primordial hylic substance and thus contradicts the doctrine of *creatio ex nihilo*. In fact, there are midrashic statements which, at least on the basis of a superficial reading, seem to support this view; Albo declares that some sages did indeed subscribe to a view akin to the Platonic doctrine of primordial substance.[5] Such an interpretation, while in error, is not heretical, so long as it is not advanced as a knowing contradiction of the biblical account. Thus, man is free to engage in philosophical speculation and is not held culpable if as a result of such endeavors he espouses a false doctrine. False beliefs, if sincerely held as the result of honest error, do not occasion loss of eternal bliss. This position is also assumed by Abraham ben David of Posquières (Ra'avad) in a gloss to Maimonides' *Mishneh Torah*[6] and received wide circulation through Albo's exposition in his *Sefer ha-Ikkarim*.[7]

In his introduction to *Ḥovot ha-Levavot*, Bahya seeks to establish, on the basis of reason, that it is entirely logical that G-d should impose duties upon the intellect. Man is a composite of body and soul, i.e., corporeal substance and intellect. As was to be stressed by later thinkers, it is the intellectual component which is uniquely human, and which constitutes the essence of man. The corporeal aspect of man is consecrated to the service of G-d by virtue of commandments imposed upon, and fulfilled by means of, the physical organs of man. It is to be anticipated that the intellect should also be impressed into the service of G-d in a like manner through imposition of commandments specifically binding upon the mind.

It is axiomatic that G-d does not impose obligations which cannot be fulfilled. Quite apart from questions of theodicy which would arise from the imposition of such obligations, it simply does not make sense to speak of an obligation which cannot under any circumstances be discharged. Jewish philosophers have repeatedly stressed that G-d cannot command man to accept the illogical or the irrational. The human intellect, no matter how much it may desire to do so, cannot affirm the absurd. Man may, if prompted by a sufficiently compelling reason, postulate the existence of unicorns or mermaids, but he cannot affirm the existence of a geometric object which is at one

and the same time endowed with the properties of both a square and a circle. He cannot fathom the concept of a square circle, much less affirm the ontological existence of such an object.

Propositions which constitute objects of belief must, then, first and foremost do no violence to human credulity. They must be readily apprehended and accepted by human thought. Yet belief implies more than hypothesization. Belief connotes unequivocal affirmation of that which is regarded as certain, rather than speculative postulation of the contingent. The latter is compatible with a state of doubt; the former is not. And herein lies a dilemma: the intellect need not be commanded to recognize the possible. An open, honest, and inquiring mind must of necessity recognize the ontological contingency of that which is affirmed by any proposition which does not violate the canons of logic. Recognition of the contingent nature of such propositions need not at all be commanded and does not constitute belief. Belief, by virtue of its very nature, entails positive affirmation of the veracity of a proposition. But how can intellectual certainty be commanded? Certainty is a psychological state of mind. It would appear that such certainty is either present or it is absent. If present, the commandment to believe is superfluous; if absent, the commandment to believe poses an obligation which cannot be fulfilled.

This paradox is presented and discussed forthrightly in the essay by Rabbi Elchanan Wasserman cited above.[8] Rabbi Wasserman's thesis is that an unbiased and unimpeded mind cannot escape an awareness and affirmation of the existence of a Creator. The Midrash presents what is probably the oldest, and certainly one of the most eloquent, formulations of the argument from design. A heretic approached Rabbi Akiva and asked him, "Who created the universe?" R. Akiva answered, "The Holy One, blessed be He." Thereupon, the heretic demanded a demonstrative proof that this was indeed so. R. Akiva responded by posing a question of his own: "Who wove your coat?" he inquired of the heretic. "A weaver," replied the latter. "Present me a demonstrative proof!" demanded Rabbi Akiva. The exchange concludes with R. Akiva's simple but forceful formulation of the teleological argument. Addressing his students, he declared: "Just as the garment testifies to [the existence of] the weaver, just as the door testifies to [the existence of] the carpenter, and just as the house testifies to [the existence of] the builder, so does the universe testify to [the existence of] the Holy One, blessed be He, who created it."[9]

A different version of the teleological argument is recorded by Bahya with the comment that experience teaches that intelligent writing never results from overturning an inkwell onto a piece of paper.[10] To put it in a different idiom, the mathematical odds militating against the probability that a chimpanzee seated at a typewriter might peck at the keys in a random manner and in the process produce the collected works of Shakespeare are so great as to render the prospect preposterous. Bahya categorizes one who seriously entertains such a belief as either a simpleton or a lunatic. Yet, on the cosmic level, there are many who find it possible to dismiss evidence of intelligence and design and to attribute the ordered nature of the universe to random causes.

Rabbi Wasserman endeavors to explain this denial by pointing to the stated consideration underlying the prohibition against bribery. This prohibition is not limited to accepting a bribe for purposes of favoring one litigant over another. Such conduct is independently forbidden by the injunction "Thou shalt not bend judgment" (Deuteronomy 16:19). The prohibition against bribe-taking encompasses even instances in which the gift is presented on the express condition that a lawful and just verdict be issued. It also applies to situations in which both the plaintiff and the defendant present the judge with gifts of equal value. And the prohibition stands no matter how upright and incorruptible the judge might be. The reason for this extreme and all-encompassing ban is spelled out clearly in Scripture: "For a bribe blinds those who have sight and perverts the words of the righteous" (Exodus 23:8).

A judge, if he is to be entirely objective, must remain detached and emotionally uninvolved in the controversy between the litigants who appear before him. Justice is assured only when evidence can be examined in a cool and dispassionate manner. Human emotions cloud judgment. No matter how honest and objective a person may strive to be, once personal interests are introduced, objectivity is compromised. Receipt of a favor creates a bond of friendship. When a judge receives a gift from a litigant, the litigant's concern becomes, in a measure, that of the judge himself. When he accepts gifts from both parties, the concerns of both become his concerns, and he can no longer dispassionately adjudicate between competing claims solely on

the basis of evidence and applicable law. The Torah testifies that all men are affected in this way at least to some extent.

All of mankind, points out Rabbi Wasserman, is subject to a subtle form of bribery. With the pleasure experienced in imbibing mother's milk, we begin to enjoy sensual gratification. Pleasure is addictive in nature; our desire for pleasure is, in a very real sense, insatiable. The need for gratification is very real, very human, and very constant.

Recognition of the existence of the Deity entails acknowledgment of His authority over us. Acceptance of other cardinal beliefs entails an awareness that our freedom to seek pleasure may be drastically curtailed. As beneficiaries of the gift of sensual gratification even before attaining the age of reason, human beings are never capable of entirely dispassionate analysis of the evidence substantiating basic religious beliefs. The sages put it succinctly in their statement, "Israel engaged in idol worship solely in order to permit themselves public licentiousness."[11] Worship of pagan gods surely involves an ideological commitment. Yet, psychologically speaking, the sages testify, intellectual conviction did not serve as the impetus for idolatry. Rather, the acknowledgment of pagan gods on the part of the worshippers of the golden calf was born of a desire for unbridled sexual gratification. Passion prevented a reasoned adjudication between the claims of idolatrous cults and monotheistic belief. Man is a logical animal; he finds it difficult to lead a life of self-contradiction. It is hard for him to accept certain concepts intellectually and then to act in a manner inconsistent with those affirmed principles. Denial of basic theological principles prevents such contradictions from arising. Certainly man has strong, albeit unconscious, motives for such denial. It is Rabbi Wasserman's thesis that many non-believers close themselves off from faith-commitments in order to avoid tension between a desire for untrammeled sensual gratification and acknowledgment of divinely imposed restraints.

The notion of a commandment concerning belief can be understood in a different manner on the basis of a statement of Ḥananiah Kazis, contained in his *Kinat Soferim*, one of the classic commentaries on Maimonides' *Sefer ha-Mitzvot*.[12] *Kinat Soferim* understands the commandment affirming the existence of G-d as bidding us to disseminate knowledge of G-d's existence and to impart the knowledge upon which this belief is predicated to future generations. His argument is both conceptual and textual. The community of Israel that experienced a beatific vision of G-d at Mount

Sinai did not need to be commanded to believe in Him; they *knew* Him. Moreover, the preamble to the Decalogue, "And G-d spoke all these words, *saying*" (Exodus 20:1), employs the Hebrew term *leimor*. In rabbinic exegesis, this term is customarily understood as meaning not simply "saying," but connoting that the person addressed is bidden "to say," that is, to convey to others the information which follows. Most frequently, this formula is employed in reporting that G-d addressed Moses bidding him to convey divine commandments to the Children of Israel. In light of the tradition which teaches that the first two commandments of the Decalogue were not transmitted to the assembled populace by Moses but were received by them directly from G-d,[13] the use of the term *leimor* in this context seems incongruous. *Kinat Soferim* argues that the connotation of the phrase in this instance is that those to whom the commandment was addressed were instructed to convey this information to succeeding generations for all of eternity. The commandment, then, is to *teach* in order that belief be possible.

Extending this concept, it certainly seems feasible to understand that the commandment as formulated delineates the *telos*, or goal, to which man is commanded to aspire. Although belief itself, while obligatory, cannot be commanded, nevertheless, activities through which belief is acquired may properly constitute the object of divine commandment. Thus, in defining the commandment, "And you shall love the L-rd, your G-d" (Deuteronomy 6:5), Maimonides writes:

One only loves G-d with the knowledge with which one knows Him. According to the knowledge will be the love. If the former be little, the latter will be little; if the former be much, the latter will be much. Therefore, a person must devote himself to the understanding and comprehension of those sciences and studies which will inform him concerning his Master, as far as is the power within man to understand and comprehend, as indeed we have explained in the Laws of the Foundations of the Torah.[14]

Bahya also posits an obligation to engage in philosophical investigation directed to the rational demonstration of the objects of belief:

. . . Scripture expressly bids you to reflect and exercise your intellect on such themes. After you have attained knowledge of them by the method of tradition which covers all the precepts of the law, their principles and details, you should investigate them with your reason, understanding,

and judgment, till the truth becomes clear to you and false notions dispelled; as it is written, "Know this day and take it to your heart that the L-rd, He is G-d" (Deuteronomy 4:39).[15]

Man is endowed with the capacity for knowledge and, hence, for belief. To state this is not at all to assume that the task is a facile one or that faith is immediately within the grasp of man. The hasidic sage, Rabbi Menaḥem Mendel of Kotzk, explained the matter by means of an allegory. G-d prepares a ladder by means of which souls descend from heaven to earth. The soul alights from the ladder and steps upon the ground. The ladder is immediately withdrawn and a voice calls out to the soul bidding it to return. Some souls do not even attempt what appears to be an impossible task. Some jump and fall; becoming disillusioned, they make no further attempt. Others try and try again, leaping time after time, refusing to become discouraged, until G-d Himself draws them nigh to Him. "You must understand," concluded the Rabbi of Kotzk, "That G-d does not extend mercy on the basis of a single leap!"[16] Judaism does not teach that G-d requires of man a "leap of faith" in the Kierkegaardian sense, i.e., blind faith to the extent of acceptance of the absurd. It teaches, rather, that G-d's beneficence assures man that his diligence and perseverance will ultimately lead to understanding and intellectual satisfaction.

Every age has witnessed the presence of both believers and doubters. Intellectual doubt and the questioning of fundamental beliefs have always been present in one form or another. It is nevertheless axiomatic that man has the ability to rise above such inner conflict and to experience faith. A just and beneficent G-d could not demand belief without bestowing upon man the capacity for faith. Abiding belief must, however, be firmly rooted in knowledge. Study has the unique effect of dispelling doubt. There is a story of a group of Jewish students in Berlin during the *Haskalah* period who, as a result of their encounter with secular society, began to experience religious doubts. Questioning the faith claims of Judaism, they were on the verge of rejecting fundamental theological beliefs. But before making a final break with Judaism they resolved to send one of their company to the Yeshiva of Volozhin, which at the time was the foremost Torah center of the world, to determine whether or not there existed satisfactory answers to the questions which troubled them. The young man to whom they delegated this task spent a period of time as a student in the Yeshiva and immersed himself completely in that institution's program of studies. Upon his return to Berlin he was met by his friends, who eagerly awaited his report. The young man described his experiences and related that he had never before experienced such intellectual delight. "But," they demanded, "have you brought answers to the questions which we formulated?" "No," he replied. "I have brought no answers – but the questions no longer plague me."

Centuries ago the sages provided an explanation for this phenomenon. They depict the Almighty as declaring, "I have created an evil inclination but I have created the Torah as its antidote."[17] With acquisition of Torah knowledge doubt recedes and ultimately dissipates. This is the essence of Jewish belief with regard to the dilemma of faith. *"Ve'idakh perusha; zil gemor—*the rest is explanation; go and study!"

ENDNOTES

[1] See his *"Betrachtungen über Bonnets Palingenesie," Gesammelte Schriften*, III (Berlin, 1843), 159-166.

[2] In medieval usage the heart is frequently spoken of as the seat of knowledge and the word *lev* is used as a synonym for "intellect."

[3] *Kovetz Ma'amarim* (Jerusalem, 1963), no. 11, sec. 14.

[4] *Teshuvot Ḥatam Sofer, Yoreh De'ah* no. 356.

[5] *Sefer ha-Ikkarim*, Book I, chap. 2.

[6] *Hilkhot Teshuvah* 3:7.

[7] Book I, chap. 2.

[8] *Loc. cit.*, secs. 1-7.

[9] *Midrash Temurah*, chap. 3, published in *Bet ha-Midrash*, ed. Adolf Jellinek, I (Leipzig, 1853), 114, and in *Otzar ha-Midrashim*, ed. J.D. Eisenstein (New York, 1915), II, 583.

[10] *Ḥovot ha-Levavot, Sha'ar ha-Yiḥud*, chap. 6.

[11] *Sanhedrin* 63b.

[12] *Mitzvot aseh*, no.1.

[13] *Makkot* 24a.

[14] *Hilkhot Teshuvah* 10:6.

[15] *Ḥovot ha-Levavot,* Introduction.

[16] See Yehudah Leib Lewin, *Bet Kotzk: Ha-Saraf* (Jerusalem, 1958), p. 98.

[17] *Kiddushin* 30b; *Sifre, Parshat Eikev* 11:18; see also *Bava Batra* 16a.

The Philosophical Quest: Of Philosophy, Ethics, Law and Halakhah, chap. 1 (Jerusalem, Koren, 2013)

Reprinted with permission of Koren Press and J. David Bleich

Maimonides, Commentary on the Mishnah [Sanhedrin],

Introduction to Ḥelek

Rabbi Moshe ben Maimon

RABBI MOSHE BEN MAIMON (MAIMONIDES, RAMBAM) 1135–1204

Halachist, philosopher, author, and physician. Maimonides was born in Córdoba, Spain. After the conquest of Córdoba by the Almohads, he fled Spain and eventually settled in Cairo, Egypt. There, he became the leader of the Jewish community and served as court physician to the vizier of Egypt. He is most noted for authoring the *Mishneh Torah*, an encyclopedic arrangement of Jewish law; and for his philosophical work, *Guide for the Perplexed*. His rulings on Jewish law are integral to the formation of halachic consensus.

The First Principle of Faith

The existence of the Creator (praised be He!), i.e. that there is an existent Being invested with the highest perfection of existence. He is the cause of the existence of all existent things. In Him they exist and from Him emanates their continued existence. If we could suppose[1] the removal of His existence then the existence of all things would entirely cease and there would not be left any independent existence whatsoever.[2] But if on the other hand we could suppose the removal of all existent things but He, His existence (blessed be He!) would not cease to be, neither would it suffer any diminution. For He (exalted be He!) is self-sufficient, and His existence needs the aid of no existence outside His. Whatsoever is outside Him, the intelligences (i.e. the angels) and the bodies of the spheres, and things below these,[3] all of them need Him for their existence. This is the first cardinal doctrine of faith, which is indicated by the commandment, "I am the L-rd thy G-d"[4] אנכי ה' אלקיך.

The Second Principle of Faith

The Unity of G-d. This implies that this cause of all is one; not one of a genus nor of a species, and not as one human being who is a compound divisible into many unities; not a unity like the ordinary material body which is one in number but takes on endless divisions and parts. But He, the exalted one, is a unity in the sense that there is no unity like His in any

way. This is the second cardinal doctrine of faith which is indicated by the assertion, "Hear, O Israel, the L-rd our G-d the L-rd is one ה' שמע ישראל אלקינו ה' אחד".[5]

The Third Principle of Faith

The removal of materiality from G-d. This signifies that this unity is not a body nor the power of a body nor can the accidents of bodies overtake Him, as e.g. motion and rest, whether in the essential or accidental sense. It was for this reason that the Sages (peace to them!) denied to Him both cohesion and separation of parts, when they remarked לא ישיבה ולא עמידה ולא עורף ולא עפוי,[6] i.e. "no sitting and no standing, no division[7] (עורף) and no cohesion[8] (עפוי) [according to the verse ועפו בכתף פלשתים, i.e. they will push them with the shoulder in order to join themselves to them]. The prophet again said.[9] "And unto whom will ye liken G-d,"&c., "and[10] unto whom will ye liken me that I may be like, saith the Holy One." If G-d were a body He would be like a body. Wherever in the scriptures G-d is spoken of with the attributes of material bodies, like motion standing, sitting, speaking, and such like, all these figures of speech, as the Sages said, דברה תורה. כלשון בני אדם"[11] The Torah speaks in the language of men." People[12] have said a great deal on this point. This third fundamental article of faith is indicated by the scriptural expression,[13] כי לא ראיתם כל תמונה "for ye have seen no likeness," i.e. you have not comprehended him as one who possesses a likeness, for, as we have remarked, he is not a body nor a bodily power.

The Fourth Principle of Faith

The priority of G-d. This means that the unity whom we have described is first in the absolute sense. No existent thing outside Him is primary in relation to Him. The proofs of this in the Scriptures are numerous. This fourth principle is indicated by the phrase [14] מעונה אל׳ קדם "The eternal G-d is a refuge."

The Fifth Principle of Faith

That it is He (be He exalted!) who must be worshipped, aggrandized, and made known by His greatness and the obedience shown to Him. This must not be done to any existing beings lower than He—not to the angels nor the spheres nor the elements, or the things which are compounded from them. For these are all fashioned in accordance with the works they are intended to perform. They have no judgement or freewill, but only a love for Him (be He exalted!). Let us adopt no mediators to enable ourselves to draw near unto G-d, but let the thoughts be directed to Him, and turned away from whatsoever is below Him. This fifth principle is a prohibition of idolatry. The greater part of the Torah is taken up with the prohibition of idol-worship.

The Sixth Principle of Faith

Prophecy. This implies that it should be known that among this human species there exist persons of very intellectual natures and possessing much perfection. Their souls are predisposed for receiving the form of the intellect. Then this human intellect joins itself with the active intellect, and an exalted emanation[15] is shed upon them. These are the prophets. This is prophecy, and this is its meaning. The complete elucidation of this principle of faith would be very long, and it is not our purpose to bring proofs for every principle or to elucidate the means of comprehending them, for this affair includes the totality of the sciences. We shall give them a passing mention only. The verses of the Torah which testify concerning the prophecy of prophets are many.

The Seventh Principle of Faith

The prophecy of Moses our Teacher. This implies that we must believe that he was the father of all the prophets before him and that those who came after him were all beneath him in rank. He (Moses) was chosen by G-d from the whole human kind. He comprehended more of G-d than any man in the past or future ever comprehended or will comprehend. And we must believe that he reached a state of exaltedness beyond the sphere of humanity, so that he attained to the angelic rank and became included in the order of the angels. There was no veil which he did not pierce. No material hindrance stood in his way, and no defect whether small or great mingled itself with him. The imaginative and sensual powers of his perceptive faculty were stripped from him. His desiderative power was stilled and he remained pure intellect only. It is in this significance that it is remarked of him that he discoursed with G-d without any angelic intermediary. We had it in our mind to explain this strange subject here and to unlock the secrets firmly enclosed in scriptural verses; to expound the meaning of פה אל פה "mouth to mouth"; and the whole of this verse and other things belonging to the same theme. But I see that this theme is very subtle; it would need abundant development and introductions and illustrations. The existence of angels would first have to be made clear and the distinction between their ranks and that of the Creator. The soul would have to be explained and all its powers. The circle would then grow wider until we should have to say a word about the forms which the prophets attribute to the Creator and the angels. The שעור קומה and its meaning would consequently have to enter into our survey. And even if this one subject were shortened into the narrowest compass it could not receive sufficient justice, even in a hundred pages. For this reason I shall leave it to its place, either in the book of the interpretation of the [16]דרשות "discourses,"which I have promised, or in the book on prophecy which I have begun, or in the book which I shall compose for explaining these fundamental articles of faith.

I shall now come back to the purpose of this seventh principle and say that the prophecy of Moses differs from that of all other prophets in four respects:–

(1)   Whosoever the prophet, G-d spoke not with him but by an intermediary. But Moses had no intermediary, as it is said, [17]פה אל פה אדבר בו "mouth to mouth did I speak with him."

(2)   Every other prophet received his inspiration only when in a state of sleep, as it is asserted in various parts of

scripture, בחלום הלילה[18] "in a dream of the night."[19] חזיון הלילה "in a dream of a vision of a night,"and many other phrases with similar significance; or in the day when deep sleep has fallen upon the prophet and his condition is that in which there is a removal of his sense-perceptions, and his mind is a blank like a sleep. This state is styled מחזה and מראה, and is alluded to in the expression במראות אלקים= "in visions of G-d." But to Moses the word came in the day-time when "he was standing between the two cherubim," as G-d had promised him in the words ונועדתי לך שם ודברתי אתך[20] "And there I will meet with thee and I will commune with thee." And G-d further said, אם יהיה נביאכם ה' במראה אליו אתודע בחלום אדבר בו לא כן עבדי משה... פה אל פה אדבר בו[21] "If there be a prophet among you, I the L-rd will make myself known unto him in a vision and will speak unto him in a dream. My servant Moses is not so, who is faithful in all mine house. With him I will speak mouth to mouth. . . ."

(3) When the inspiration comes to the prophet, although it is in a vision and by means of an angel, his strength becomes enfeebled, his physique becomes deranged. And very great terror falls upon him so that he is almost broken through it, as is illustrated in the case of Daniel. When Gabriel speaks to him in a vision, Daniel says: ולא נשאר בי כח והודי נהפך עלי למשחית ולא עצרתי כח[22] "And there remained no strength in me; for my comeliness was turned in me into corruption and I retained no strength." And he further says: ואני הייתי נרדם על פני ופני ארצה[23] "Then was I in a deep sleep on my face, and my face towards the ground." And further: במראה[24] נהפכו צירי עלי "By the vision my sorrows are turned upon me." But not so with Moses. The word came unto him and no confusion in any way overtook him, as we are told in the verse[25] ודבר ה' אל משה פנים אל פנים כאשר ידבר איש אל רעהו "And the L-rd spake unto Moses face unto face as a man speaketh unto his neighbour." This means that just as no man feels disquieted when his neighbour talks with him, so he (peace to him!) had no fright at the discourse of G-d, although it was face to face; this being the case by reason of the strong bond uniting him with the intellect, as we have described.

(4) To all the prophets the inspiration came not at their own choice but by the will of G-d. The prophet at times waits a number of years without an inspiration reaching him. And it is sometimes asked of the prophet that he should communicate a message [he has received], but the prophet waits some days or months before doing so or does not make it known at all. We have seen cases where the prophet prepares himself[26] by enlivening his soul and purifying his spirit,[27] as did Elisha in the incident when he declared ועתה קחו לי מנגן[28] "But now bring me a minstrel!" and then the inspiration came to him. He does not necessarily receive the inspiration at the time that he is ready for it. But Moses our teacher was able to say at whatsoever time he wished, עמדו ואשמעה מה יצוה ה' לכם[29] "Stand, and I shall hear what G-d shall command concerning you." It is again said, דבר אל אהרן אחיך ואל יבא בכל עת אל הקדש[30] "Speak unto Aaron thy brother that he come not at all times into the sanctuary;" with reference to which verse the Talmud remarks "that only Aaron is יבא בבל, but Moses is not בבל יבא. The prohibition ("That he come not at all times") applies only to Aaron. But Moses may enter the sanctuary at all times.

The Eighth Principle of Faith

That the Torah has been revealed from heaven. This implies our belief that the whole of this Torah found in our hands this day is the Torah that was handed down by Moses and that it is all of divine origin. By this I mean that the whole of the Torah came unto him from before G-d in a manner which is metaphorically called "speaking"; but the real nature of that communication is unknown to everybody except to Moses (peace to him!) to whom it came. In handing down the Torah, Moses was like a scribe writing from dictation the whole of it, its chronicles, its narratives and its precepts. It is in this sense that he is termed מחוקק= "law-giver." And there is no difference between verses like ובני[31] חם כוש ומצרים ופוט וכנען "And the sons of Ham were Cush and Mizraim, Phut and Canaan," or ושם אשתו מהיטבאל בת מטרד[32] "And his wife's name was Mehatabel, the daughter of Matred," or ותמנע היתה פילגש[33] "And Timna was concubine," and verses like אנכי ה' אלקיך[34] "I am the L-rd thy G-d," and שמע ישראל[35] "Hear, O Israel." They are all equally of divine origin and all belong to the תורת ה' תמימה טהורה וקדושה אמת "The Law of G-d which is perfect, pure, holy, and true." In the opinion of the Rabbis, Manasseh was the most renegade and the greatest of all infidels because he thought that in the Torah there were a kernel and a husk, and that these histories and anecdotes have no value and emanate from Moses. This is the significance of the expression אין תורה מן השמים "The Torah does not come from heaven," which, say the Rabbis,[36] is the remark of one who believes that all the Torah is of divine origin save a certain verse which (says he) was not spoken by G-d but by Moses himself. And of such a one the verse says [37] כי דבר ה' בזה "For he hath despised the word of the L-rd." May G-d be exalted far above and beyond the speech of the infidels! For truly in every letter of the Torah there reside wise maxims and admirable truths for him to whom G-d has given understanding. You cannot grasp the uttermost bounds of its wisdom. "It is larger in measure than the earth, and wider than the sea."[38] Man has but to follow in the footsteps of the anointed one of the G-d of Jacob, who prayed [39] גל עיני ואביטה נפלאות מתורתך "Open my eyes and I shall behold wonderful things from thy Law." The interpretation of traditional law is in like manner of divine origin. And that which we know today of the nature of succah, lulav, shofar, fringes, and phylacteries (סוכה, לולב, שופר, ציצית, תפילין) is essentially the same as that which G-d commanded Moses, and which the latter told us. In the success of his mission Moses realized the mission of a [40] נאמן (a faithful servant of G-d). The text in which the eighth principle of faith is indicated is: [41] בזאת תדעון כי ה' שלחני לעשות את כל המעשים האלה כי לא מלבי "Hereby ye shall know that the L-rd hath sent me to do all these works; for I have not done them of mine own mind."

The Ninth Principle of Faith

The abrogation of the Torah. This implies that this Law of Moses will not be abrogated and that no other law will come from before G-d. Nothing is to be added to it nor taken away from it, neither in the written nor oral law, as it is said [42] לא תוסף עליו ולא תגרע ממנו "Thou shalt not add to it nor diminish from it." In the beginning of this treatise we have already explained that which requires explanation in this principle of faith.

The Tenth Principle of Faith

That He, the exalted one, knows the works of men and is not unmindful of them. Not as they thought who said, עזב ה' את הארץ[43] "The L-rd hath forsaken the earth," but as he

declared who exclaimed [44] גדול העצה ורב העליליה אשר עיניך פקו־חות על כל דרכי בני אדם "Great in counsel, and mighty in work; for thine eyes are open upon all the ways of the sons of men." It is further said, [45] וירא ה' כי רבה רעת האדם בארץ "And the L-rd saw that the wickedness of man was great in the earth." And again, [46] זעקת סדום ועמורה כי רבה "the cry of Sodom and Gomorrah is great." This indicates our tenth principle of faith.

The Eleventh Principle of Faith

That He, the exalted one, rewards him who obeys the commands of the Torah, and punishes him who transgresses its prohibitions. That G-d's greatest reward to man is עולם הבא "the future world," and that his strongest punishment is כרת "cutting off." We have already said sufficient upon this theme. The scriptural verses in which the principle is pointed out are. [47] אם תשא חטאתם ואם אין מחני נא מספרך "Yet now if Thou wilt forgive their sin –; but if not, blot me out of Thy book." And G-d replied to him, [48] מי אשר חטא לי אמחנו מספרי "Whosoever hath sinned against Me, him will I blot out of My book." This is a proof of which the obedient and the rebellious each obtain.[49] G-d rewards the one and punishes other.

The Twelfth Principle of Faith

The days of the Messiah. This involves the belief and firm faith in his coming, and that we should not find him slow in coming. [50] אם יתמהמה חכה לו "Though he tarry, wait for him." No date must be fixed for his appearance,[51] neither may the scriptures be interpreted with the view of deducing the time of his coming. The Sages said, [52] תפח רוחן של מחשבי קצין "A plague on those who calculate periods" (for Messiah's appearance). We must have faith in him, honouring and loving him, and praying for him according to the degree of importance with which he is spoken of by every prophet, from Moses unto Malachi. He that has any doubt about him or holds his authority in light esteem imputes falsehood to the Torah, which clearly promises his coming in [53] פרשת בלעם "the chapter of Balaam," and in [54] אתם נצבים "Ye stand this day all of you before the L-rd your G-d." From the general nature of this principle of faith we gather that there will be no king of Israel but from David and the descendants of Solomon exclusively. Every one who disputes the authority of this family denies G-d and the words of his prophets.

The Thirteenth Principle of Faith

The resurrection of the dead.[55] We have already explained this.

ENDNOTES

[1] To accord with the Arabic קדרנא we should expect נעלה על לב, and not the third pers. sing. יעלה.

[2] The Arabic מסתקל בוגודה "that which is independent, absolute, in its existence," is rather loosely and inaccurately rendered by נמצא שיתקים מציאותי.

[3] The Hebrew has ומה שיש בתוכם "and what is inside them," which is not represented in the Arabic, unless the translator understood דון (دون) to contain this meaning among the many others which it possesses in Arabic. I cannot, however, find this meaning indicated in the dictionaries.

[4] Exod. xx. 2.

[5] Deut. vi. 4.

[6] *Hagiga,* 15a.

[7] עורף The Arabic ערף means "to divide." In Hebrew we get this meaning in וערפתו (Exod. xiii. 13) "and thou shall break its neck," i.e. separate, divide the head from the trunk. In Hosea x. 2 we get the phrase הוא יערף מזבחותם "he shall break down their altars," i.e. take them to pieces, separate stone from stone.

[8] This translation is in accord with the *Targum* of Jonathan which renders the verse Isa. xi. 14 ויתחברון כתף חד.

[9] Isa. xi. 18.

[10] Isa. xi. 25.

[11] *Berachoth,* 31b.

[12] For the Arabic אלנאס "people" the Hebrew has החכמים "the sages." The reason for this change is not clear.

[13] Deut. iv. 15.

[14] Deut. xxxiii. 27.

[15] The Arabic פאץ literally signifies "to flow" (of water, blood, &c.), and is usually represented in Hebrew by שפע which has an exactly similar significance. This whole subject is thoroughly discussed in the *Moreh,* II, 12. Everything that happens in the world is influenced by the פיץ of the Divine Creator. It is that that is shed upon the prophets, enabling them to prophesy. נאמר שהעולם נתחדש משפע הבורא עליו ושהוא המשפיע עליו כל מה שיתחדש בו וכן יאמר שהוא השפיע חכמתו על הנביאים "It is said that the universe renews itself by the emanation of the Creator, and that it is He who is the cause of the emanation of everything that renews itself in it. Similarly, it is said that He causes His wisdom to emanate to the prophets. "Maimonides instances the usage of this idea in the prophetical books of the Bible by quoting Jeremiah xvii, 13 אותי עזבו מקור מים חיים "They have forsaken me, the fountain of living waters."

[16] This promised work was left undone by Maimonides. His son Abraham wittily alluded to the fact in the words וירא משה מגשת אליו "And Moses was afraid to draw near to it" (a slight alteration of Exod. xxxiv. 30).

[17] Num. xii. 8.

[18] Gen. xx. 3.

[19] Job xxxiii. 15.

[20] Exod. XXV. 22.

[21] Num. xii. 6-8.

[22] Dan. x. 8.

[23] Dan. x. 9.

[24] Dan. x. 16.

[25] Exod. xxxiii. 11. For the full discussion of all the meanings of פנים, see *Moreh,* I, 37. He there explains שמיעת הקול בפנים as פנים מבלתי אמצעיות מלאך "the perception of the Divine voice without the intervention of an angel."

[26] The Arabic word פאטר is only found in the sense of "Creator," which cannot possibly fit in here. Holzer suggests that it may be meant by Maimonides for פטרת, which means "religious sentiment," "natural disposition." As an instance of the necessity for previous self-preparation on the part of a prophet one would have thought that Maimonides would have mentioned the case of the severe ordeal of Isaiah (chap. vi) which is far more striking than the instance he quotes in the life of Elisha.

[27] The Arabic נפסה יבסט does not seem to be rendered in the Hebrew version.

[28] 2 Kings iii. 15.

[29] Num. ix. 8.

[30] Lev. xvi. 2.

[31] Gen. x. 6.

[32] Gen. xxxvi. 39.

[33] Gen. xxxvi. 12.

[34] Exod. xx. 2.

[35] Deut. vi. 4.

[36] *Sanhedrin,* 99a.

[37] Num. xv. 31.

[38] Job xi. 9.

[39] Ps. cxix. 18.

[40] Num. xii. 7.

[41] Num. xvi. 28.

[42] Deut. xiii. 1.

[43] Ezek. viii. 12; ix. 9.

[44] Jer. xxxii. 19.

[45] Gen. vi. 5.

[46] Gen. xviii. 20.

[47] Exod. xxxii. 32.

[48] Exod. xxxii. 33.

[49] For the Arabic תחציל (II. infin. of חצל) the Hebrew has שיודע "that he knows." The word חצל signifies "to obtain," either in the material sense or figuratively in the sense of grasping or comprehending some scientific idea. The Hebrew gives the second signification. I have translated, however, in its first meaning.

[50] Hab. ii. 3.

[51] Many computations were made by Jews in the middle ages with regard to the time of the Messiah's appearance. It was one such computation by a Jewish enthusiast in Yemen (about 1172) that caused Maimonides to compose his famous אגרת תימן in which he says: "It is wrong to calculate the Messianic period, as the Yemen enthusiast thinks he has succeeded in doing; for it can never be exactly determined, it having been purposely concealed, as a deep

secret, by the prophets" (Graetz, *History of the Jews,* English transl., vol. III, p. 478).

[52] *Sanhedrin* 97b.

[53] Num. xxiii-xxiv. In the אגרת תימן Maimonides derives the exact date of the coming of the Messiah from the verse כעת יאמר ליעקב וכו' (Num. xxiii. 23). This is most strangely inconsistent with the advice given in this essay, and in the *Iggereth Teman,* against calculating the date of the Messiah's appearance. (See Dr. Friedlander's *Introduction to Translation of Moreh* vol. I.)

[54] Deut. XXX. 1-10.

[55] From the briefness with which Maimonides dismisses this thirteenth article concerning the Resurrection of the Dead, it has been inferred by many that he was really opposed to classing it among the fundamental dogmas of Judaism, and only did so as an unwilling concession to the current orthodox views of his day. His *Moreh Nebuchim* is quite silent on the point. Maimonides was attacked on this very question by his opponents during his lifetime. They complained that whereas he had made an exhaustive examination of the question of immortality, he had passed over the doctrine of Resurrection with little notice. Maimonides vindicated himself by writing his famous מאמר תחיית המתים in Arabic in the year 1191. He says there that he "firmly believes in the Resurrection as a miracle whose possibility is granted with the assumption of a temporal Creation" (Graetz, English transl., vol. III, p.503). Maimonides seems to have looked on the Resurrection as a secondary consideration. [See the General Introduction to this book in which I have attempted to place Maimonides' views on resurrection in proper perspective. J.D.B.]

Rabbi J. David Bleich (ed.), *With Perfect Faith: The Foundations of Jewish Belief* (New York: Ktav Publishing House, Inc., 1983), pp. 36–43, chapter translation by J. Abelson.

Reprinted with permission of Rabbi J. David Bleich and the publisher

G-d in the World

By Rabbi Adin Even-Israel Steinsaltz

RABBI ADIN EVEN-ISRAEL (STEINSALTZ)
1937–2020

Talmudist, author, and philosopher. Rabbi Even-Israel (Steinsaltz) is considered one of the foremost Jewish thinkers of the 20th century. Praised by *Time* magazine as a "once-in-a-millennium scholar," he has been awarded the Israel Prize for his contributions to Jewish study. He lives in Jerusalem and is the founder of the Israel Institute for Talmudic Publications, a society dedicated to the translation and elucidation of the Talmud.

According to the Sages, the purpose of Creation is to establish a place for G-d to live in the world. As a certain folk story described it: Whatever for? Why should the Almighty ever want to dwell in this nether world? And the answer is that like so many other desires and cravings, it should not be inquired into. True, the philosophers have not added much to this half-joking explanation, but it may be appropriate to investigate it a little further.

First, there is a certain technical difficulty to be overcome. If we say that G-d wishes to live here on earth, it may imply that He is actually somewhere else. Thus, we are confronted with the paradox of above and below, because for the Infinite there can be no such thing—neither place nor time nor difference in dimension. Even though there is a matter of levels in relation to Divine essence, higher and lower levels, we are still baffled by the fact that He occupies all places and levels equally.

Before He created the world, only G-d may be said to have existed, without limits or distinct forms, and there was nothing else. But nothing actually changed in this respect by virtue of Creation. He is still everywhere. And the relationship with His creatures is a one-way relationship. Even the person who claims to have seen the Divine essence can be said to be looking into a dark glass that does not transmit light; the only possible exception is Moses, who is said to have seen G-d in a "luminous (transparent) glass." Nevertheless, the general truth holds fast that no man may see G-d and live. For the "luminous glass" is also a transparent window through which one "looks" and is looked at by oneself. Thus the prophets, in peering into this "glass," were able to see only as much as the dazzling luminosity permitted–the less light there was, the more they could see. In any event, this is a most complex matter in itself. For our purposes, suffice it to say that those who receive anything of the Divine essence are invariably caught in the paradox of seeing and of not seeing, of being confronted with a one-way concealment in which they are themselves made transparent and yet are unable to penetrate beyond a certain depth.

Even the angels may not see G-d; no one and nothing can pierce the veil of Divine hiddenness. What can be observed is an unfolding of worlds, a process of descent, or generation, which creates that which we call a lower world, a world of levels that are ever more dense, more wrapped in the Divine hiddenness and less exposed to G-d. Even in individuals on earth one may detect such differences of density or "concealment."

The lower world, created by the process of Divine emanation, is physical and of substance, and, in certain respects, it is also an end product of the Divine Will. That is to say, it is a world that can be measured, and it has distinctiveness and form; it can be touched. Man, too, is a part of this world of matter, and no small part of man's struggle in life consists of the effort to gain release from the physical limitations of his being. It is not only a question of making contact with genuine holiness; it is also a question of freeing oneself from images and pictures, from the sense of touch and the bondage that comes from the attachment to that which is of substance.

Moreover, there is still another part of this world, even lower than all the rest, containing shells of imagined independence; that is to say, they are so far removed from G-d that they can even deny Him. Just as at the highest level of this lower world of ours there are those with minimal wrappings separating them from G-d; so too, at the lowest level of this lower world, there are those who claim individual independence; that is, they do not acknowledge their own creatureliness, their status as a product of Creation. This lowest level is the source of evil as opposed to good and is recognized when a person says: "I and none else." There are, thus, two poles of being. One admits that there is G-d in the world and that alongside Him, throughout the whole world, nothing else can exist. And there is the other, which does not only fail to see G-d everywhere, but which sees itself as the basis for everything, the beginning and the end of all existence. In other words, the shell, as a category, is merely a matter of level of existence between these two poles. Anyone, whether man or angel, who says "I and G-d" or "G-d and I" includes the shell in his being.

The question here is: What nourishes the shell and sustains its existence? And the answer is: G-d Himself, even at the extremity of the shell's impudence, when the shell is allowed to repudiate G-d. The greater the gap, the harder it is to see the direct connection between Creation and the world; one sees only the links. As Maimonides said, all idolatry is a degeneration of one's faith in the unity of the linked system of Creation. The first step in this degeneration of faith is to consider the desirability of establishing some relation with these links, channels, or instruments of Divine power, in order to ensure their proper functioning for one's own benefit. And as happens whenever one learns to deal with the lesser officials of government and forgets that there is a sovereign power who is really in charge, one begins to depend on oneself. The slogan of "I and none other" steals its way into the soul.

All of this explains what is meant by above and below, upper and lower—the "lower" being not what is further removed from G-d but what is less open to the knowledge of the fact that G-d is present within it. The upper worlds are open to Divine influence and transmit everything easily, without taking or gaining anything for themselves. The ultimate purpose seems to be the worlds below, the lower levels of being. If this is true, then this world of ours has two essences built into its very structure. It is the lowest of the low. It is also charged with a purpose—to reach a certain level of consciousness, so that it is sufficiently able to receive the Infinite light. When this is achieved, the very depths of darkness and the *Sitra Achra* will shine and radiate more powerfully and brightly than the upper worlds. For the light of the upper worlds is still clothed and hidden somewhat—being, of necessity, separate from the Divine and not altogether nullified in Him. The point is that G-d and the world are, in essence, opposites; they are contradictions in terms of being. They can exist together only when there is a state of ignorance, when the world does not know the Divine essence and cannot even recognize its presence. Because as soon as the world feels G-d, it cannot continue to be anything, much less itself. That is to say, all the world lives on the basis of the fiction that it has some sort of independent being. Where there is a knowledge of the truth, the world ceases to exist.

Our world is no more than a variety of such false relations; and although it may feel the absurdity of its position, it does not suffer unduly from the urge to nullify itself before the absolute Divine light. To be sure, there have been instances of men who experienced the rapture of the kiss of death, uniting with the Divine essence. It is told of Rabbi Moshe Zechut (HaRamaz), for instance, that in a state of religious ecstasy, he crumpled to earth and ceased to breathe. The fact is that, throughout history, there have been many more such instances than are known, even until fairly recent times.

All of this readiness for self-nullification does not, however, characterize the World of Action as it does the higher worlds. In fact, our world is characterized by grossness and evil, and is, therefore, very different from the many thousands of spiritual worlds. Nevertheless, this becomes an advantage in that it enables one to reach Divine consciousness by following a certain path in life without the risk of self-nullification in the Infinite light. The very fact that it is so structured, based on gross matter, which is relatively impervious to the Divine, makes it possible to become a vessel to contain the Divine light. The spiritual worlds have no such covering or protection; they remain one-dimensional. Nevertheless, we may well wonder why we have to struggle against grossness, cruelty, and insensitivity. As Rabbi Nachman said: "People maintain that this world exists, and I am quite willing to believe it; but from what we can all see, it looks more like Hell." The point is that we somehow manage to live in this world because, notwithstanding all its horrors, it has the capacity to absorb what the higher worlds cannot assimilate.

Our world is, therefore, the place where the ultimate Divine revelation will occur, precisely because of its limitations and restrictions. Without delving into the matter deeply, we may say that the theory behind this is the process of generation or involution (as opposed to evolution). Among other things, it explains the descent of G-d in terms of levels, and further explains His withdrawal as whatever makes it possible for something that is not G-d (Divine absence) to exist. It does not explain the development of matter. And ultimately, the whole process of physical creation seems to point to a lower frontier, the edge of existence. Only the infinite power of the Divine can create matter which is finite, which puts a limit to G-d, and this contrast has its emotional implications. We tend to relate to matter and spirit as two levels or degrees of the same thing, with matter, since it is more dense, being of lower value. But the truth is that matter is simply what is more hidden or concealed from Divine light; it is not necessarily of lesser or lower value.

Furthermore, matter can be a vessel to contain the Infinite, which the spirit, with its greater vulnerability, cannot be. That is to say, the physical Torah is a way to achieve a certain Divine love and unity, while pure love of G-d and ecstatic experiences are not able to contain the Infinite because of their human personal limitations. In other words, the Divine hiddenness is not seriously affected by the presence of G-d in matter, whereas in the realm of the spiritual, it is difficult, if not impossible, for Divine hiddenness to be maintained. It is only at the end of days that the revelation of G-d will eliminate all the barriers marking His hiddenness in the world. It will be the end of the Divine experiment that began with Creation—could a world exist in the light of G-d without the protection afforded by His hiddenness.

This brings us to the problem of the resurrection of the dead. In contrast to Maimonides, the Baal HaTanya maintains that it is impossible to achieve a complete spiritual union of the human with the Divine; thus, the ultimate revelation cannot take place in Paradise; it has to be realized through and within the physical world. Therefore, there has to be a physical body, because the body can undergo all sorts of modifications. We cannot conceive of all the possible transmutations that can occur in the body as a result of the mutual relations between body and soul. The existence of the body, or of matter, is a part, not only of reward and punishment, but also of that which makes it possible to experience a true revelation and to see G-d in spite of the fact that "no man shall see Me and live." Moreover, it is said: "Eye to eye will they see G-d." All of this is, perhaps, to be interpreted to mean that G-d cannot be seen now, when man has to divest himself of his outer (physical) garments in order to approach G-d, a state in which there is no desire for life and no possibility for life to continue. On the other hand, in the time of G-d's revelation, there will be a transformation in all the world, the change toward which we aspire.

All our efforts to serve and worship Him are intended to bring about the upheaval involved in Divine revelation, beyond anything that was or could be in the past. Indeed, the whole world was created for that purpose. And life after that, the life of immortality, is thus the aim of this life. It is appropriate to mention that the ultimate reward will be given in the seventh millennium, within the reality of this world, and not in Paradise. That is to say, Paradise and Hell are no more than stations along the way. A person lives a certain span, doing his share of good and evil. If the evil predominates, his soul is corrupted, and he needs purification and correction. He is therefore sent for a while to some such place where this can be done for him. Another person, who does not require such a transition period and special corrective conditions for the purification of the soul, is sent somewhere else, according to his level of being. Such a one, according to the Baal HaTanya, is not yet seated with the righteous and the saintly in blissful enjoyment of Heaven: he simply waits for the end of days, which is a real time in the concrete history of man; during this period, his entire being has to pass through a great modification.

A precedent for this may be seen in the experience of the giving of the Torah (*Matan Torah*), which was a revelation of G-d, a breaking of all the barriers and concealments, while at the same time sustaining the world intact. The Almighty said, "I am that I am," and added, "and the world may also be." The people were brought into contact with the reality of Divine existence; it was not a matter of intellectual proof or even signs and miracles; their very senses apprehended G-d. His voice filled all of one's being. The Revelation at Sinai left no part of a person separate from the utterance "I am." There could be no such thing as hesitation or doubt.

The Revelation at Sinai was thus a manifestation of the innermost light, and for this reason, it was said: "We, the people, were nullified and then, by G-d, revived." It was a momentary bursting of all normal bounds, an intimation of the sublime reality of the end of days. Yet, what is being described is speech, the words of the Ten Commandments, hewn in the stone of the tablets. And the Hebrew word for "hewn" is similar to the root of the word for freedom, *cherut,* freedom from the angel of death. As it is said of the end of days, "And death shall be swallowed forever" (Isaiah 25:8). At a certain moment in history, the end of history came and went, and this was the flash of revelation.

However—and this seems to be the point of the dissertation—this was in part necessary only because the people did not yet have the Torah—they did not possess the means of protecting themselves from the Divine light and were, therefore, unable to know G-din any other way than by the miracle of His descent. The Torah, among other things, provides man with the tools to experience the Divine, even if, at times, in a very rudimentary fashion. As some Chasidim used to say: "We study the secret lore, learn about the existence of other worlds, angels, seraphs, and heavenly beings; but I don't see any angels or heavenly beings, and I don't believe that anyone who studies more is able to see more. Nevertheless, the difference between the one who studies and the one who does not study is that, in the future, when these things are made manifest, the one who studies will be able to recognize them better, to relate them to what he has learned."

This hints at a concept of what is to be expected in the ultimate time. It will not be a total nullification of matter, but a purification of matter, a metamorphosis of all physical density making it transparent. Matter is now the densest and heaviest of all the forms of existence. At the End of Days it will become purified and luminous; the reality of the world will become transparent, completely receptive to the Divine light.

It is written in Isaiah 60:2: "For though darkness covers the earth and dark night the nations, the L-rd shall shine upon you and over you shall His glory appear; and the nations shall march towards your light and their kings to your sunrise." This is possible because the Torah is a structure that the soul can aspire to and attain; it is a code of the spirit, a many-layered message concerning the manner of relating to the highest holiness. This relation is something we build up for generations, constructing and tearing down and continually striving to form something lasting. When we do reach some kind of closeness with G-d, when we begin to make proper use of the code—in Torah, in *mitzvot,* or in deeds—much of what had been secret wisdom and hidden lore becomes something that reveals Him. As Rabbi Nachman of Bratslav saw it: The whole of Torah and mitzvot may be apprehended as a new arrangement of the world, making the world into a means of communication between G-d and man; and it is one's task in the world to make the necessary changes that are integral to this new arrangement, changes that transform a disorderly world into an orderly one.

This can be illustrated in various other realms of existence where human intervention is crucial—like in the magnetization of iron—all man does is place a particular substance in certain positions and thereby he induces movement; and the innate force in the substance, the atoms and the molecular structure of its reality, arrange themselves in a new order, augmenting the nature of the substance and transforming it. It is a process of creating some order out of the ordinary lack of order which is chance. As it is described by the modem science of communications: The world is full of sounds and all we have to do is put these sounds together in some coherent fashion. What does G-d say? What does the Divine want to communicate by this or that "noise?" When we sort out the sounds, we can begin to understand and eventually to respond. The basic element of experience, which is made up of matter and the combinations of matter, is not a fundamental creation; it only points to something else that is not apparent to us, which, with the proper grasp, can become an instrument for our own use. It is like a problem to be solved, a puzzle to be clearly worked out; the change one introduces makes it into a vessel for something that is needed. In this respect, Torah can be conceived of as that which changes the world by means of wisdom, speech, and actions; it enables life to achieve a higher level of communication, thereby allowing light to enter. "For My mouth has spoken."

The Long Shorter Way: Discourses on Chasidic Thought (New Milford, Conn.: Toby-Koren Press LLC, 2014), ch. 36

Biblical Prophecies Regarding the Messianic Era

Editor's note:

Text 1 of this lesson (p. 45) cites Maimonides's description of the messianic world. Below are some of the biblical prophesies on which this description is based.

Ezekiel 36:24–36

I will take you from the nations, gather you from the countries, and bring you to your land. . . . From all your contaminations, from all your idols, I will cleanse you.

I will give you a new heart, and a new spirit I will place within you. I will remove the heart of stone from your flesh and give you a heart of flesh.

I will place My spirit within you. I will make that you follow My edicts, and keep and do My laws. And you will dwell in the land that I gave to your forefathers. And you will be My people, and I will be your G-d.

I will call unto the grain and I will multiply it. . . . I will multiply the fruit of the tree and the produce of the field, so that you shall no more have to accept the shame of famine among the nations. . . .

I will settle the cities; the ruins will be rebuilt. The desolate land will be cultivated, instead of lying desolate in the sight of all who pass by. . . . And the nations that remain about you will know that I, G-d, have rebuilt the ruins and have planted the desolation; I, G-d, have spoken and done it.

Ibid., 37:24–27

My servant David shall be king over them, and one shepherd will be for them all. . . . My servant David will be their prince forever.

I will form a covenant of peace for them, an everlasting covenant shall be with them. . . . and I will set My Sanctuary in their midst forever. My dwelling shall be upon them; I will be their G-d, and they will be My people.

Isaiah 11:1–9

A shoot shall come forth from the stem of Jesse; and a twig shall sprout from his roots.

The spirit of G-d will rest upon him; a spirit of wisdom and understanding, a spirit of counsel and might, a spirit of knowledge and fear of G-d. . . . He will judge the poor with equity, and decide with justice for the lowly of the land. . . . Righteousness will be the girdle of his loins, and faith the girdle of his waist.

The wolf will dwell with the lamb, and the leopard will lie with the kid. . . . the lion, like cattle, will eat straw. . . . A suckling child will play on the cobra's hole. . . . They shall neither harm nor destroy. . . . for the world will be filled with knowledge of G-d as waters cover the sea.

Ibid., 1:24–27

Therefore, says the Master, the L-rd of Hosts, the champion of Israel. . . . I will purge away your dross as with lye. . . . I will restore your judges as of yore, and your counselors as in the beginning; after that you shall be called city of righteousness, a faithful city. Zion shall be redeemed through justice, and her returnees through righteousness.

Ibid., 11:11–12

And it shall come to pass that on that day, G-d shall again apply His hand a second time to acquire the remnants of His people who will remain from Assyria and from Egypt and from Pathros and from Ethiopia and from Elam and from Sumeria and from Hamath and from the islands of the sea.

And He will raise a banner to the nations, and He will gather the lost of Israel, and the scattered ones of Judah He will gather from the four corners of the earth.

Ibid., 27:1

It shall come to pass on that day that a great shofar shall be sounded, and they will come, those lost in the land of Assyria and those exiled in the land of Egypt; and they will bow to G-d on the holy mountain, in Jerusalem.

Ibid., 4:2–4

It shall come to pass in the last days, that the mount of the house of G-d will be established atop the mountains, and be exalted above the hills; and all nations will stream to it.

Many nations will go, and say: "Come, let us go up to the mountain of G-d, to the house of the G-d of Jacob; and he will teach us of His ways and we will walk in His paths." For from Zion shall go forth Torah, and the word of G-d from Jerusalem.

And he will judge between the nations, and he will reprove many peoples. And they will beat their swords into plowshares, and their spears into pruning hooks. Nation will not lift up sword upon nation, neither will they learn war any more.

Joel 2:24–26

The granaries will be filled with grain, and the vats will roar with wine and oil. . . . You will eat and be sated, and you will praise the name of your G-d Who has performed wonders with you; and My people shall never be ashamed.

Isaiah 60:18

Violence will no longer be heard in your land, nor robbery and destruction within your borders.

Malachi 3:23–24

Behold, I am sending you Elijah the prophet, before the great and awesome day of G-d will come. He will restore the hearts of fathers to their children and the hearts of children to their fathers.

Isaiah 35:5–6

Then the eyes of the blind will be opened, and the ears of the deaf will be unstopped. Then the lame will skip like a deer, and the tongue of the mute will sing.

Ibid., 65:20

There will no longer be from there a youth or an old man who will not fill his days.

Ibid., 25:18

G-d will annihilate death forever, and He will wipe off the tears from every face.

Amos 8:11

"Behold, days are coming," says G-d, "when I will send a famine upon the earth; not a famine for bread, nor a thirst for water, but to hear the word of G-d."

Zechariah 13:2

I will remove the spirit of impurity from the world.

Jeremiah 31:32–33

For this is the covenant that I will form with the house of Israel after those days, says G-d: I will place My Torah in their innards, and I will inscribe it upon their hearts; and I will be their G-d and they will be My people. No longer will a person teach their fellow . . . for all will know Me, from their smallest to their greatest.

Joel 3:1

And it will come to pass afterwards that I will pour out My spirit upon all flesh, and your sons and daughters will prophesy.

Isaiah 30:20

No longer will your Master be cloaked; your eyes will behold your Master.

Isaiah 40:20

The glory of G-d will be revealed; and all flesh will see that the mouth of G-d has spoken.

Zechariah 14:9

And G-d will be king over the entire world; on that day, G-d will be one, and His name will be one.

Zephaniah 3:8–9

Therefore, await Me, says G-d, for the day that I will arise to meet [with you]. . . . For then I will convert the nations to a pure language, that all of them call in the name of G-d, to serve Him of one accord.

30

PROUN (PROJECT FOR PROGRESS SERIES)
before 1924, El Lissitzky, watercolor, Stedelijk
Van Abbemuseum, Eindhoven, Netherlands

SUPERHUMAN VS. SUPER HUMANS

*Waiting for a Messiah to come to save humanity feels a little . . . un-Jewish. But what if Redemption is a natural reaction to humanity's own cumulative actions? Let's discover the effect we've **already** had on the reality of the world.*

I. WHY DO YOU DO A MITZVAH?

The previous lesson defined our overall mission in life. We learned that G-d created the world, deliberately placed us in it, and provided us with the Torah—all for the sake of empowering us to bring the world to its messianic state. Put in ancient terms that are both poetic and precise, we are to "make a home for G-d in the lowest world," referring to our tangible reality. In this lesson, we will discuss *how* to accomplish this goal.

It is first necessary to clarify that the messianic era is not simply a *reward* for following G-d's commandments, but rather, it is the actual *result* of our mitzvah acts.

WHY DO YOU DO A MITZVAH?

Choose a mitzvah that you do regularly (attend Shabbat services, keep kosher, give charity, put on *tefilin*, study Torah, etc.). Why do you do this mitzvah? Select one or more of the following:

- Because G-d said so.
- It makes my life more orderly and stable.
- It makes my life more spiritual.
- It strengthens my Jewish identity.
- It feels right.
- It makes the world a better place.
- I believe that G-d will reward me for doing *mitzvot*.
- I'm afraid to disobey G-d.
- Other

TEXT 1

No Good Deed Goes Unrewarded

Leviticus 26:3–4

אִם בְּחֻקֹּתַי תֵּלֵכוּ וְאֶת מִצְוֹתַי תִּשְׁמְרוּ וַעֲשִׂיתֶם אֹתָם.
וְנָתַתִּי גִשְׁמֵיכֶם בְּעִתָּם וְנָתְנָה הָאָרֶץ יְבוּלָהּ וְעֵץ הַשָּׂדֶה יִתֵּן פִּרְיוֹ.

If you follow My statutes and keep My commandments
and observe them, I will provide your rains in their
proper time, the earth will give its produce, and
the trees of the field will yield their fruits.

ABUNDANCE
France, Eurilda Loomis,
1885–1931, oil on canvas,
University of California, San Diego

TEXT 2

The Result of Our *Mitzvot*

Rabbi Shne'ur Zalman of Liadi, *Tanya*, chapter 37

וְהִנֵּה תַּכְלִית הַשְּׁלֵמוּת הַזֶּה שֶׁל יְמוֹת הַמָּשִׁיחַ וּתְחִיַּת הַמֵּתִים, שֶׁהוּא גִּלּוּי אוֹר אֵין סוֹף בָּרוּךְ הוּא בָּעוֹלָם הַזֶּה הַגַּשְׁמִי, תָּלוּי בְּמַעֲשֵׂינוּ וַעֲבוֹדָתֵנוּ כָּל זְמַן מֶשֶׁךְ הַגָּלוּת.

כִּי הַגּוֹרֵם שְׂכַר הַמִּצְוָה הִיא הַמִּצְוָה בְּעַצְמָהּ.
כִּי בַּעֲשִׂיָּתָהּ מַמְשִׁיךְ הָאָדָם גִּלּוּי אוֹר אֵין סוֹף בָּרוּךְ הוּא מִלְמַעְלָה לְמַטָּה לְהִתְלַבֵּשׁ בְּגַשְׁמִיּוּת עוֹלָם הַזֶּה.

This ultimate perfection of the age of Mashiach and the Resurrection—namely, the revelation of the infinite radiance of G-d in this physical world—depends on our actions and our work throughout the duration of Exile.

For the reward of a mitzvah is the result of the mitzvah itself. This is because with the performance of a mitzvah, one elicits G-d's infinite radiance so that it descends into, and is integrated within, the physical matter of this world.

RABBI SHNE'UR ZALMAN OF LIADI (ALTER REBBE) 1745–1812

Chasidic rebbe, halachic authority, and founder of the Chabad movement. The Alter Rebbe was born in Liozna, Belarus, and was among the principal students of the Magid of Mezeritch. His numerous works include the *Tanya*, an early classic containing the fundamentals of Chabad Chasidism; and *Shulchan Aruch HaRav*, an expanded and reworked code of Jewish law.

Mrs. Shimona Tzukernik delivers the mystical spin on why "What You Do Matters": *myjli.com/canhappen*

II. HOW A MITZVAH CHANGES REALITY

Each mitzvah that is performed serves to further penetrate the divine concealment that blankets our physical reality. It thereby reveals the G-dly truth that breathes within material existence.

To be more specific, each mitzvah plays a dual role in accomplishing this goal: One of its impacts is universal—meaning that no matter which of the countless varieties of *mitzvot* is performed, a similar impact on the world's receptivity to divine overtness will be generated. At the same time, each mitzvah also wields an utterly unique footprint on reality, depending on the spiritual properties and tangible elements of the particular mitzvah. This second element explains why the Torah provides such a broad spectrum of *mitzvot*.

**REJOICING IN
THE ETROG FRUIT**
2nd half, 19th cent., Beregi,
oil on cardboard. Judaica
Collection Max Berger, Vienna

TEXT 3

Parchment, a Fruit, and Money

Rabbi Shne'ur Zalman of Liadi, *Tanya*, chapter 37

בַּעֲשִׂיָּתָהּ מַמְשִׁיךְ הָאָדָם גִּלּוּי אוֹר אֵין סוֹף בָּרוּךְ
הוּא מִלְמַעְלָה לְמַטָּה, לְהִתְלַבֵּשׁ בְּגַשְׁמִיּוּת עוֹלָם
הַזֶּה בְּדָבָר שֶׁהָיָה תְּחִלָּה תַּחַת מֶמְשֶׁלֶת קְלִפַּת נֹגַהּ
וּמְקַבֵּל חַיּוּתָהּ מִמֶּנָּה, שֶׁהֵם כָּל דְּבָרִים הַטְּהוֹרִים
וּמֻתָּרִים שֶׁנַּעֲשִׂית בָּהֶם הַמִּצְוָה מַעֲשִׂית.

כְּגוֹן קְלַף הַתְּפִלִּין וּמְזוּזָה וְסֵפֶר תּוֹרָה . . . וְכֵן אֶתְרֹג
שֶׁאֵינוֹ עָרְלָה, וּמְעוֹת הַצְּדָקָה שֶׁאֵינָן גֵּזֶל, וְכַיּוֹצֵא בָּהֶם.
וְעַכְשָׁו שֶׁמְּקַיֵּם בָּהֶם מִצְוַת ה' וּרְצוֹנוֹ, הֲרֵי הַחַיּוּת שֶׁבָּהֶם
עוֹלָה וּמִתְבַּטֵּל וְנִכְלָל בְּאוֹר אֵין סוֹף בָּרוּךְ הוּא.

Through the performance of a mitzvah, a person causes a flood of G-d's infinite light to descend from Above and be enclothed within the corporeality of the world—within an object that was previously under the dominion of, and whose existence depended upon, the spiritual forces that obscure the G-dly reality. This includes all things that are kosher and permissible with which a mitzvah is then performed.

For example: The parchment used in *tefilin,* a *mezuzah,* or a Torah scroll . . . ; an *etrog* [citron], so long as it is not *orlah* [fruit from a tree's first three years, which are biblically proscribed]; money given to charity, so long as it had not been dishonestly acquired; and similarly with other [material] things. When one uses these objects to perform G-d's mitzvah and thereby fulfill His expressed desire, their vivifying force ascends and is absorbed within G-d's infinite light.

THE TZADDIK
IS PROTECTING
ERETZ YISRAEL
(*REVACH VEHATZALA*)
Yehoshua Wiseman, Israel

TEXT 4

The Dual Function of a Mitzvah

The Rebbe, Rabbi Menachem Mendel Schneerson,
Likutei Sichot 4, pp. 1193–1194

**RABBI MENACHEM
MENDEL SCHNEERSON
1902-1994**

The towering
Jewish leader of
the 20th century, known
as "the Lubavitcher
Rebbe," or simply as "the
Rebbe." Born in southern
Ukraine, the Rebbe escaped
Nazi-occupied Europe,
arriving in the U.S. in June
1941. The Rebbe inspired
and guided the revival of
traditional Judaism after
the European devastation,
impacting virtually every
Jewish community the
world over. The Rebbe
often emphasized that
the performance of just
one additional good deed
could usher in the era of
Mashiach. The Rebbe's
scholarly talks and writings
have been printed in more
than 200 volumes.

אִין דִי מִצְוֹת גוּפָא (אוּן אִין זֵייעֶר קִיוּם)
זַיינֶען פַארַאן עֶנלֶעכֶע צְווֵיי עִנְיָנִים.

אֵיין עִנְיָן אִיז ווָאס מִיט יֶעדֶער מִצְוָה אִיז מֶען מְקַיֵים
דֶעם אוֹיבֶּערְשְׁטְנְס רָצוֹן, ווָאס אִין דֶעם אִיז נִיט פַארַאן
קֵיין חִלוּק צְווִישְׁן אֵיין מִצְוָה אוּן אַ צְווֵייטֶער; עֶר אִיז
מְקַיֵים אַ מִצְוָה נִיט צוּלִיב דֶער פְּרָטִיוּת'דִיקֶער מַעֲלָה
אוּן סְגֻלָה ווָאס אִיז דָא אִין דֶער מִצְוָה, נָאר בִּכְדֵי צוּ
מְקַיֵים זַיין דֶעם רָצוֹן הָעֶלְיוֹן, וְכַמַאֲמָר "אֵלוּ נִצְטַוָּה
לַחְטוֹב עֵצִים" (לקוטי תורה שלח מ, א) ווָאלְטְן מִיר
עֶס גֶעטָאן מִיטן זֶעלְבְּן חַיוּת (פוּן קַבָּלַת עוֹל) ווִי מִיר
הָאבְּן בַּיי מְקַיֵים זַיין דִי מִצְוָה פוּן הֲנָחַת תְּפִלִּין.

אוּן אַ צְווֵייטֶער עִנְיָן אִיז דָא אִין מִצְוֹת, ווָאס יֶעדֶער
מִצְוָה טוּט אוֹיף אַ זְכוּךְ אִין דֶעם מֶעֶנטְשְׁן ווָאס אִיז אִיר
מְקַיֵים . . . אוֹיךְ אִין דִי גַשְׁמִיוּת'דִיקֶע זַאכְן מִיט ווֶעלְכֶע
דִי מִצְוָה ווֶערְט גֶעטָאן, בִּיז - אוֹיךְ אַ זְכוּךְ אִין וֶועלְט.

דֶער חִלוּק צְווִישְׁן דִי צְווֵיי עִנְיָנִים אִיז: אִין דֶעם עֶרְשְׁטְן
עִנְיָן אִיז נִיט נוֹגֵעַ דֶער **פְּרָט** פוּן דֶער מִצְוָה; אִין דֶעם
זַיינֶען אַלֶע מִצְוֹת גְלַייךְ, ווַייל אַלֶע מִצְוֹת זַיינֶען דָאךְ
רְצוֹנוֹ יִתְבָּרֵךְ. מַה שֶׁאֵין כֵּן אִין צְווֵייטְן עִנְיָן אִיז נוֹגֵעַ דִי
מִצְוָה **פְּרָטִית**, ווַייל יֶעדֶער מִצְוָה ווֶערְט אַן אַנְדֶער לְבוּשׁ
צוּ דֶער נְשָׁמָה אוּן פּוֹעֶל'ט אַן אַנְדֶער זְכוּךְ אִין וֶועלְט.

we live in a concealed world we don't see G-dliness.

Survival Ego

Doing a mitzvah penetrates the concealment so something else breaks the world we experience.

There are two aspects to every mitzvah:

One aspect is the fact that with every mitzvah that we do, we fulfill G-d's will. In this regard, there is no difference between one mitzvah and the next. An individual fulfills a mitzvah not because of its unique qualities and its unique effects, but simply to carry out G-d's will. This aspect of the mitzvah is aptly demonstrated in the observation of Rabbi Shne'ur Zalman of Liadi (*LIKUTEI TORAH*, SHELACH, P. 40A) that if we were commanded to chop wood we would do it in obedience to the divine will *with the same enthusiasm* as we fulfill the mitzvah of *tefilin*.

The second aspect of a mitzvah is that each mitzvah brings a spiritual refinement to the individual performing the mitzvah. . . . Similarly, the mitzvah brings a spiritual refinement to the objects with which it is performed, and ultimately refines the world.

The difference between these two elements is that with the first aspect, the specifics of the mitzvah are irrelevant. All *mitzvot* are equal, for they are all equally G-d's will. By contrast, the second element highlights the significance of each mitzvah's specific details, for each mitzvah brings a dissimilar branch of spiritual enhancement to the soul, and it refines the world in a different way.

King Solomon compares *mitzvot* to light. In this two-minute clip, **Rabbi Shais Taub** explains the profound connection: *myjli.com/canhappen*

TEXT 5

It's about Our Benefit

Midrash, *Bereishit Rabah* 44:1

וְכִי מַה אִיכְפַּת לֵיהּ לְהַקָדוֹשׁ בָּרוּךְ הוּא
לְמִי שֶׁשּׁוֹחֵט מִן הַצַּוָּאר אוֹ מִי שֶׁשּׁוֹחֵט מִן הָעוֹרֶף?
הֱוֵי, לֹא נִתְּנוּ הַמִצְוֹת אֶלָא לְצָרֵף בָּהֶם אֶת הַבְּרִיּוֹת.

Does G-d truly mind if a person slaughters an animal from the throat or slaughters it from the back of the neck? Rather, the *mitzvot* were given only to refine the individuals who perform them.

Printless
m.nd Rl

BEREISHIT RABAH

An early rabbinic commentary on the Book of Genesis. This Midrash bears the name of Rabbi Oshiya Rabah (Rabbi Oshiya "the Great"), whose teaching opens this work. This Midrash provides textual exegeses and stories, expounds upon the biblical narrative, and develops and illustrates moral principles. Produced by the sages of the Talmud in the Land of Israel, its use of Aramaic closely resembles that of the Jerusalem Talmud. It was first printed in Constantinople in 1512 together with 4 other Midrashic works on the other 4 books of the Pentateuch.

TEXT 6

The Variety of *Mitzvot*

Midrash, *Tanchuma*, Shelach 15

וְלֹא הִנִּיחַ דָּבָר בָּעוֹלָם שֶׁלֹּא נָתַן בּוֹ מִצְוָה לְיִשְׂרָאֵל.

יָצָא לַחֲרוֹשׁ, שֶׁנֶּאֱמַר, "לֹא תַחֲרֹשׁ
בְּשׁוֹר וּבַחֲמֹר" (דברים כב, י).

לִזְרוֹעַ, "לֹא תִזְרַע כַּרְמְךָ כִּלְאָיִם" (שם, ט).

לִקְצוֹר, "כִּי תִקְצֹר קְצִירְךָ בְשָׂדֶךָ" (שם כד, יט).

בְּדִישָׁה, "לֹא תַחְסֹם שׁוֹר בְּדִישׁוֹ" (שם כה, ד).

בָּעִיסָה, "רֵאשִׁית עֲרֹסֹתֵכֶם" (במדבר טו, כ) . . .

קַן צִפּוֹר, "שַׁלֵּחַ תְּשַׁלַּח" (דברים כב, ז).

חַיָּה וָעוֹף, "וְשָׁפַךְ אֶת דָּמוֹ וְכִסָּהוּ בֶּעָפָר" (ויקרא יז, יג).

נָטַע, "וַעֲרַלְתֶּם עָרְלָתוֹ" (שם יט, כג).

קָבַר מֵת, "לֹא תִתְגֹּדְדוּ" (דברים יד, א).

מְגַלֵּחַ שְׂעַר רֹאשׁ, "לֹא תַקִּפוּ פְּאַת רֹאשְׁכֶם" (ויקרא יט, כז).

בָּנָה בַיִת, "וְעָשִׂיתָ מַעֲקֶה" (דברים כב, ח). בִּמְזוּזָה,
"וּכְתַבְתָּם עַל מְזֻזוֹת בֵּיתֶךָ וּבִשְׁעָרֶיךָ" (שם ו, ט).

נִתְכַּסָּה בְּטַלִּית, "וְעָשׂוּ לָהֶם צִיצִת" (במדבר טו, לח).

TANCHUMA

A Midrashic work bearing the name of Rabbi Tanchuma, a 4th-century Talmudic sage quoted often in this work. "Midrash" is the designation of a particular genre of rabbinic literature usually forming a running commentary on specific books of the Bible. *Tanchuma* provides textual exegeses, expounds upon the biblical narrative, and develops and illustrates moral principles. *Tanchuma* is unique in that many of its sections commence with a halachic discussion, which subsequently leads into nonhalachic teachings.

G-d did not leave anything in the world without providing the people of Israel with a means of performing a mitzvah with it:

A person proceeding to plow must heed, "Do not plow with an ox and a donkey together" (DEUTERONOMY 22:10).

[Similarly, if one wishes to . . .]

Sow—"Do not sow *kilayim* [hybrid plantings] in your vineyard" (IBID., V. 9).

Reap—"When you reap your harvest in your field [leave any forgotten sheaves for the poor]" (DEUTERONOMY 24:19).

Thresh—"Do not muzzle an ox while it is threshing" (IBID., 25:4).

Knead dough—"From the first of your kneading bowl [separate some as *challah*, as a gift to the priest]" (NUMBERS 15:20). . . .

Remove eggs from a nest—"Send away the mother bird" (DEUTERONOMY 22:7).

Slaughter a wild animal or a fowl—"Cover its blood with soil" (LEVITICUS 17:13).

Plant a tree—"Observe its *orlah* [by abstaining from its fruit for its first three years]" (IBID., 19:23).

Bury a deceased relative—"Do not [mourn excessively by] slashing yourself [in grief]" (DEUTERONOMY 14:1).

Take a haircut—"Do not shave the corners of your head" (LEVITICUS 19:27).

Build a house—"Install a [safety] fence [around its roof]" (DEUTERONOMY 22:8) and "Inscribe [these words] on the doorposts of your home and on your city gates" (IBID., 6:9).

Wear a garment [that has four corners]— "They shall make for themselves *tsitsit*" (NUMBERS 15:38).

FIGURE 3.1

 The Mitzvah's Dual Impact

Performing *mitzvot* transforms the world into a "home for G-d," an environment in which the divine reality is fully expressed, with a two-pronged approach:

 In a general way: every mitzvah-action counteracts the inherently "selfish" self-perception of physical reality and reinforces that truth— that it exists only to serve a higher purpose.

 In a specific way: each mitzvah makes a particular part of the world more spiritually refined: more generous, more aware, more respectful, more loving, more connected, etc.

III. THE PARTNER MENTALITY

The materials presented until this point add up to an awesome realization: G-d created the world for a reason, and we are His partners in bringing all that exists to its ultimate purpose and destination. We are not low-level (or even high-level) employees; we are *partners*—with G-d Himself!—in the largest, most critical, and most beautiful enterprise that ever existed.

To fully absorb this revelation, it is necessary to define "a partner" in this context, as well as to explore the implications of this realization.

THE SHOFAR (LE SHOFAR)
1914–15, Marc Chagall, graphite, watercolor, gouache on gray paper, mounted on red paper, Musée National d'Art Moderne, Paris

TEXT 7

A Partner in the Work of Creation

Talmud, Shabbat 119b

כָּל הַמִתְפַּלֵּל בְּעֶרֶב שַׁבָּת וְאוֹמֵר "וַיְכֻלּוּ", מַעֲלֶה עָלָיו הַכָּתוּב כְּאִלּוּ נַעֲשָׂה שֻׁתָּף לְהַקָּדוֹשׁ בָּרוּךְ הוּא בְּמַעֲשֵׂה בְרֵאשִׁית.

The Torah considers those who recite the passage of *vayechulu* during the eve of Shabbat prayers as if they have become partners with G-d in the work of creation.

QUESTION

What are some of the key distinctions between an *employee* and a *partner*?

Equal in + equal out

Manager Grant
not equal py or work

BABYLONIAN TALMUD

A literary work of monumental proportions that draws upon the legal, spiritual, intellectual, ethical, and historical traditions of Judaism. The 37 tractates of the Babylonian Talmud contain the teachings of the Jewish sages from the period after the destruction of the 2nd Temple through the 5th century CE. It has served as the primary vehicle for the transmission of the Oral Law and the education of Jews over the centuries; it is the entry point for all subsequent legal, ethical, and theological Jewish scholarship.

Just Following Orders

Rabbi Yoel Kahn, *Shiurim Betorat Chabad*
(Netanya, Israel: Mayenotecha, 2006), p. 149

RABBI YOEL KAHAN
B. 1930

Lead expert on Chabad
philosophy. Rabbi
Kahan served as the
senior member and
leader of the team that
would memorize and
transcribe the Rebbe's
talks and discourses
that were delivered on
Shabbat and holidays,
when audio recordings
and taking notes is
proscribed. The leading
authority on Chabad
philosophy and the
Rebbe's teachings, he is
in the midst of publishing
a comprehensive
encyclopedia on Chabad
Chasidism, of which 10
volumes have already
appeared. He also
serves as the senior
educator of Chasidic
teachings at the Central
Lubavitcher Yeshiva.

לִכְאוֹרָה יְהוּדִי יָכוֹל לִטְעוֹן: לְמַאי נַפְקָא מִינָהּ בַּעֲבוֹדָתִי לָדַעַת שֶׁיּוֹם יָבוֹא וְהַגְּאֻלָּה תַּגִּיעַ? עָלַי לַעֲשׂוֹת אֶת עֲבוֹדָתִי וּלְקַיֵּם אֶת מִצְווֹתָיו שֶׁל הַקָּדוֹשׁ בָּרוּךְ הוּא, וְאֵין זֶה מֵעִנְיָנִי לָדַעַת מַהִי הַמַּטָּרָה בָּזֶה וּמַהִי תּוֹצָאַת הָעֲבוֹדָה.

מוּבָן מֵאֵלָיו שֶׁזּוֹ גִּישָׁה בִּלְתִּי נְכוֹנָה. מָשָׁל לְמָה הַדָּבָר דּוֹמֶה, לְחַיָּל בְּאֶמְצַע הַמִּלְחָמָה שֶׁיָּקוּם וְיֹאמַר, שֶׁאֵין זֶה מֵעִנְיָנוֹ לָדַעַת מַדּוּעַ הַמְפַקֵּד נָתַן פְּקֻדָּה לִירוֹת. לְדַעְתּוֹ, בִּזְמַן מִלְחָמָה הָעִקָּר הוּא לִהְיוֹת מְמֻשְׁמַע לַהוֹרָאוֹת, וְאֵין לוֹ צוֹרֶךְ לָדַעַת שֶׁעַל יְדֵי פְּעֻלּוֹתָיו הוּא מַרְחִיק אֶת הָאוֹיֵב וּמְקָרֵב אֶת נִצְחוֹן הַמִּלְחָמָה. חַיָּל שֶׁיֹּאמַר כַּךְ, אֲפִלּוּ יַעֲשֶׂה אֶת כָּל הַמֻּטָּל עָלָיו, יֶחְסַר לוֹ מוֹרַל וְחֵשֶׁק בַּמִּלְחָמָה, וּבְמִדָּה מְסֻיֶּמֶת הַדָּבָר גַּם יַשְׁפִּיעַ עַל צוּרַת הַלְחִימָה שֶׁלּוֹ, שֶׁלֹּא תִהְיֶה כְּפִי הַנִּדְרָשׁ.

כְּמוֹ כֵן בַּעֲבוֹדָתוֹ שֶׁל יְהוּדִי בְּתוֹרָה וּמִצְווֹת: יְהוּדִי אֵינוֹ יָכוֹל לוֹמַר שֶׁאֵין זֶה מֵעִנְיָנוֹ לָדַעַת שֶׁעַל יְדֵי קִיּוּם הַמִּצְווֹת הוּא מְקָרֵב אֶת הַנִּצָּחוֹן הַמְיֻחָל. יְהוּדִי בְּהֶחְלֵט צָרִיךְ לָדַעַת שֶׁמִּתְנַהֶלֶת כָּאן מִלְחָמָה בֵּין צַד הַקְּדֻשָּׁה לְצַד הַ'קְלִפָּה', וְעָלֵינוּ לְנַצֵּחַ בְּמִלְחָמָה זוֹ. הוּא צָרִיךְ לָדַעַת שֶׁעַל יְדֵי כָּל מִצְוָה נוֹסֶפֶת שֶׁהוּא מְקַיֵּם הוּא מֵבִיא עוֹד אֱלֹקוּת לָעוֹלָם וּבְכַךְ מְקָרֵב אֶת הַנִּצָּחוֹן.

A Jew can argue, "Practically, why is it important for me to know that the Redemption will arrive someday? I need to do my work and fulfill that which G-d instructs me to do. It's not my business to know or be concerned with the greater objectives and the results of my service!"

The fallacy of this approach should be self-understood, but here is an illustration: Imagine a soldier in the midst of battle standing up and saying, "It's not my business to know why my commanding officer gave me an order to fire my weapon. All that is important is that I meticulously follow the orders handed down by the chain of command. The fact that my actions impact the outcome of the battle—causing the enemy to retreat and bringing my side closer to victory—is irrelevant to me. I just need to shoot my rifle!" This soldier, even if he dutifully executes every order he is given, will lack morale and passion. Moreover, without a doubt, to one degree or another, it will negatively impact his performance on the battlefield.

The same is true regarding our service of G-d through Torah and mitzvah observance. We cannot claim that it is not our concern whether or not our service affects the long-awaited victory. We must know that there is a campaign underway and that it is our mission to bring it to its successful conclusion. We must be keenly aware of the reality that with each additional mitzvah, we reveal more G-dliness in this world, thereby moving a step closer to the ultimate triumph.

THE SEVEN AGES OF MAN: THE SOLDIER (SHAKESPEARE'S *AS YOU LIKE IT*, ACT II, SC. VII)
Robert Smirke (1752–1845), oil on panel

FIGURE 3.2

Employee vs. Partner I

EMPLOYEE MINDSET	**PARTNER MINDSET**
Focused on the *job description*	Focused on the company *mission statement*

TEXT 9

Altruistic Service

Ethics of the Fathers 1:3

אַנְטִיגְנוֹס אִישׁ סוֹכוֹ קִבֵּל מִשִּׁמְעוֹן הַצַּדִּיק. הוּא הָיָה אוֹמֵר: אַל תִּהְיוּ כַּעֲבָדִים הַמְשַׁמְּשִׁין אֶת הָרַב עַל מְנָת לְקַבֵּל פְּרָס, אֶלָּא הֱווּ כַּעֲבָדִים הַמְשַׁמְּשִׁין אֶת הָרַב שֶׁלֹּא עַל מְנָת לְקַבֵּל פְּרָס.

Antignos of Socho received the tradition from Shimon the Righteous. He would say, "Do not be as servants who serve their master for the sake of reward. Rather, be as servants who serve their master not for the sake of reward."

ETHICS OF THE FATHERS (PIRKEI AVOT)

A 6-chapter work on Jewish ethics that is studied widely by Jewish communities, especially during the summer. The first 5 chapters are from the Mishnah, tractate Avot. Avot differs from the rest of the Mishnah in that it does not focus on legal subjects; it is a collection of the sages' wisdom on topics related to character development, ethics, healthy living, piety, and the study of Torah.

FIGURE 3.3

Employee vs. Partner II

EMPLOYEE MINDSET	**PARTNER MINDSET**
Focused on the *job description*	Focused on the company *mission statement*
Reward-oriented	*Results*-oriented

A PUBLIC SERVANT
Arnold Friedman (1879–1946),
undated, oil on canvas,
The Phillips Collection,
Washington, D.C.

TEXT 10A

Don't Expect Delay

Maimonides, Mishnah, Sanhedrin, Ch. 10, Introduction

RABBI MOSHE BEN MAIMON (MAIMONIDES, RAMBAM) 1135-1204

Halachist, philosopher, author, and physician. Maimonides was born in Córdoba, Spain. After the conquest of Córdoba by the Almohads, he fled Spain and eventually settled in Cairo, Egypt. There, he became the leader of the Jewish community and served as court physician to the vizier of Egypt. He is most noted for authoring the *Mishneh Torah*, an encyclopedic arrangement of Jewish law; and for his philosophical work, *Guide for the Perplexed*. His rulings on Jewish law are integral to the formation of halachic consensus.

הַיְסוֹד הַשְּׁנֵים עָשָׂר: יְמוֹת הַמָּשִׁיחַ. וְהוּא לְהַאֲמִין וּלְאַמֵּת שֶׁיָּבֹא וְלֹא יַחֲשֹׁב שֶׁיִּתְאַחֵר, "אִם יִתְמַהְמֵהּ חַכֵּה־לוֹ" (חבקוק ב, ג).

The twelfth foundation [of Jewish belief] is the era of Mashiach. That is, to believe and affirm that he will come, and not to think that he will be delayed. [In the words of the prophet, Habakkuk 2:3,] "If he tarries, expectantly await him."

TEXT 10B

A Denial of Torah

Maimonides, *Mishneh Torah*, Laws of Kings 11:1

וְכָל מִי שֶׁאֵינוֹ מַאֲמִין בּוֹ, אוֹ מִי שֶׁאֵינוֹ מְחַכֶּה לְבִיאָתוֹ, לֹא בִּשְׁאָר נְבִיאִים בִּלְבַד הוּא כּוֹפֵר, אֶלָּא בַּתּוֹרָה וּבְמשֶׁה רַבֵּנוּ.

Anyone who does not believe in Mashiach or does not expectantly await his coming denies not only the other prophets, but also the Torah and our teacher Moses.

TEXT 10C

Although He May Tarry

Siddur, "Ani Maamin" Declaration of Faith

אֲנִי מַאֲמִין בֶּאֱמוּנָה שְׁלֵמָה בְּבִיאַת הַמָּשִׁיחַ. וְאַף עַל
פִּי שֶׁיִּתְמַהְמֵהַּ, עִם כָּל זֶה אֲחַכֶּה לוֹ בְּכָל יוֹם שֶׁיָּבוֹא.

I believe with complete faith in the coming of Mashiach. Although he may tarry, I expectantly await his coming each day.

SIDDUR

The siddur is the Jewish prayer book. It was originally developed by the sages of the Great Assembly in the 4th century BCE, and later reconstructed by Rabban Gamliel after the destruction of the Second Temple. Various authorities continued to add prayers, from then until contemporary times. It includes praise of G-d, requests for personal and national needs, selections of the Bible, and much else. Various Jewish communities have slightly different versions of the siddur.

A DAY DREAM
1877, Eastman Johnson, oil on paperboard, Fine Arts Museums of San Francisco

"I'm on My Way...."

Talmud, Sanhedrin 98a

רַבִּי יְהוֹשֻׁעַ בֶּן לֵוִי אַשְׁכַּח לְאֵלִיָּהוּ . . .
אָמַר לֵיהּ, "אֵימַת אָתֵי מָשִׁיחַ?"

אָמַר לֵיהּ, "זִיל שַׁיְילֵיהּ לְדִידֵיהּ".

"וְהֵיכָא יָתֵיב?"

"אַפִּיתְחָא דְקַרְתָּא".

"וּמַאי סִימָנֵיהּ?"

"יָתֵיב בֵּינֵי עַנְיֵי סוֹבְלֵי חֳלָאִים. וְכֻלָּן שָׁרוּ
וַאֲסִירִי בְּחָד זִימְנָא, אִיהוּ שָׁרֵי חַד וְאָסִיר חַד.
אָמַר: דִּילְמָא מִבָּעֵינָא, דְּלָא אֲעַכֵּב".

אָזַל לְגַבֵּיהּ. אָמַר לֵיהּ, "שָׁלוֹם עָלֶיךָ רַבִּי וּמוֹרִי!"

אָמַר לֵיהּ, "שָׁלוֹם עָלֶיךָ בַּר לֵיוָאי".

אָמַר לֵיהּ, "לְאֵימָת אָתֵי מַר?"

אָמַר לֵיהּ, "הַיּוֹם".

אָתָא לְגַבֵּי אֵלִיָּהוּ . . . אָמַר לֵיהּ, "שַׁקּוּרֵי קָא
שַׁקַּר בִּי! דְּאָמַר לִי הַיּוֹם אָתֵינָא, וְלֹא אָתָא".

אָמַר לֵיהּ, "הָכִי אָמַר לָךְ: 'הַיּוֹם - אִם
בְּקֹלוֹ תִשְׁמָעוּ (תהילים צה, ז)'".

Rabbi Yehoshua ben Levi met with
Elijah the Prophet . . . and asked
him, "When will Mashiach come?"

Elijah responded, "Go and ask him."

"Where is he located?"

"At the gateway of the city [of Rome]."

"By what sign [can I recognize] him?"

"He is sitting among the poor who suffer from
illnesses. All the others untie all their bandages
at once, and then rebandage all their wounds
together—whereas he unties and rebandages
each wound separately, thinking, 'Perhaps
I will be needed [immediately to bring the
Redemption], and I must not be delayed.'"

Rabbi Yehoshua ben Levi went to him and greeted
him, "Peace upon you, my master and teacher."

Mashiach responded, "Peace upon you, son of Levi."

"Master! When will you come?"

"Today."

Rabbi Yehoshua came [back] to Elijah . . . and complained, "He lied to me. He told me that he is coming today, and he didn't come."

Elijah responded, "This is what he told you, 'Today— if you will listen to His voice' (PSALMS 95:7)."

A VIEW OF ROME THE COLOSSEUM
1816, Fyodor Matveyev, oil on canvas, Tretyakov Gallery, Moscow

What was the purpose of Mashiach's "trick answer"? Why did the Redeemer not provide a straightforward response—that he will arrive when we listen to G-d's voice?

TEXT 12

Mashiach Is On Call

Rabbi Yaakov Sekili, *Torat Haminchah* 59

וּכְתִיב "וְרוּחַ אֱלֹקִים מְרַחֶפֶת", וְהוּא . . . רוּחוֹ שֶׁל מָשִׁיחַ . . .
לְלַמֶּדְךָ שֶׁהַמָּשִׁיחַ מוּכָן וּמְזוּמָּן מִשֵּׁשֶׁת יְמֵי בְרֵאשִׁית,
וְהוּא מְרַחֵף עַל פְּנֵי הַמַּיִם וְאֵינוֹ מִתְעַכֵּב אֶלָּא בִּשְׁבִיל
הַתְּשׁוּבָה . . . הֲדָא הוּא דִכְתִיב, "הַיּוֹם אִם בְּקוֹלוֹ תִשְׁמָעוּ".

The Torah (GENESIS 1:2) states that
"the spirit of G-d hovered [over the surface of the
waters]" . . . referring to the soul of Mashiach. . . .
This informs us that the soul of Mashiach has
been standing at the ready ever since the six
days of Creation. It hovers over the waters, held
back only until we return to G-d. . . . As it is
stated, "Today—if you will listen to His voice."

**RABBI YAAKOV SEKILI
14TH CENTURY**

Rabbi and preacher.
Little is known about the
life of Rabbi Sekili, but
it appears that he was
raised in Spain, where
he studied under Rabbi
Shlomo ibn Aderet
(Rashba), and later lived
in the Middle East. His
book of philosophically
oriented sermons on the
weekly Torah portion,
Torat Haminchah,
was published from
manuscript in 1991.

FIGURE 3.4

Employee vs. Partner III

EMPLOYEE MINDSET   **PARTNER MINDSET**

Focused on the   Focused on the company
job description   *mission statement*

Reward-oriented   *Results*-oriented

Does not need to believe in   Certain of and anticipates
the enterprise's success   the success of the enterprise

THE DOUBLE DREAM OF SPRING
Paris, January–May 1915,
Giorgio de Chirico, Oil on canvas,
The Museum of Modern Art, N.Y.

Dream vs. Reality

The Rebbe, Rabbi Menachem Mendel Schneerson,
Torat Menachem 5744:4, pp. 2210–2213

בְּהֶמְשֵׁךְ לְהַמְזְכָּר לְעֵיל אוֹדוֹת עִנְיַן הַגְּאֻלָּה, יֶשְׁנָם כָּאֵלּוּ שֶׁמִּתְעוֹרֶרֶת אֶצְלָם תְּמִיהָה וּפְלִיאָה (אַף שֶׁמִּטְעָמִים מוּבָנִים אֵינָם מַעֲלִים תְּמִיהָה זוֹ עַל דַּל שְׂפָתָם):

הֲיִתָּכֵן, מְהַרְהְרִים הֵם, שֶׁיּוֹשֵׁב לוֹ יְהוּדִי לְדַבֵּר בָּרַבִּים, וּבְכָל הִתְוַעֲדוּת וְהִתְוַעֲדוּת מַכְרִיז לְלֹא הֶרֶף וְאֵינוֹ מַפְסִיק לְדַבֵּר אוֹדוֹת נוֹשֵׂא אֶחָד: בִּיאַת מְשִׁיחַ צִדְקֵנוּ. וּבְהַדְגָּשָׁה שֶׁאֵין זֶה דָּבָר שֶׁנִּדְפַּס בִּלְבַד, אֶלָּא הַכַּוָּנָה לְבִיאַת מְשִׁיחַ צִדְקֵנוּ בְּפוֹעַל מַמָּשׁ, לְמַטָּה מֵעֲשָׂרָה טְפָחִים וְתֵיכֶף וּמִיָּד מַמָּשׁ בְּיוֹם זֶה עַצְמוֹ. וּבְנִדּוֹן דִּידָן, יוֹם הַשַּׁבָּת פָּרָשַׁת פִּינְחָס תשד"מ! וּכְמוֹ כֵן אוֹמְרִים בְּכָל פַּעַם שֶׁיִּבָּנֶה "שֶׁיִּבָּנֶה בֵּית הַמִּקְדָּשׁ בִּמְהֵרָה בְיָמֵינוּ" וּמַדְגִּישִׁים שֶׁאֵין הַכַּוָּנָה 'בִּמְהֵרָה בְיָמֵינוּ' מָחָר, אֶלָּא הַיּוֹם מַמָּשׁ!

וַדַּאי מַאֲמִין כָּל יְהוּדִי שֶׁמְּשִׁיחַ צִדְקֵנוּ יָכוֹל לָבוֹא בְּכָל רֶגַע - "אֲחַכֶּה לוֹ בְּכָל יוֹם שֶׁיָּבוֹא". אֲבָל אַף עַל פִּי כֵן, מְהַרְהְרִים הֵם, מַהוּ פֵּשֶׁר הַהַנְהָגָה לְדַבֵּר לְלֹא הֶרֶף עַל עִנְיָן זֶה, וּלְהַדְגִּישׁ בְּכָל פַּעַם שֶׁבְּרֶגַע זֶה מַמָּשׁ יָכוֹל לָבוֹא מְשִׁיחַ צִדְקֵנוּ - דָּבָר שֶׁקָּשֶׁה לִפְעוֹל בְּרֶגֶשׁ שֶׁל הָאָדָם שֶׁיִּתְיַחֵס לְכַךְ כְּאֶל דָּבָר מְצִיאוּתִי. מַהוּ פֵּשֶׁר הַדִּבּוּר וְהַלַּהַט בְּעִנְיָן זֶה לְלֹא הֶרֶף בְּכָל הִתְוַעֲדוּת וְהִתְוַעֲדוּת כְּאִלּוּ הָיוּ רוֹצִים לְהַכְנִיס אֶת הַדָּבָר בְּרֹאשָׁם שֶׁל הַשּׁוֹמְעִים בְּכֹחַ.

אֶלָּא מַאי - מְסִיקִים הֵם - עִנְיָן זֶה הוּא בְּגֶדֶר שֶׁל
חֲלוֹם . . . חֲלוֹם טוֹב וְיָפֶה, וּבְנוּסַח הַתְּפִלָּה שֶׁאוֹמְרִים
בְּעֵת בִּרְכַּת כֹּהֲנִים: "שֶׁיִּהְיוּ כָּל חֲלוֹמוֹתַי עָלַי וְעַל כָּל
יִשְׂרָאֵל לְטוֹבָה", אֲבָל לֹא דָבָר מְצִיאוּתִי. וְאִם כֵּן, טוֹעֲנִים
הֵם, לְשֵׁם מָה צְרִיכִים לְדַבֵּר אוֹדוֹת עִנְיְנֵי חֲלוֹמוֹת?

אָמְנָם לַאֲמִיתוֹ שֶׁל דָּבָר הַהֵיפֶךְ הוּא הַנָּכוֹן:

יֶשְׁנוֹ דְרוּשׁ בְּתוֹרָה אוֹר (דִּבּוּר הַמַּתְחִיל שִׁיר הַמַּעֲלוֹת בְּשׁוּב
כו' הָיִינוּ כְּחוֹלְמִים) שֶׁבּוֹ מְבוֹאָר שֶׁכְּלָלוּת עִנְיַן הַגָּלוּת הוּא
בְּדֻגְמַת הַחֲלוֹם. שֶׁהַחֲלוֹם הוּא מְחַבֵּר שְׁנֵי הֲפָכִים בְּנוֹשֵׂא אֶחָד.

כְּלוֹמַר, אַדְרַבָּה. מְצִיאוּת הַגָּלוּת הִיא חֲלוֹם.
וְאִלּוּ הַגְּאֻלָּה, זוֹהִי מְצִיאוּתוֹ הָאֲמִתִּית שֶׁל יְהוּדִי! . . .

הֲרֵי בְּרֶגַע אֶחָד יָכוֹל הַמַּצָּב לְהִתְהַפֵּךְ מִן הַקָּצֶה אֶל
הַקָּצֶה, הַיְינוּ שֶׁיּוֹצְאִים מֵ"חֲלוֹם" הַגָּלוּת וּבָאִים
לַמְצִיאוּת הָאֲמִתִּית - גְּאֻלָּה בְּפוֹעַל מַמָּשׁ.

אִם כֵּן בְּוַדַּאי שֶׁבְּיָדוֹ שֶׁל כָּל אֶחָד וְאַחַת לִפְעוֹל שֶׁהַגְּאֻלָּה
תָּבוֹא בִּמְהֵרָה בְּיָמֵינוּ. וְלֹא רַק מָחָר אוֹ לְאַחַר זְמַן, אֶלָּא הַיּוֹם
מַמָּשׁ, שַׁבָּת פָּרָשַׁת פִּינְחָס שְׁנַת תשמ"ד, וּבְשַׁבָּת זוֹ עַצְמָהּ
לִפְנֵי תְּפִלַּת מִנְחָה. וּבְפַשְׁטוּת - שֶׁבְּרֶגַע זֶה מַמָּשׁ פּוֹתְחִים אֶת
הָעֵינַיִם וְרוֹאִים שֶׁמְּשִׁיחַ צִדְקֵנוּ נִמְצָא עִמָּנוּ בְּבֵית כְּנֶסֶת וּבֵית
מִדְרָשׁ זֶה, בָּשָׂר וָדָם, נְשָׁמָה בַּגּוּף, לְמַטָּה מֵעֲשָׂרָה טְפָחִים.

We have been discussing the Redemption and the
era of Mashiach. Some in the audience are genuinely
astounded at this (although, for obvious reasons,

they do not openly voice their amazement): How
can an individual appear in public, week after week,
and repeatedly and unceasingly discuss a single
subject—the coming of Mashiach? Moreover, this
individual emphasizes that he is not merely discussing
the published Torah materials on this topic; rather,
he is discussing our righteous Mashiach's *actual
coming*—in our *tangible* reality, here on physical
earth! And *immediately*—on this very day—Shabbat
Parshat Pinchas, 5744! This individual further
instructs others to sing, on each and every occasion:
Sheyiboneh Beit Hamikdash—"May the Holy Temple
be rebuilt *speedily in our days*!" And he points out
that "speedily in our days" does not refer to the very
near future; it means quite literally, "speedily, *today*"!

Certainly, every Jew believes that Mashiach can
come at any moment, [in keeping with one of the
fundamentals of Jewish faith that states,] "I await his
coming every day." Nevertheless—they wonder—how
is it justifiable to discuss this topic without letup, and
to emphasize on each occasion that Mashiach can
come *at that very moment*? Is it not rather challenging
to expect people to relate to Mashiach's imminence
as if it were a tangible fact of our reality? So why does
this individual speak incessantly about this, on every
occasion, and with such single-minded intensity, as if to
forcefully ram the idea into the minds of his listeners?

Their conclusion is that all this is a beautiful dream (and, as we recite in our prayers, "May all my dreams be positively fulfilled for me and for all of Israel")—nice, but not realistic. If so, they claim, there is truly no point in discussing one's dreams at such length and with such frequency.

The truth, however, is precisely the opposite:

Rabbi Shne'ur Zalman of Liadi delivered a discourse based on the verse, "When G-d returns the exiles of Israel, we shall be as those who have dreamed" (PSALMS 126:1). He explained that our current state of Exile is comparable to a dream—because in a dream, one's sense of perception can tolerate the most contradictory and irrational things.

In other words, our current "reality" is a dream, whereas the world of Mashiach is our true reality. In a single moment, the situation can be reversed from one extreme to the other. We can awaken from the dream of Exile and enter the true reality—the actual state of Redemption. . . .

If so, each and every individual present in this room certainly has the ability to make the Redemption come immediately: not tomorrow or in the near future, but right now, on this Shabbat *Parshat Pinchas*, 5744, before we even have a chance to recite the afternoon prayers. Simply stated: at this very moment, we open our eyes and see Mashiach, in the flesh, with us, here in this room.

KEY POINTS

1   The purpose of Creation, according to Chasidic
    teachings, is G-d's desire for a home in our
    material world and corporeal reality.

2   The physical world is referred to as the "lowly world"
    because it obscures the truth that G-d pervades
    every aspect of existence. Making the world a "home
    for G-d" means to penetrate this concealment
    and transform physical reality into a place that
    expresses the divine goodness and perfection.

3   The messianic world is not only a reward for doing
    mitzvot, but it is the actual result of these actions:
    A mitzvah transforms the object with which it is
    performed from a self-defined existence into an
    instrument of G-d's will. In addition, each mitzvah
    makes a particular part of the world more receptive
    to spirituality, bringing it one step closer to
    expressing the divine goodness and perfection.

4   The *mitzvot* directly engage with only a small
    percentage of the physical universe and of each
    individual life. But each mitzvah-action is the product
    of countless other actions and processes. In this way,
    the whole of creation is ultimately transformed.

5   The sages teach us that by doing *mitzvot*, we become "a partner with G-d in the work of creation." There are a number of distinctions between a partner mentality and an employee mentality: (a) An employee is driven primarily by his or her job description, whereas for the partner, the company's mission statement is the driving force. (b) An employee is motivated by reward, whereas a partner is results-driven. (c) A partner is confident of the success of the enterprise.

6   The twelfth foundation of Judaism (by Maimonides's count) is not only the belief that Mashiach will come, but also the daily anticipation of the Redemption. When we understand that the true nature of reality is the divine goodness and perfection, the expectation of Mashiach's imminent coming is more realistic than the concealment that obscures this truth.

ADDITIONAL READINGS

Mitzvot / Their Spiritual Role and Function

By Rabbi Faitel Levin

RABBI FAITEL LEVIN

Chasidic scholar, halachist, and author. Born in England, Rabbi Levin is the author of *Halacha, Medical Science and Technology: Perspectives on Contemporary Halacha Issues* and *Heaven on Earth: Reflections on the Theology of Rabbi Menachem M. Schneerson, the Lubavitcher Rebbe*; and is the founding editor of *The Australian Journal of Torah Thought*. He is currently the rabbi of the Brighton Hebrew Congregation in Melbourne, Australia, and a most sought-after lecturer on halachic issues.

It is now time to devote a chapter to bring the central role and spiritual function of physical mitzvot into sharper relief. We first step back to look at the views of previous thought systems.

Mitzvot in Classic Jewish Writings

Various classic scholars have provided insight into the question of the role of physical mitzvot within Judaism. Maimonides[1] understands mitzvot as a type of springboard designed to aid the masses to overcome their carnality, to free their minds from their bodies towards true spiritual endeavor. That is, the true arena for religious endeavor is indeed the mind. According to Maimonides, man's highest goal in life is metaphysical speculation. G-d is Supreme Logic and in the human too, logic reigns supreme. Thus, religious experience, or communication between man and G-d, is achieved specifically by way of a rational interchange: man's mind contemplates Divine ideas. It is only as a type of necessary evil as it were, to provide a cure to help get the body out of the way, that mitzvot enter the picture.

Sefer HaChinuch, a classic medieval compilation, generally offers some philosophical insight into the six hundred and thirteen mitzvot collated in the work. Generally, it might be said that *Chinuch* regards mitzvot as performing a pedagogic, conditioning role.[2] Man's heart is influenced by his actions. Accordingly, each mitzvah

aims to have a particular positive effect on the person performing it, refining him, elevating him. In this system then, too, mitzvot are not the primary arena for religious endeavor, not man's ultimate mode for relating to G-d, rather a vehicle by which to enhance man's true religious standing.

Chasidic literature, too, stresses the value inherent in refining man through the performance of mitzvot (as discussed in chapter ten. It has been in fact erroneously portrayed as anti-legal, as a system that somewhat disregards the externalities of Judaism, in search of the core.

In fact, there is much in Chasidic theology, however, that serves to establish a most significant religious role for mitzvot (subsequently receiving particular emphasis and focus in the Dirah Betachtonim system). Indeed, a very basic argument from general Chasidic literature aims to emphasize the importance of the strict adherence to the minutiae of physical mitzvot.

The Physical Is No Further From G-d

Let us return once again to the very start, to the prevalent notion that meditation rather than physical mitzvot—activities of the mind rather than of the hand, the abstract rather than the concrete, the transcendent rather than the real—are closer to G-d. Upon analysis, apart from all we have said till this point, this attitude is based in part on an erroneous extrapolation from what is common in the human world.

A freshman, for example, would attempt to display nothing but his highest intellectual acumen when speaking to a world authority on his subject. An ordinary person would attempt to display nothing but his best behavior in the presence of a saint. Such is the nature of much of our experience: the knowing, not the ignorant, consult meaningfully with the expert; the talented, rather than the mediocre, can collaborate with the truly gifted; the strong, not the feeble, can spar with the mighty; the bright, rather than the dull, can converse with the brilliant; the noble, rather than the ordinary, can approach the sublime. Extrapolating from this, it is assumed that, if anything, for communicating with transcendent G-d Himself, only man's most sublime features—only his spiritual faculties—can be of use, whereas his more mundane dimensions must be suppressed and hidden. As it were, if only rungs eight and nine of the ladder are appropriate for communicating with rung ten, it is certainly they that are appropriate for communicating with rung one hundred.

But all of this assumes that man and G-d are in fact on the same ladder, that G-d is at the loftier end of the same continuum as man. But as we have seen earlier,[3] a great divide separates all of man's faculties, including his heart and mind, from G-d. It is, as we have seen, even inappropriate to say that G-d cannot be comprehended by the human mind. G-d is separated from man by a chasm, a "quantum leap." Moreover, a great divide separates G-d Himself from even *Divine* wisdom, and kindness—that is, from the very "operating systems" of wisdom and kindness. For all specific features and defined entities, however lofty, are meaningless to G-d Himself as He stands prior to tzimtzum.[4] It follows, that the notion that man's mental and emotional endeavors enjoy a *natural* relationship with G-d is mistaken. Human capabilities and G-d are not on the same ladder. Man's loftiest ideas and most sublime sentiments are incomparably further removed from G-d than are a child's intellectual displays from a world authority's thinking, his most refined behavior is further removed than is a crude person's behavior

from a saint—for indeed, in the latter cases the distance is relative, in the former it is absolute.

Moreover, upon reflection it can be seen that man's lower and higher faculties are in fact, inherently, equidistant from G-d. Where two arenas exist as totally detached frames of references, the highs and lows in one arena are meaningless in the other. By way of analogy, to a deaf person, there is no difference between particularly pleasing and uplifting harmony, or particularly dissonant and irritating cacophony. An outstanding musical symphony and particularly unpleasant noise will elicit precisely the same response—the same lack of response. Unlike the hard of hearing, the deaf have no access to the world of sound at all, their exclusion is not relative but absolute, excluded by an unnegotiable chasm; hence, the intense differences the hearing discern and insist on affirming in the world of sound, not only lose their prominence with regard to the deaf, but lose their values altogether. Similarly (though in reverse), since man is removed from G-d by an *absolute* chasm, since G-d operates on an "operating system" which has no relationship, no channels of discourse with man's "operating system," the human's loftier side and mundane side are equidistant from G-d—they are equally irrelevant and meaningless.

But if man, by his very nature, has no faculties which relate meaningfully to G-d—does this mean that all religious activities lose their inherent value? If man is separated from G-d as the deaf are from sound, if man's lofty side elicits the same response in G-d as does his mundane side—zero—then what is the value of religious endeavor on his part?

Chasidut maintains that, indeed, it is solely the fact that G-d's inscrutable Will calls for a certain form of behavior that imbues this behavior with significance. If not for G-d's command, no form of human behavior would, in fact, be meaningful at all to Him.[5]

It follows, then, that though the criteria of the human frame of reference judge prayer and meditation more lofty and spiritual than physical mitzvot, there is no such preference in terms of G-d. Prima facie—if not for G-d's command—both are equally meaningless; if G-d chooses, he can will either, and thereby imbue His desired choice with meaning.

The analogy of the deaf, used differently, further elucidates our position in relation to mitzvot.

A deaf person enters your room where an audio system is blaring out of control. You motion to him to improve it. He goes over, studies the dial and turns it—all the way up! He argues that he's fixed the stereo—the dial *looks* better this way! From his unfortunate point of view he cannot discern the values and preferences at the other side of the chasm. So his attempts to bring satisfaction to the hearing, using the criteria of vision available to him, result in the precise reverse.

Nevertheless, the deaf are in truth able to satisfy the criteria of those fortunate to have access to the world of sound. The hearing can prescribe to them how to act. If the instructions are followed correctly, the deaf will perform in a way that is of value to the world of sound.

In similar fashion, though man's activities cannot relate to G-d along the terms of his own frame of reference, they can be of value to G-d along lines plotted out by Him, on terms man can never apprehend.

This insight, in turn, reinforces the notion that we ought not assert that physical mitzvot are inherently inferior to prayer or meditation. Since G-d's instructions are our only clue to meaningful communication with Him, if G-d declares that physical mitzvot are meaningful to Him, we must acquiesce, as we have no faculties with which to make an alternative assessment. Indeed, if we insist upon offering G-d a prayer when He has requested wearing woolen strings (*tzitzit*), we might be acting no more appropriately than the deaf person who turns the stereo all the way up.

In sum, in light of general Chasidic teachings we dismiss the *a-priori* inferiority of physical mitzvot and set them on an inherently equal footing with man's spiritual activities as possible candidates for G-d's instructions. But these insights themselves do not yet ascribe *positive* qualities specific to physical mitzvot. We now return to Dirah Betachtonim where, in a final fleshing out of the basic ideas of the Dirah Betachtonim system, we elaborate upon the dimension of physical mitzvot which in fact justifies and warrants their predominance within Judaism.

Physical Mitzvot and the Essence of G-d

As amply dwelt upon in previous chapters, in addition to the notion that physical mitzvot uniquely express the infinity of G-d and the "infinity" of man's connection with Him (*manifestations*), more importantly, it is in particular they that provide an avenue to the Essence of G-d; whereas prayer and meditation, as lofty as they may seem, give expression only to *manifestations* of man and similarly relate merely to *manifestations* of G-d, but do not touch the essence, the *être*, of man or the Essence of G-d.

Put somewhat differently, more profoundly as well as more radically, "spiritual" religious activities are in a very subtle sense almost an insult to G-d. For they seem to ignore the fact that G-d is greater than humans *absolutely*, as they focus on areas in which man and G-d share. The types of *difference* between the worshiper and He who is worshipped that are at the fore during such forms of worship, as well as the modes of *communication* between the worshiper and the Worshipped that are involved, are not unique to the man-G-d relationship. Take prayer for example. This experience highlights that, unlike man, G-d is "Great, Powerful and Awesome," and that man is the mere beneficiary of all good that emanates from G-d the provider. But amongst human beings too there are differences in terms of greatness, power and awe, as well as benefactor-recipient relationships. Similarly with regard to the mode of communication involved, forms of praise similar to prayer can be utilized in communication even amongst humans, as was, for example, the case with serfs and monarchs of old. Moreover, similar forms of expression, such as passionate, humble or poetic statements, may be suitable in relation to awesome natural wonders or aesthetically overwhelming scenes. Neither the character of the highlighted differences nor the communication experience is uniquely man-G-d oriented.

Thus, these forms of worship are in a subtle sense almost an affront to G-d.[6] For communicating with G-d (only) on wavelengths that are appropriate for non-Divine beings regards Him, by implication, as belonging within the same framework.

More profoundly, it is true that once existence is a fact, there is a continuum of character and quality, ranging, for example, from the lowly to the great, or from the powerless to the mighty. "Spiritual" forms of worship occur along this continuum. Man at the lower end of the continuum of greatness, power and awe communicates with G-d who is at its apex. But this means that here is communication within the frame of reference of the existing, addressing *qualities* of things that exist—concerned with *manifestations* of existence—whilst the fact that things exist is taken for granted. This is in fact the reason why this experience can be enjoyed by even two non-Divine entities, two created beings: the experience is not created-Creator oriented, as it addresses issues that arise once existence is a fact.

Here lies the difficulty in confining man's communication with G-d through a spiritual medium. G-d is implicitly experienced as within the framework of the existing, whereas the deepest mystery of all, the deepest Divinity of all—the plane unique to G-d that stands outside this frame of reference, i.e. essence, *being*—is overlooked. It is forgotten here that G-d straddles reality's non-existence and existence, that G-d is the Master of being, that He called all into being (catered for the being of all)—including the frame of reference, existence itself. Relating to G-d's *qualities*, however sublime, with heart and mind via prayer and meditation is a rejection, as it were, of the Being of G-d that lies beyond.

But worship through physical mitzvot is different. Unlike the mind and heart, the hands, or moreover pieces of leather (*tefillin*), are not vehicles one would naturally choose for prayerful expression or for other forms of devotional experience. Nor are they appealing to the Love or Wisdom of G-d. No emotional quality, no logical idea, is expressed by mere hands or hide. Or, in other words, within the frame of reference of the rational, emotional and devotional these are totally unresponsive, meaningless, zero. Indeed, even the humility felt in prayer before the greatness, power and awesomeness of G-d is not applicable here, as that too is experiential, meaningless in the world of indifferent, hard and fast objects. Thus, when the worshiper does in fact take a piece of leather in his hand proposing to make it a vehicle for communicating with G-d—no intellectual, emotional or other religiously *meaningful* channels are available. But yet, even this religiously opaque object is part of G-d's world. In which way? Its being, and nothing else. Its being was catered for by G-d, it partakes in the Divine *Being*, and moreover, its very spiritual indifference represents transparency to

and oneness with its core, the in-itself of the Divine Being. Hence, when the worshiper attempts to make a connection with G-d—it occurs on the wavelength of Being.

The introduction of physical entities into worship, then, forces the worshiper beyond the continuum, beyond the frame of reference of qualities or features, to that plane unique to G-d—to the mystery of existence itself. Here, as it were, the very frame itself communicates with G-d: essence to Essence. In the absence of meaning and significance man is brought before the Essence of G-d.

True, then, as it appeared at the very outset, leather, wool or food appear uninspiring; certainly, an initial evaluation of Judaism may find it bogged down with minutiae and restrictions—but it is specifically the dark, finite, restrictive nature of physical mitzvot, maintains Dirah Betachtonim, that frees worship of the qualities that color existence, enabling man's essence as well as the essence of the physical objects involved to be bare of coverings, superimpositions and taintings, and be at one with the Essence of G-d, as it stands uncompromised beyond His most sublime qualities.

ENDNOTES

[1] In, for example, *Guide for the Perplexed* III, 51 and III, 27.
[2] See, inter alia, Mitzvah 545.
[3] Chapters 2, 6 and 11.
[4] Though, as we have seen, the 'laser apparition,' despite its manifest great difference from light, is inherently light. See above, Chapter 6.
[5] Put differently: Mitzvot are an expression of the Will of G-d. The Will of G-d transcends both human logic and even Divine logic, as it were. And in this transcendence, the a priori notion of material mitzvot being inferior to man's spiritual self, or even totally immaterial to G-d, which is ultimately the product of a rational assessment, loses itself. Thus, human acts that are inherently meaningless to G-d assume value—due to His Will. As explained at length in Chasidut, human experience provides an analogy: humans too can, in a limited way, will things that have no meaning for them when a purely rational or emotional assessment is undertaken—whereupon they assume meaning for them.
[6] See Megillah 25:a.

Heaven on Earth: Reflections on the Theology of Rabbi Menachem M. Schneerson, the Lubavitcher Rebbe (Brooklyn, N.Y.: Kehot Publication Society, 2002)

Reprinted with the permission of the publisher

Moshiach Means That the Torah Is for Real

by Rabbi Yanki Tauber

RABBI YANKI TAUBER
1965–

Chasidic scholar and author. A native of Brooklyn, N.Y., Rabbi Tauber is an internationally renowned author who specializes in adapting the teachings of the Lubavitcher Rebbe. He is a member of the JLI curriculum development team and has written numerous articles and books, including *Once Upon a Chassid* and *Beyond the Letter of the Law*.

In his famed introduction to his commentary on the Talmudic chapter known as Chelek [Ch. 10 of Talmud Tractate Sanhedrin], Maimonides enumerates the thirteen basic principles of the Jewish faith.

The first four principles deal with the belief in G-d: that G-d is the Original Cause upon which every creation is utterly dependent for its existence; that He is absolutely one and singular; that He is non-corporeal and timeless. The fifth principle establishes man's duty to serve Him and fulfill the purpose for which he was created. Principles six to eleven establish that G-d relates to humanity: that He communicates His will to man; that every word of the Torah was transmitted by G-d to Moses; that G-d observes and is concerned with the behavior of man; that He punishes the wicked and rewards the righteous.

The final two principles deal with the era of Moshiach: the belief that there will arise a leader who will bring the entire world to recognize and serve the Creator, ushering in an era of universal peace and Divine perfection.

What does it mean when we say that something is a "basic principle" in Judaism? A simple definition would be that in order to qualify as a "believing Jew" one must accept the truth of these thirteen precepts. But the Torah clearly makes no such distinctions. As Maimonides himself writes in his eighth principle:

> . . . This entire Torah, given to us by Moses, is from the mouth of the Almighty—namely, that it was communicated to him by G-d. . . . In this, there is no difference between the verses, 'The sons of Ham were Kush and Mitzrayim,' 'The name of his wife was Meithavel' and 'Timna was a concubine,' and the verses, 'I Am the L-rd your G-d' and 'Hear O Israel, [the L-rd is our G-d, the L-rd is One]': all are from the mouth of the Almighty, all is the Torah of G-d, perfect, pure, holy and true. . . . Our sages have said: Anyone who believes that the entire Torah is from the mouth of the Almighty, except for a single verse, is a heretic. . . .

So a "basic principle" is more than a required set of beliefs; that would apply to each and every word in the Torah. Rather, these are thirteen principles upon which everything else rests. The Hebrew word Maimonides uses is *yesodot*, "foundations": different parts of an edifice could conceivably exist independently of each other, but without the foundation, the entire building would collapse. So, too, each of these thirteen principles is a "foundation" to the entire Torah.

In other words, while every word in the Torah is equally important to the believer as a person, these principles are crucial to the faith itself. To deny that "Do not steal" is a divine commandment is no less heretical than to deny the existence of G-d; but belief in the rest of the Torah is not dependent upon the fact that G-d said not to steal. On the other hand, things like the existence of G-d, His absolute and exclusive power, His involvement in human affairs, and His communication of the Torah to man, obviously prerequire the whole of Judaism. Without these "foundations" the rest is virtually meaningless.

One difficulty, however, remains with this explanation: Why is the belief in Moshiach included among the foundations of the Jewish faith? Obviously, the concept of Moshiach is an important part of Judaism. The Torah speaks of it (in Deuteronomy 30 and Numbers 24, among others); the prophets are full of it. But could one not conceivably believe in the rest of the Torah without accepting its vision of a future perfect world?

Not in Heaven

The Torah details a most exacting and demanding code of behavior, governing every hour of the day, every phase of life, and every aspect of the human experience. It takes a lifetime of committed labor, tremendous self-discipline, and every iota of man's intellectual, emotional and spiritual prowess to bring one's life into utter conformity with the Torah's edicts and ideals.

Thus, there are two possible ways in which to view the Torah's vision of life.

One may conceivably argue that the level of perfection expected by Torah is beyond feasible reach for a majority of people. From this perspective, Torah is an ideal to strive towards, a vision of absolute goodness designed to serve as a point of reference for imperfect man. A person ought to seek attaining this ideal—says this view—although he will probably never reach it, for he will much improve himself in the process.

The second view takes the Torah at its word: each and every individual is capable of, and expected to attain, the perfectly righteous and harmonious life it mandates. Torah is not an abstract ideal, but a practical and implementable blueprint for life.

The Torah itself leave no room for doubt on its own view of the matter: "For the mitzvah which I command you this day," it states, "it is not beyond you nor is it remote from you. It is not in heaven. . . . nor is it across the sea. . . . Rather,

it is something that is very close to you, in your mouth, in your heart, that you may do it" (Deuteronomy 30:11–14).

Underlying Perspectives

These two views reflect two different ways of looking at the essence of G-d's creation. If man is inherently or even partially evil, then obviously he can go either way. There is no reason to assume that he will, or even can, attain a state of perfect righteousness. A world community that is utterly committed to goodness, in which every single individual acts in concert with the purpose for which he was created, can only be the dream of a chronic optimist, or of one who is hopelessly out of touch with "reality."

Yet if one believes that the world is intrinsically good—that G-d has imbued His every creation with the potential to reflect His absolute goodness and perfection—then, one's concept of reality is completely different. Then, our currently harsh reality is the anomalous state, while the reality of Moshiach is the most natural thing in the world.

In other words, where a person stands on Moshiach expresses his attitude vis-a-vis the entire Torah. Is Torah's formula for life a pipe dream, or is it a description of the true nature of creation? If the Torah is nothing more than a theoretical utopia, then one does not expect a world free of greed, jealousy and hate any time in the near future. But if the Torah mirrors the essence of man, then one not only believes in a "future" Moshiach, but understands that the world is capable of instantaneously responding to his call.

This explains why belief in Moshiach entails not only the conviction that he will "eventually" arrive, but the anticipation of his imminent coming. In the words of Maimonides: "The Twelfth Principle concerns the era of Moshiach: to believe and to validate his coming; not to think that it is something of the future—even if he tarries, one should await him. . . ." And in his Mishneh Torah, Maimonides states: "One who does not believe in him, or one who does not anticipate his coming, not only denies the prophets, he denies the Torah itself" (*Mishneh Torah*, Laws of Kings, 11:1).

When Moshiach is that very realistic possibility, for another moment to go by without the Redemption taking place is far, far more "unrealistic" (that is, less in keeping with the true nature of things) than the prospect of its immediate realization.

The Nature and Definition of Truth

Of course, man has been granted freedom of choice. But the choice between good and evil is not a choice of what to be—he cannot change his quintessential self—but the choice of how to act. Man can choose to express his true essence in his behavior, or choose to suppress it.

Ultimately, the truth, by nature and definition, always comes to light. So, while man can choose how to act in any given moment, the very nature of humanity, and of G-d's creation as a whole, mandates that it not only can, but will attain the perfection of the era of Moshiach.

Moshiach means that the true nature of creation will ultimately come to light. That "evil" is but the shallow distortion of this truth, and has no enduring reality. That man will free himself of hate and ignorance. That every human being will fulfill his divinely ordained role as outlined in the Torah, transforming the world into a place suffused with the wisdom, goodness and perfection of its Creator.

Moshiach means that the Torah is for real.

Week in Review: www.meaningfullife.com

Reprinted with permission from The Meaningful Life Center

4

LESSON

WE'RE GETTING THERE

Judaism sees all of history as one connected journey toward a single desired destiny. In this lesson, we look back to identify four distinct epochs that show us how far we've traveled on the way to a truly good world.

I. UNPACKING THE PRIMORDIAL DESIRE

Based on our discussions in the previous lessons of this course, it would be reasonable to assume that we could review the millennia of our nation's history and map an observable spiritual progression. Is that the case? Has the world been steadily spiritually progressing?

In this lesson, we explore some of our nation's major ups and downs to see if and how they moved the world toward its desired messianic state.

To do so accurately, it is necessary to revisit the central idea discussed in the previous lessons—G-d's desire for a home in this world. There are several key components to this divine aspiration, and defining them will allow us to measure any messianic progress.

QUESTION

In a single word, how would you characterize the journey of Jewish history?

TEXT 1

G-d's Primordial Desire

Midrash, *Tanchuma,* Naso 16

בְּשָׁעָה שֶׁבָּרָא הַקָּדוֹשׁ בָּרוּךְ הוּא אֶת הָעוֹלָם,
נִתְאַוָּה שֶׁיְּהֵא לוֹ דִירָה בְּתַחְתּוֹנִים.

When the Holy One, blessed be He, created the universe, He desired to have a home in the lowest realm.

TANCHUMA

A Midrashic work bearing the name of Rabbi Tanchuma, a 4th-century Talmudic sage quoted often in this work. "Midrash" is the designation of a particular genre of rabbinic literature usually forming a running commentary on specific books of the Bible. *Tanchuma* provides textual exegeses, expounds upon the biblical narrative, and develops and illustrates moral principles. *Tanchuma* is unique in that many of its sections commence with a halachic discussion, which subsequently leads into nonhalachic teachings.

Home Is Where the Essence Is

The Rebbe, Rabbi Menachem Mendel Schneerson,
Sefer Hasichot 5748:1, pp. 139–140

דִי הַדְגָּשָׁה אִין "דִירָה (בְּתַחְתּוֹנִים)" אִיז, אַז דֶער גִילוּי
אֱלֹקוּת דָא לְמַטָּה (בְּתַחְתּוֹנִים) זָאל זַיין אִין אַזַא אוֹפֶן וְוִי
אַ מֶענְטְשׁ (לְהַבְדִּיל) גֶעפִינְט זִיךְ בַּא זִיךְ אִין זַיין דִירָה.

בְּשְׁעַת אַ מֶענְטְשׁ גֵייט אִין גַאס אָדֶער עֶר גֶעפִינְט
זִיךְ בַּא אַ צְוֵוייטְן, מוּז עֶר זַיין בַּאשְׁרֵיינְקְט (מְצֻמְצָם)
לוֹיט דֶעם אָרְט וְואוּ עֶר גֶעפִינְט זִיךְ. מַה שֶׁאֵין כֵּן
בַּא זִיךְ אִין דִירָה - אִיז עֶר בְּגִלוּי וּבְהַרְחָבָה. וְואס
דָאס אִיז דֶער פֵּרוּשׁ פוּן "נִתְאַוָּה הַקָּדוֹשׁ בָּרוּךְ
הוּא לִהְיוֹת לוֹ יִתְבָּרֵךְ דִירָה בְּתַחְתּוֹנִים", אַז דֶער
גִלוּי אֱלֹקוּת לְמַטָּה זָאל זַיין בְּגִלוּי וּבְהַרְחָבָה.

אוּן נָאכְמֶער: דֶער דִין בַּא אַ מֶלֶךְ אִיז "אֵין רוֹאִין אוֹתוֹ
כוּ' כְּשֶׁהוּא עָרוֹם" (ס'אִיז הֵפֶךְ כְּבוֹד הַמַּלְכוּת), אוּן
אַף עַל פִּי כֵן בַּא זִיךְ אִין דִירָה, אִיז פַארַאן (בִּזְמַנִּים
שׁוֹנִים) דֶער מַצָּב וְוִי דֶער מֶלֶךְ אִיז עָרוֹם.

דֶער טַעַם פוּן דֶעם . . . וַוייְלֶע דִי כַּוָנָה פוּן "דִירָה
לוֹ יִתְבָּרֵךְ בְּתַחְתּוֹנִים" אִיז, אַז דִי הִתְגַּלוּת פוּן
אוֹיבֶּערְשְׁטְן לְמַטָּה (בְּתַחְתּוֹנִים) זָאל סוֹף סוֹף זַיין
"בְּלִי שׁוּם לְבוּשׁ" (תַּנְיָא פֶּרֶק ל"ו), וְוִי עֶס שְׁטֵייט
אוֹיף לֶעָתִיד לָבוֹא (וְואס דַאן וֶועט זִיךְ דוּרְכְפִירְן דִי
כַּוָנָה פוּן דִירָה בְּתַחְתּוֹנִים) "וְלֹא יִכָּנֵף עוֹד מוֹרֶיךָ"
(יְשַׁעְיָהוּ ל, כ), "שֶׁלֹּא יִתְכַּסֶּה מִמְּךָ בְּכָנָף וּלְבוּשׁ".

**RABBI MENACHEM
MENDEL SCHNEERSON
1902-1994**

The towering
Jewish leader of
the 20th century, known
as "the Lubavitcher
Rebbe," or simply as "the
Rebbe." Born in southern
Ukraine, the Rebbe
escaped Nazi-occupied
Europe, arriving in
the U.S. in June 1941.
The Rebbe inspired
and guided the revival
of traditional Judaism
after the European
devastation, impacting
virtually every Jewish
community the world
over. The Rebbe often
emphasized that the
performance of just
one additional good
deed could usher in
the era of Mashiach.
The Rebbe's scholarly
talks and writings have
been printed in more
than 200 volumes.

In "What Does G-d Want?
A Vision of Our Future,"
Rabbi Manis Friedman
explores our nation's past to
arrive at answers about our
future: *myjli.com/canhappen*

The emphasis on transforming this material world specifically into a "home" for G-d informs us that the ultimate goal is for G-dliness to be revealed here, in the tangible reality of this world, to the extent and naturalness that is analogous to the way a person is when found within his or her own home.

When we take a stroll or pay a visit to a friend, we are forced to limit our self-expression to the degree that is appropriate for our present location. By contrast, when we are in our own homes, we can be ourselves openly and to the fullest extent. Similarly, the revelation of G-dliness must be overt and with full expression, for "G-d desired a *home* in the lowest realm."

Furthermore, Jewish law insists that "we must not view a king while he is without clothing," for that would undermine respect for the monarchy. Despite that, *when he is in his own home*, there are specific instances in which the king will indeed be without clothing.

Similarly . . . the ultimate purpose for G-d's desire to transform our material reality into a home, specifically, is that (as Rabbi Shne'ur Zalman of Liadi explains in *Tanya*, ch. 36) G-d longs to finally reveal and express Himself "without any garment." G-d conveyed this desire to us through a prophecy regarding the future Redemption—at which point the goal of establishing a dwelling for G-d in the material reality will have been achieved: "No longer will your Teacher garb Himself" (ISAIAH 30:20), which means [per Rashi's commentary] that "He will no longer conceal Himself from you with a robe or garment."

TEXT 3

By Invitation Only

The Rebbe, Rabbi Menachem Mendel Schneerson,
Likutei Sichot 12, p. 73

הַכַּוָּנָה בְּ"דִירָה בְּתַחְתּוֹנִים" הִיא שֶׁהַ"תַּחְתּוֹנִים" מִצַּד **עִנְיָנָם הֵם** יִהְיוּ דִירָה לוֹ יִתְבָּרַךְ, וְלָכֵן צָרִיךְ שֶׁהַ"דִירָה" תֵּעָשֶׂה עַל יְדֵי הָעֲבוֹדָה דְנִשְׁמוֹת יִשְׂרָאֵל הַמְלֻבָּשׁוֹת בְּגוּפִים, כִּי דַוְקָא אָז נַעֲשִׂים הַ"**תַּחְתּוֹנִים**" דִירָה לוֹ יִתְבָּרַךְ. מַה שֶׁאֵין כֵּן אִם הַ"דִירָה" הָיְתָה נַעֲשֵׂית מִצַּד הַגִּלּוּי שֶׁ**מִלְמַעְלָה** הֲרֵי אָז, הַתַּחְתּוֹנִים עַצְמָם, מִצַּד עִנְיָנָם הֵם, לֹא נַעֲשׂוּ דִירָה לוֹ יִתְבָּרַךְ.

G-d's intention in having "a home in the lowest realm" is for the lowest realm to become a home for G-d *on its own terms*. For that reason, the home must be achieved through the efforts of human beings—the souls of Israel in *corporeal bodies*—for only then are the *lowest* realms themselves reformed into a home for G-d. By contrast, if the home would be imposed through a transformative revelation *from Above*, the lowest realms themselves would *not* be—on their own terms—a home for G-d.

FIGURE 4.1

G-d's Tripartite Desire:

A.   To be present here *in the lowliest of realms*

B.   To be *fully at home* in this lowest of realms

C.   To have a home in the lowest of realms *created by the inhabitants of the lowest realm*

FIGURE 4.2   The Peaks and Valleys: A Timeline

▲ **ABRAHAM IS BORN**
  1948 (1813 BCE)

▲ **CREATION**
  1 (3760 BCE)

▼ **EXPULSION FROM THE GARDEN OF EDEN**
  1 (3760 BCE)

JACOB AND HIS FAMILY DESCEND TO EGYPT
2238 (1523 BCE)
▼

THE SIN OF THE
GOLDEN CALF

2448 (1313 BCE)

EXODUS AND THE
GIVING OF THE TORAH
AT MOUNT SINAI

2448 (1313 BCE)

THE TABERNACLE AND
THE HOLY TEMPLES

2448–3829 (1313 BCE–69 CE)

EXILE

3829–Present (69 CE–Present)

PRESENT

II. THE GARDEN OF EDEN AND
THE TREE OF KNOWLEDGE

▲ 1 (3760 BCE)

Now that we have gained a more detailed understanding of G-d's purpose for creation, we can begin to make sense of history's spiritual highs and lows. In this lesson, we will focus on four major historical "acts"—four primary peaks-and-plummets.

The first act is the stage-setting episode of the Garden of Eden and the sin of the Tree of Knowledge.

THE GARDEN OF EDEN (DETAIL)
Thomas Cole, oil on canvas, 1828
(Amon Carter Museum of American Art, Fort Worth, Texas)

TEXT 4

Planted in Paradise

Genesis 2:8

וַיִּטַּע ה׳ אֱלֹקִים גַּן בְּעֵדֶן מִקֶּדֶם,
וַיָּשֶׂם שָׁם אֶת הָאָדָם אֲשֶׁר יָצָר.
וַיַּצְמַח ה׳ אֱלֹקִים מִן הָאֲדָמָה כָּל עֵץ
נֶחְמָד לְמַרְאֶה וְטוֹב לְמַאֲכָל.

G-d planted a garden in the eastern side of Eden,
and He placed there the man whom He had
formed. G-d caused to sprout from the ground
every tree that was pleasant to see and good to eat.

TEXT 5

A Divine Garden

Midrash, *Shir Hashirim Rabah* 5:1

SHIR HASHIRIM RABAH

A midrashic text and
exegetical commentary on
the book of Song of Songs.
This Midrash explicates
this biblical book based
on the principle that its
verses convey an allegory
of the relationship between
G-d and the people of
Israel. It was compiled and
edited in the Land of Israel
during the 6th century.

"בָּאתִי לְגַנִּי" (שִׁיר הַשִּׁירִים ה, א) . . . "בָּאתִי לְגַן"
אֵין כְּתִיב כָּאן, אֶלָּא "לְגַנִּי", לִגְנוּנִי, לְמָקוֹם שֶׁהָיָה
עִקָּרִי מִתְּחִלָּה, וְעִקַּר שְׁכִינָה לֹא בַּתַּחְתּוֹנִים הָיְתָה?

"I have come to My garden" (SONG OF SONGS 5:1).
. . . The verse does not speak of "a garden" [*gan* in
Hebrew], but rather, "*My* garden" [*ganni*], for the
sake of implying *genuni*, "My marital home"—the
location that originally served as My primary
residence. For was not G-d's primary presence
originally located within the lowest realm?

QUESTION

Based on our earlier clarification of the purpose of creation, was the divine goal fulfilled with the existence of the Garden of Eden? Why or why not?

TEXT 6A

The Expulsion

Genesis 3:23–24

וַיְשַׁלְּחֵהוּ ה' אֱלֹקִים מִגַּן עֵדֶן לַעֲבֹד אֶת הָאֲדָמָה אֲשֶׁר לֻקַּח מִשָּׁם. וַיְגָרֶשׁ אֶת הָאָדָם.

G-d expelled Adam from the Garden of Eden; He sent Adam out to work the earth whence he had been taken.

▼ **1 (3760 BCE)**

EXPULSION FROM PARADISE
Thomas Cole, Oil on canvas, 1828 (Museum of Fine Arts, Boston)

TEXT 6B

Purposeful Eviction

The Rebbe, Rabbi Menachem Mendel Schneerson,
Sefer Hamaamarim Melukat 6 (classic edition), p. 18

הַטַּעַם (בִּפְנִימִיּוּת הָעִנְיָנִים) עַל זֶה שֶׁהָאָדָם גֵּרַשׁ מִגַּן עֵדֶן הוּא,
כִּי הַכַּוָּנָה דְּדִירָה בְּתַחְתּוֹנִים הִיא שֶׁדִּירָה תִּהְיֶה בְּהַתַּחְתּוֹן שֶׁאֵין
תַּחְתּוֹן לְמַטָּה מִמֶּנּוּ, וְשֶׁהַדִּירָה בּוֹ תִּהְיֶה מִצַּד עִנְיָנוֹ (דְּתַחְתּוֹן זֶה),

וְלָכֵן, "וַיְשַׁלְּחֵהוּ ה' אֱלֹקִים מִגַּן עֵדֶן לַעֲבֹד אֶת הָאֲדָמָה גו'"
(בְּרֵאשִׁית ג, כג), לַעֲשׂוֹת הַמָּקוֹם דְּעוֹלָם (תַּחְתּוֹן בְּיוֹתֵר)
מֻכְשָׁר לְהַגִּילּוּי, בִּכְדֵי שֶׁגַּם הַתַּחְתּוֹן שֶׁאֵין תַּחְתּוֹן לְמַטָּה
מִמֶּנּוּ יִהְיֶה דִּירָה לוֹ יִתְבָּרַךְ, וְשֶׁהַדִּירָה בּוֹ תִּהְיֶה מִצַּד עִנְיָנוֹ.

The deeper, spiritual reason for Adam's eviction from
the Garden of Eden is because G-d's ultimate goal [for
Creation] is that He should have "a home in the lowest
realm." This goal demands that G-d's home be fashioned:
(a) within the realm that is the *absolute* lowest; and b)
using the *natural materiality* of the lowest realm itself.

Adam was therefore dispatched from the Garden
of Eden *"to work the earth"* (GENESIS 3:23),
meaning, to make the earth's *physical dimension of
space* receptive to divine revelation. This way, (a)
even the lowest plane of reality [that lacks the overt
spirituality of the Garden of Eden] will become
a home for G-d, and (b) the divine home will be
fashioned from the reality of material existence.

"The Sin of the Tree
of Knowledge: Free
Choice" explained as only
**Rabbi Adin Even-Israel
(Steinsaltz)** can:
myjli.com/canhappen

FIGURE 4.3

G-d's Home, Chart I

	GARDEN OF EDEN
LOWLY REALM	NO
G-D'S ESSENCE	NO
BUILT BY US	NO

III. ABRAHAM'S MONOTHEISTIC REVOLUTION AND THE EGYPTIAN SLAVERY

**1948
(1813 BCE)**

Banished from Paradise, humanity entered a dark and G-dless era. At the moment of greatest darkness, a bright star appeared: Abraham, who reintroduced humanity to the existence of the Creator and thereby launched the active campaign to transform the world into a place that is hospitable to the Divine.

Would this noble endeavor be sufficient to satisfy G-d's desire for a home in this world?

THE SACRIFICE OF ISAAC (DETAIL)
Mosaic by Marianos and Hanina, 6th century CE
(pavement of the synagogue Beth Alpha, Israel)

TEXT 7

The Revolutionary

Maimonides, *Mishneh Torah*, Laws of Idolatry 1:3

RABBI MOSHE
BEN MAIMON
(MAIMONIDES, RAMBAM)
1135–1204

Halachist,
philosopher,
author, and physician.
Maimonides was born
in Córdoba, Spain. After
the conquest of Córdoba
by the Almohads, he fled
Spain and eventually
settled in Cairo, Egypt.
There, he became the
leader of the Jewish
community and served
as court physician to
the vizier of Egypt.
He is most noted for
authoring the *Mishneh
Torah*, an encyclopedic
arrangement of
Jewish law; and for his
philosophical work,
Guide for the Perplexed.
His rulings on Jewish
law are integral to
the formation of
halachic consensus.

כֵּיוָן שֶׁנִּגְמַל אֵיתָן זֶה הִתְחִיל לְשׁוֹטֵט בְּדַעְתּוֹ וְהוּא
קָטָן וְהִתְחִיל לַחֲשֹׁב בַּיּוֹם וּבַלַּיְלָה . . . וְלֹא הָיָה לוֹ
מְלַמֵּד וְלֹא מוֹדִיעַ דָּבָר אֶלָּא מֻשְׁקָע בְּאוּר כַּשְׂדִּים בֵּין
עוֹבְדֵי כּוֹכָבִים הַטִּפְּשִׁים וְאָבִיו וְאִמּוֹ וְכָל הָעָם עוֹבְדֵי
כּוֹכָבִים וְהוּא עוֹבֵד עִמָּהֶם וְלִבּוֹ מְשׁוֹטֵט וּמֵבִין.

עַד שֶׁהִשִּׂיג דֶּרֶךְ הָאֱמֶת וְהֵבִין קַו הַצֶּדֶק מִתְּבוּנָתוֹ
הַנְּכוֹנָה. וְיָדַע שֶׁיֵּשׁ שָׁם אֱלוֹקַּ אֶחָד . . . וְהוּא בָּרָא
הַכֹּל וְאֵין בְּכָל הַנִּמְצָא אֱלוֹקַּ חוּץ מִמֶּנּוּ . . .

וּבֶן אַרְבָּעִים שָׁנָה הִכִּיר אַבְרָהָם אֶת בּוֹרְאוֹ. כֵּיוָן שֶׁהִכִּיר וְיָדַע
הִתְחִיל לְהָשִׁיב תְּשׁוּבוֹת עַל בְּנֵי אוּר כַּשְׂדִּים וְלַעֲרֹךְ דִּין עִמָּהֶם
וְלוֹמַר שֶׁאֵין זוֹ דֶּרֶךְ הָאֱמֶת שֶׁאַתֶּם הוֹלְכִים בָּהּ . . . כֵּיוָן שֶׁגָּבַר
עֲלֵיהֶם בִּרְאָיוֹתָיו בִּקֵּשׁ הַמֶּלֶךְ לְהָרְגוֹ וְנַעֲשָׂה לוֹ נֵס וְיָצָא לְחָרָן.

וְהִתְחִיל לַעֲמֹד וְלִקְרֹא בְּקוֹל גָּדוֹל לְכָל הָעוֹלָם וּלְהוֹדִיעָם
שֶׁיֵּשׁ שָׁם אֱלוֹקַּ אֶחָד לְכָל הָעוֹלָם וְלוֹ רָאוּי לַעֲבֹד.
וְהָיָה מְהַלֵּךְ וְקוֹרֵא וּמְקַבֵּץ הָעָם מֵעִיר לְעִיר וּמִמַּמְלָכָה
לְמַמְלָכָה עַד שֶׁהִגִּיעַ לְאֶרֶץ כְּנַעַן וְהוּא קוֹרֵא שֶׁנֶּאֱמַר,
"וַיִּקְרָא שָׁם בְּשֵׁם ה' אֵ-ל עוֹלָם" (בראשית כא, לג).

וְכֵיוָן שֶׁהָיוּ הָעָם מִתְקַבְּצִין אֵלָיו וְשׁוֹאֲלִין לוֹ עַל דְּבָרָיו
הָיָה מוֹדִיעַ לְכָל אֶחָד וְאֶחָד כְּפִי דַּעְתּוֹ עַד שֶׁיַּחֲזִירֵהוּ

Rabbi Yitzchak
Schochet's brief
commentary on "Abraham
and the Quest for Truth":
myjli.com/canhappen

לְדֶרֶךְ הָאֱמֶת עַד שֶׁנִּתְקַבְּצוּ אֵלָיו אֲלָפִים וּרְבָבוֹת וְהֵם
אַנְשֵׁי בֵּית אַבְרָהָם וְשָׁתַל בְּלִבָּם הָעִקָּר הַגָּדוֹל הַזֶּה.

After this mighty personage [Abraham] was weaned,
he began to ponder deeply. Though he was a young
child, he began to contemplate by day and by night. . . .
He had no teacher, nor was there anyone to inform him.
Rather, he was mired in Ur Kasdim's population of
foolish idolaters. His father, mother, and all the people
around him worshipped idols. He would worship
along with them, but his heart was busy analyzing
everything, and he gained a clear understanding.

Ultimately, he arrived at the true way and understood
the path of righteousness through his accurate
comprehension. He realized that there was one
G-d . . . that He created everything, and that
there is no other G-d among all that exists. . . .

Abraham was forty years old when he became fully
aware of his Creator. He then used his recognition
and knowledge of the Creator to formulate
presentations for the population of Ur Kasdim, and
to debate them, informing them that they were
not following the true path. . . . When he won
them over with the strength of his arguments, the

king desired to execute him. His life was spared through a miracle, and he relocated to Charan.

He then began a public campaign, loudly proclaiming to all humanity and informing them that in all the universe there is but one G-d, and that to Him alone is it appropriate to worship. He traveled to publicize his message everywhere, rallying people in city after city, kingdom after kingdom, until he arrived in the land of Canaan. At every location he proclaimed G-d's existence, as it is stated: "Abraham proclaimed there in the name of the eternal G-d" (GENESIS 21:33).

When the people would rally to him, questioning him regarding his statements, he would explain to each individual, according to their understanding, until he had brought that individual back to the true path. Eventually, thousands and myriads rallied around Abraham; they are the folk referred to [in the Torah] as "the people of the House of Abraham" (GENESIS 17:23), in whose hearts he firmly planted this great fundamental principle.

Did Abraham's efforts (and the efforts of the subsequent Patriarchs) to bring divine awareness to the world constitute the fulfillment of G-d's intention of having a home in the lowest realm? Why or why not?

TEXT 8

Not Defined by Creation

Rabbi Shne'ur Zalman of Liadi, *Torah Or*, *Megilat Esther* 99b

RABBI SHNE'UR ZALMAN OF LIADI (ALTER REBBE) 1745–1812

Chasidic rebbe, halachic authority, and founder of the Chabad movement. The Alter Rebbe was born in Liozna, Belarus, and was among the principal students of the Magid of Mezeritch. His numerous works include the *Tanya*, an early classic containing the fundamentals of Chabad Chasidism; and *Shulchan Aruch HaRav*, an expanded and reworked code of Jewish law.

דְּבְחִינַת מְמַלֵּא וְסוֹבֵב הוּא רַק הֶאֱרָה לְבַד מִמֶּנּוּ יִתְבָּרֵךְ, אֲבָל מַהוּתוֹ וְעַצְמוּתוֹ יִתְבָּרֵךְ אֵינוֹ בְּגֶדֶר עָלְמִין כְּלָל אֲפִלּוּ לִהְיוֹת סוֹבֵב וּמְמַלֵּא לְעָלְמִין.

כִּי לֹא זֶה הִיא עִקַּר הָאֱלֹקוּת מַה שֶּׁהָעוֹלָמוֹת מִתְהַוִּים מִמֶּנּוּ וּמְקַבְּלִים חַיּוּתָם מִמֶּנּוּ יִתְבָּרֵךְ. שֶׁהֲרֵי, "אַתָּה הוּא עַד שֶׁלֹּא נִבְרָא הָעוֹלָם וּלְאַחַר שֶׁנִּבְרָא" בְּשָׁוֶה מַמָּשׁ.

An intimate form of Creation-sustaining divinity, referred to as *memale* ("filling" the universe), breathes within each item of existence. Far beyond that, a highly intense and abstract form of divinity, referred to as *sovev* ("encompassing" the universe), uniformly envelops all of existence. However, G-d Himself—the Essence—is utterly beyond the entire concept of a universe. We cannot possibly refer to G-d Himself as pervading existence, or even as encompassing it.

The fact that the universe is brought into existence and is actively sustained through G-d's divinity is *not* a primary feature of G-d Himself. Rather, [as we recite in our daily prayers,] "You were *before* the creation of the universe and You are *since* the creation of the universe"—with no change whatsoever.

QUESTION

In a world that perceives G-d "merely" as the Creator of nature, what might need to happen to open a new vista of perception of G-d's true Essence?

JACOB AND HIS FAMILY DESCEND TO EGYPT

2233 (1523 BCE) ▼

ISRAELITES IN BONDAGE IN EGYPT (DETAIL)

The Tegernsee Haggadah, Joseph son of R. Ephraim; black and brown ink, gold leaf and different shades of blue, magenta, green, red, yellow, brown and white; before 1489 (Bayerische Staatsbibliothek [BSB], Munich, Germany)

TEXT 9

A Noble Principle on Life Support

Maimonides, *Mishneh Torah*, Laws of Idolatry 1:3

וְהָיָה הַדָּבָר הוֹלֵךְ וּמִתְגַּבֵּר בִּבְנֵי יַעֲקֹב וּבַנִּלְוִים עֲלֵיהֶם
וְנַעֲשֵׂית בָּעוֹלָם אֻמָּה שֶׁהִיא יוֹדַעַת אֶת ה'.

עַד שֶׁאָרְכוּ הַיָּמִים לְיִשְׂרָאֵל בְּמִצְרַיִם וְחָזְרוּ לִלְמֹד מַעֲשֵׂיהֶן
וְלַעֲבֹד כּוֹכָבִים כְּמוֹתָן חוּץ מִשֵּׁבֶט לֵוִי שֶׁעָמַד בְּמִצְוַת אָבוֹת.

וּמֵעוֹלָם לֹא עָבַד שֵׁבֶט לֵוִי עֲבוֹדַת כּוֹכָבִים.
וְכִמְעַט קָט הָיָה הָעִקָּר שֶׁשָּׁתַל אַבְרָהָם נֶעֱקַר
וְחוֹזְרִין בְּנֵי יַעֲקֹב לְטָעוּת הָעוֹלָם וּתְעִיּוֹתָן.

The concept [of monotheism introduced by Abraham] proceeded and gathered strength among the descendants of Jacob and those who rallied to them, until there became a nation within the world that knew G-d.

This lasted until the Jews' extended stay in Egypt. There they regressed; they learned from the Egyptians' ways and began worshipping idols as they did (with the exception of the tribe of Levi, who clung to the *mitzvot* of the Patriarchs and never served false gods).

The fundamental principle that Abraham planted came awfully close to being uprooted, whereby the descendants of Jacob would have returned entirely to the world's erroneous perception [of G-d] and adopted their crooked [ways].

FIGURE 4.4

G-d's Home, Chart II

	 GARDEN OF EDEN	PATRIARCHS
LOWLY REALM	NO	YES
G-D'S ESSENCE	NO	NO
BUILT BY US	NO	YES

IV. EXODUS, REVELATION, AND THE GOLDEN CALF

▲ **2448**
(1313 BCE)

In ancient Egypt, the Jews hit rock bottom—spiritually and materially. At this point, G-d reveals Himself with awesome miraculous might and extracts them from Egypt and gives them the Torah. G-d thereby demonstrates that He is present in this world, and not only as Creator, but as the One Who is beyond creation and the rules that He put in place to govern it.

Are we there yet? Have we arrived at the ultimate destination? Is anything more needed?

GALUT
Samuel Hirszenberg, colorized Rosh Hashanah postcard version of original 1904 lithograph

Allow Me to Introduce Myself!

TEXT 10A

Exodus 20:2

אָנֹכִי ה' אֱלֹקֶיךָ אֲשֶׁר הוֹצֵאתִיךָ מֵאֶרֶץ מִצְרַיִם מִבֵּית עֲבָדִים.

I am your G-d, Who extracted you from the
land of Egypt—from the house of bondage.

A Greater Feat

TEXT 10B

The Rebbe, Rabbi Menachem Mendel Schneerson,
Torat Menachem 5742:2, p. 515

יָדוּעַ קֻשְׁיַת הַמְפָרְשִׁים - מַדּוּעַ נֶאֱמַר
"אָנֹכִי ה' אֱלֹקֶיךָ אֲשֶׁר הוֹצֵאתִיךָ מֵאֶרֶץ מִצְרַיִם
מִבֵּית עֲבָדִים", וְלֹא נֶאֱמַר עִנְיָן גָּדוֹל יוֹתֵר (לִכְאוֹרָה)
- "אָנֹכִי ה' אֱלֹקֶיךָ אֲשֶׁר בָּרָאתִי שָׁמַיִם וָאָרֶץ".

וְיָדוּעַ הַבֵּאוּר בָּזֶה - שֶׁכְּלָלוּת הָעִנְיָן דִּיצִיאַת מִצְרַיִם מוֹרֶה
עַל הַפְלָאָה גְּדוֹלָה יוֹתֵר מֵאֲשֶׁר בְּרִיאַת שָׁמַיִם וָאָרֶץ,
כִּי גַם לְאַחֲרֵי שֶׁנִּבְרְאוּ שָׁמַיִם וָאָרֶץ בְּהַגְבָּלַת הַטֶּבַע,
הֲרֵי בְּכֹחוֹ שֶׁל הַקָּדוֹשׁ בָּרוּךְ הוּא לְשַׁנּוֹת אֶת סִדְרֵי הַטֶּבַע,
וּלְהַנְהִיג אֶת הָעוֹלָם בְּאֹפֶן שֶׁלְּמַעְלָה מֵהַטֶּבַע.

The Biblical commentators wonder why G-d
emphasized, "I am your G-d, Who *extracted you*

from the land of Egypt," instead of, "I am your G-d, Who *created heaven and earth.*" Surely the latter demonstrates a far greater feat?

The explanation is that the Exodus demonstrates something far more wondrous than creation. The Exodus demonstrates that after creating heaven and earth with a defined set of rules of nature, G-d is nevertheless able to alter the natural order and to conduct the universe in an entirely supernatural manner.

QUESTION

Do the Exodus and Revelation at Mount Sinai constitute the complete fulfillment of G-d's intention and purpose in having a home in the lowest realm? Why or why not?

A Temporary Injection of Holiness

The Rebbe, Rabbi Menachem Mendel Schneerson,
Likutei Sichot 15, p. 77

בְּמַתַּן תּוֹרָה גוּפָא אִיז אָבֶּער גֶעוֶועזן דֶער גִלוּי אִין אַן
אוֹפֶן פוּן מִלְמַעְלָה לְמַטָה, דָאס הֵייסְט, דֶער מַטָה אִיז
נִיט גֶעוֶועזן קֵיין כְּלִי צוּ דֶעם גִלוּי אוֹר, אוּן דֶערְפַאר אִיז
אָט דֶער אוֹר אוֹר נִיט אַרָאפְגֶעקוּמֶען אִין אִים בְּאוֹפֶן גָלוּי.

וְכַיָדוּעַ אַז דֶער גִלוּי אוֹר אֱלֹקִי וָואס אִיז גֶעוֶועזן בְּמַתַּן
תּוֹרָה אִיז גֶעוֶועזן לְפִי שָׁעָה אוּן דֶערְנָאךְ אִיז עֶר נִפְסַק
גֶעוָוארֶן - "בִּמְשׁוֹךְ הַיּוֹבֵל הֵמָה יַעֲלוּ בָהָר" (שְׁמוֹת יט, יג).

The divine revelation at the Giving of the Torah
occurred in a top-down manner: Our lower reality
was unprepared to receive this revelation of divine
light, and consequently, it was unable to internalize,
to a noticeable degree, the light that it did receive.

For that reason, the revelation of divine light at the
Giving of the Torah was temporary; it ended abruptly,
as described in the verse, "When an extended blast
is sounded with the ram's horn they may ascend
the mountain" (EXODUS 19:13) [for the divinity
dissipated entirely, leaving the mountain unchanged].

Watch "A Lesson from the
Story of the Golden Calf"
by **Mrs. Sharon Freundel**:
myjli.com/canhappen

THE SIN OF
THE GOLDEN CALF

2448
(1313 BCE)

**THE ADORATION
OF THE GOLDEN
CALF (DETAIL)**
Nicolas Poussin,
oil on canvas, c. 1634,
(National Gallery,
London, UK)

TEXT 12

To Facilitate *Teshuvah*

The Rebbe, Rabbi Menachem Mendel Schneerson,
Sefer Hamaamarim Melukat 5 (classic edition), p. 205

הַכַּוָּנָה (דִלְמַעְלָה) בְּמַעֲשֵׂה הָעֵגֶל מִלְכַתְּחִלָּה הָיְתָה
בִּכְדֵי שֶׁעַל יְדֵי זֶה יַגִּיעוּ לְמַעֲלַת הַתְּשׁוּבָה.

The sin of the Golden Calf transpired due to a preceding
supernal decision that, through such an event, the
people will achieve the superiority of *teshuvah*.

FIGURE 4.5

G-d's Home, Chart III

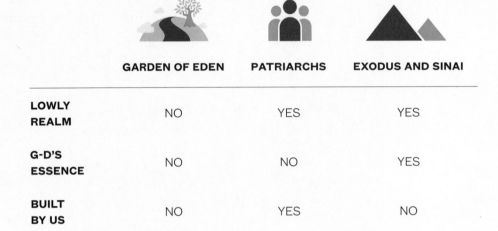

	GARDEN OF EDEN	PATRIARCHS	EXODUS AND SINAI
LOWLY REALM	NO	YES	YES
G-D'S ESSENCE	NO	NO	YES
BUILT BY US	NO	YES	NO

V. HOLY TEMPLE AND EXILE

▲ **2448**
(1313 BCE)

After the sin of the Golden Calf, the Jews built a Tabernacle and Temple—a home for the essence of G-d, seemingly built of their own efforts. However, it turns out that these were "close but no cigar."

For the sake of achieving the full completion of G-d's original desire, it was necessary for the Jewish nation to experience the destruction of the Temples and the subsequent exiles. Moreover, within exile, for G-d's plan to be fully achieved, the Jews would need to experience eras of oppression and eras of freedom.

THE TABERNACLE IN THE WILDERNESS
Artist unknown, Illustration Plate 1 from The Jewish Tabernacle and Priesthood by Rev. G. C. Needham, 1874.

Lasting Holiness

The Rebbe, Rabbi Menachem Mendel Schneerson,
Likutei Sichot 21, p. 151

דִי הַשְׁרָאַת הַשְּׁכִינָה בַּמִּשְׁכָּן אִיז גֶעקוּמֶען דּוּרְךְ "וְעָשׂוּ לִי
מִקְדָּשׁ" (שְׁמוֹת כה, ח), עַל יְדֵי עֲשִׂיַת בְּנֵי יִשְׂרָאֵל . . . אוּן
וְוִיבַּאלְד דִי הַשְׁרָאַת הַשְּׁכִינָה אִיז גֶעקוּמֶען דּוּרְךְ עֲשִׂיַת
הָאָדָם, אִיז דִי קְדֻשָּׁה נִקְבַּע גֶעוָוארְן אִין דֶער חֶפְצָא (גֶשֶׁם)
פוּן מִשְׁכָּן, סְ'אִיז גֶעוָוארְן אַ קְדֻשָּׁה אִין דֶעם מִשְׁכָּן וַחֲלָקָיו.

The divine presence was manifested within the
Tabernacle as a result of the Jewish people's tangible
efforts, in accordance with their mandate—"*They
should make* a Sanctuary for Me" (EXODUS 25:8).
. . . And because the divine presence's manifestation
occurred through human action, the sanctity became
installed within the materiality of the Tabernacle's
components. Consequently, the physical Tabernacle
and its components gained a lasting sanctity.

FIGURE 4.6

G-d's Home, Chart IV

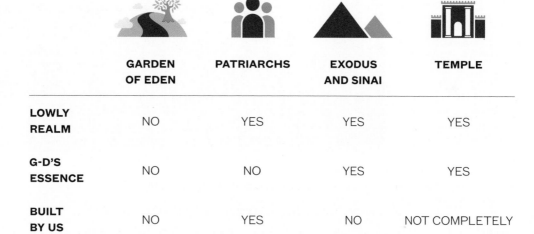

	GARDEN OF EDEN	PATRIARCHS	EXODUS AND SINAI	TEMPLE
LOWLY REALM	NO	YES	YES	YES
G-D'S ESSENCE	NO	NO	YES	YES
BUILT BY US	NO	YES	NO	NOT COMPLETELY

EXILE

3829–Present (69 CE–Present) ▼

THE ARCH OF
TITUS (DETAIL)
c. 81 CE, marble,
Forum Romanum,
Rome

TEXT 14

The Yield of Darkness

The Rebbe, Rabbi Menachem Mendel Schneerson,
Likutei Sichot 17, p. 96

דָאס וָואס דֶער גִלּוּי דְלֶעָתִיד טוּט זִיךְ אוֹיף דּוּרְךְ "מַעֲשֵׂינוּ
וַעֲבוֹדָתֵנוּ" אִיז עֶס (בְּעִקָּר) "כָּל זְמַן מֶשֶׁךְ הַגָּלוּת" (תַּנְיָא
פֶּרֶק לו) . . . בִּזְמַן הַגָּלוּת אִיז מֵאִיר דֶער כֹּחַ הַמְסִירַת נֶפֶשׁ
מֶער וְוִי בִּזְמַן הַבַּיִת, וַויְיל דַוְקָא דֶער הֶעלֶם וְהֶסְתֵּר (פוּן
זְמַן הַגָּלוּת) רוּפְט אַרוֹיס דֶעם גִלּוּי פוּן כֹּחַ הַמְסִירַת נֶפֶשׁ.

The future revelation [in the messianic era
that is the goal of creation] is generated by our

actions and divine service during these times of exile. . . . For it is during our exile, to a far greater extent than during the Temple eras, that our power of self-sacrifice shines. This is because it is specifically the spiritual darkness and divine concealment predominant during exile that mobilizes our potential for self-sacrifice.

QUESTION

Why might there be an advantage to our spiritual efforts in a time of relative freedom, as opposed to in an era of persecution?

"How Do the Negative Experiences of Our Life Bring Us to Higher Heights?"
Rabbi Mendy Cohen explains:
myjli.com/canhappen

Applying the Squeeze

The Rebbe, Rabbi Menachem Mendel Schneerson,
Sefer Hamaamarim Melukat 6 (classic edition), p. 134

בְּנוֹגֵעַ כָּתִית לַמָּאוֹר, שֶׁעַל יְדֵי הָעִנְיָן דְּכָתִית שֶׁבִּזְמַן
הַגָּלוּת מַגִּיעִים לְהַמָּאוֹר, דִּשְׁנֵי עִנְיָנִים בָּזֶה.

כְּשֶׁיִשְׂרָאֵל נִמְצָאִים בְּמַצָּב שֶׁל כָּתִית מִצַּד זֶה
שֶׁיֶּשְׁנָם גְּזֵרוֹת עַל קִיּוּם הַתּוֹרָה וּמִצְווֹת . . .

וְעוֹד עִנְיָן בְּכָּתִית לַמָּאוֹר, שֶׁגַּם כְּשֶׁיִשְׂרָאֵל נִמְצָאִים
בְּמַצָּב שֶׁל הַרְחָבָה, הַרְחָבָה בְּגַשְׁמִיּוּת וְגַם הַרְחָבָה
בְּרוּחָנִיּוּת, אֶלָּא שֶׁהֵם נִמְצָאִים בְּגָלוּתָם . . . הֵם
שְׁבוּרִים וְנִדְכָּאִים (כָּתִית) מִזֶּה שֶׁהֵם בְּגָלוּת.

וְעַל יְדֵי הַכָּתִית דְּיִשְׂרָאֵל מִזֶּה שֶׁנִּמְצָאִים
בְּגָלוּת, מַגִּיעִים לְהַמָּאוֹר.

Like an olive is crushed so that its oil can provide illumination, the "crushing" that we experience in exile causes the revelation of our soul's most essential light. However, there are two distinct degrees of crushing:

a) We are crushed by [external pressures, such as] decrees against the performance of Torah and *mitzvot*....

b) We experience freedom and prosperity in both the material and the spiritual sense . . . and nevertheless we are "crushed" and broken [internally] by the fact that we remain in a state of [spiritual] exile.

Of the two possible experiences, our brokenness over the very fact that we are in exile produces the ultimate light.

KEY POINTS

1   G-d desires "a home in the lowest realm." This has three
     specifications: It must be *the lowest* realm, receptive to
     G-d's *Essence*, and fashioned by *its mortal inhabitants*.
     All three conditions must be met fully and simultaneously.

2   The spiritual peaks and pits of our history were all
     steps *forward* toward this goal.

3   Initially, the world was physically and spiritually beautiful
     and was inhabited by G-d. The drawback: It met none
     of the specifications. It was too spiritual, unprimed for
     G-d's *Essence*, and lacking the initiative to embrace
     G-d. The sin of the Tree of Knowledge was necessary
     to ensure that our physical realm was truly the lowest.

4   Abraham discovered G-d on his own and shared G-d with
     the world, creating a quasi-home for G-d. The drawback:
     Abraham educated the world about its *Creator*, but
     G-d's Essence—*beyond* creation—was not yet revealed.

5   The Exodus and Giving of the Torah introduced
     G-d's *Essence*, transcendent of creation. The
     drawback: It was imposed by divine acts; it was
     not the result of *internal* transformation.

6   The sin of the Golden Calf removed the superimposed divine awareness. The Jews then erected the Tabernacle and, later, the Jerusalem Temples, where G-d's Essence was obvious and revealed in man-made homes. The drawback: Human initiative was undermined by strong divine dependence, because (a) these edifices were G-d's initiatives, and (b) G-d provided instant spiritual feedback.

7   In exile, we persisted in transforming this world into G-d's home *despite* every hardship and persecution. We did so *without* seeing or sensing G-d, based exclusively on our *mortal initiative*. Today's free societies offer the *ultimate*, final challenge: choosing to make a home for G-d without the influence of overt divinity and without even the external stimulus of persecution. Now it is truly *us* inviting G-d.

8   This journey is reflected in our own lives: Even our past regretful choices facilitate a plan and are steps forward in our personal *growth*.

ADDITIONAL READINGS

Overcoming Setbacks

by Rabbi Lord Jonathan Sacks

**RABBI LORD JONATHAN SACKS, PHD
1948-2020**

Former chief rabbi of the United Kingdom. Rabbi Sacks attended Cambridge University and received his doctorate from King's College, London. A prolific and influential author, his books include *Will We Have Jewish Grandchildren?* and *The Dignity of Difference.* He received the Jerusalem Prize in 1995 for his contributions to enhancing Jewish life in the Diaspora, was knighted and made a life peer in 2005, and became Baron Sacks of Aldridge in 2009.

At first, Moses' mission seemed to be successful. He had feared that the people would not believe in him, but G-d had given him signs to perform, and his brother Aaron to speak on his behalf. Moses "performed the signs before the people, and they believed. And when they heard that the L-rd was concerned about them and had seen their misery, they bowed down and worshiped." (Exodus 4:30-31)

But then things start to go wrong, and continue going wrong. Moses' first appearance before Pharaoh is disastrous. Pharaoh refuses to recognise G-d and he rejects Moses' request to let the people travel into the wilderness. Then he makes life worse for the Israelites. They must still make the same quota of bricks, but now they must also gather their own straw. The people turn against Moses and Aaron: "May the L-rd look on you and judge you! You have made us obnoxious to Pharaoh and his officials and have put a sword in their hand to kill us." (Exodus 5:21)

Moses and Aaron return to Pharaoh to renew their request. They perform a miraculous act – they turn a staff into a snake—but Pharaoh is unimpressed. His own magicians can do likewise. Next they bring the first of the 10 Plagues, but again Pharaoh is unmoved. He will not let the Israelites go. And so it goes on, nine times. Moses does everything in his power to make Pharaoh relent and finds that

nothing makes a difference. The Israelites are still slaves.

We sense the pressure Moses is under. After his first setback at the end of last week's parsha, he had turned to G-d and bitterly asked: "Why, L-rd, why have You brought trouble on this people? Is this why You sent me? Ever since I went to Pharaoh to speak in Your name, he has brought trouble on this people, and You have not rescued Your people at all." (Exodus 5:22-23)

In this week's parsha of Vaera, even when G-d reassures him that he will eventually succeed, he replies, "If the Israelites will not listen to me, why would Pharaoh listen to me, since I speak with faltering lips?" (Exodus 6:12).

There is an enduring message here. Leadership, even of the very highest order, is often marked by failure. The first Impressionists had to arrange their own art exhibition because their work was rejected by the established Paris salons. The first performance of Stravinsky's *The Rite of Spring* caused a riot, with the audience booing throughout. Van Gogh sold only one painting in his lifetime despite the fact that his brother, Theo, was an art dealer.

So it is with leaders. Lincoln faced countless setbacks during the Civil War. He was a deeply divisive figure, hated by many in his lifetime. Gandhi failed in his dream of uniting Muslims and Hindus together in a single nation. Nelson Mandela spent twenty-seven years in prison, accused of treason and regarded as a violent agitator. Winston Churchill was regarded as a spent force in politics by the 1930s, and even after his heroic leadership during the Second World War he was voted out of office at the first General Election once the war was over. Only in retrospect do heroes seem heroic and the many setbacks they faced reveal themselves as stepping-stones on the road to victory.

In our discussion of parshat Vayetse, we saw that in every field—high or low, sacred or secular—leaders are tested not by their successes but by their failures. It can sometimes be easy to succeed. The conditions may be favourable. The economic, political or personal climate is good. When there is an economic boom, most businesses flourish. In the first months after a general election, the successful leader carries with him or her the charisma of victory. In the first year, most marriages are happy. It takes no special skill to succeed in good times.

But then the climate changes. Eventually it always does. That is when many businesses, and politicians, and marriages fail. There are times when even the greatest people stumble. At such moments, character is tested. The great human beings are not those who never fail. They are those who survive failure, who keep on going, who refuse to be defeated, who never give up or give in. They keep trying. They learn from every mistake. They treat failure as a learning experience. And from every refusal to be defeated, they become stronger, wiser and more determined. That is the story of Moses' life in both parshat Shemot and parshat Vaera.

Jim Collins, one of the great writers on leadership, puts it well:

> The signature of the truly great versus the merely successful is not the absence of difficulty, but the ability to come back from setbacks, even cataclysmic catastrophes, stronger than before. . . . The path out of darkness begins with those exasperatingly persistent individuals who are constitutionally incapable of capitulation. It's one thing to suffer a staggering defeat . . . and entirely another to give up on the values and aspirations that make the protracted struggle worthwhile. Failure is not so much a physical state as a state of mind; success is falling down, and getting up one more time, without end.[1]

Rabbi Yitzhak Hutner once wrote a powerful letter to a disciple who had become discouraged by his repeated failure to master Talmudic learning:

> A failing many of us suffer is that when we focus on the high attainments of great people, we discuss how they are complete in this or that area, while omitting mention of the inner struggles that had previously raged within them. A listener would get the impression that these individuals sprang from the hand of their creator in a state of perfection. . . .

> The result of this feeling is that when an ambitious young man of spirit and enthusiasm meets obstacles, falls and slumps, he imagines himself as unworthy of being "planted in the house of G-d" (Ps. 92:13). . . .

> Know, however, my dear friend, that your soul is rooted not in the tranquillity of the good inclination, but in the battle of the good inclination . . . The English expression, "Lose a battle and win the war," applies. Certainly you have stumbled and will stumble again, and in many battles you will fall lame. I promise you, though, that after those losing campaigns you will emerge from the war with laurels of victory on your head. . . . The wisest of men said, "A righteous man falls seven times, but rises again." (Proverbs 24:16) Fools believe the intent of the verse is to teach us that the righteous man falls seven times and, despite this, he rises. But the knowledgeable are aware that the essence of the righteous man's rising again is **because** of his seven falls.[2]

Rabbi Hutner's point is that *greatness cannot be achieved without failure*. There are heights you cannot climb without first having fallen.

For many years, I kept on my desk a quote from Calvin Coolidge, sent by a friend who knew how easy it is to be discouraged. It said:

"Nothing in this world can take the place of persistence. Talent will not: nothing is more common than unsuccessful men with talent. Genius will not; unrewarded genius is almost a proverb. Education will not: the world is full of educated derelicts. Persistence and determination alone are omnipotent."

I would only add, "And *seyata diShmaya*, the help of Heaven." G-d never loses faith in us, even if we sometimes lose faith in ourselves.

The supreme role model is Moses who, despite all the setbacks chronicled in last week's parsha and this week's, eventually became the man of whom it was said that he was "a hundred and twenty years old when he died, yet his eyes were undimmed and his energy unabated." (Deut. 34:7)

Defeats, delays and disappointments hurt. They hurt even for Moses. So if there are times when we, too, feel discouraged and demoralised, it is important to remember that even the greatest people failed. What made them great is that they kept going. The road to success passes through many valleys of failure. There is no other way.

ENDNOTES

[1] Jim Collins, *How the Mighty Fall: And Why Some Companies Never Give In* (New York, Harper Collins, 2009), 123.
[2] Rabbi Yitzhak Hutner, *Sefer Pachad Yitzchak: Iggerot u-Ketavim* (Gur Aryeh, 1981), no. 128, 217–18.

Va'era, Lessons in Leadership: A Weekly Reading of the Jewish Bible, 2015 www.rabbisacks.org/vaera-5781/ or www.chabad.org/2430632

Reprinted with permission from the Office of Rabbi Sacks

To read more from Rabbi Sacks, please visit www.rabbisacks.org. You can also follow @RabbiSacks on social media.

The Thirteenth Principle

By Rabbi Noson Gurary

RABBI NOSON GURARY

Rabbi and lecturer. Rabbi Gurary is the executive director of Chabad in Buffalo, NY, servicing the local Jewish community and the University of Buffalo. He is a respected lecturer on Jewish mysticism and Chasidism.

I believe with complete faith that the dead will be brought back to life when g-d wills it to happen.

The thirteenth and last principle is the belief in the Resurrection of the Dead. That the dead will be resurrected is one of the foundations of Jewish belief handed down by Moshe. It is fundamental to the extent that one who does not believe in the Resurrection of the Dead is regarded as a heretic[1] and will be excluded from the resurrection when it takes place.[2] Moreover, the Resurrection of the Dead is meant literally and is not to be interpreted allegorically, as is stated explicitly in the Prophetic Writings (Daniel 12:12): "Many who sleep in the dust shall awaken, some to everlasting life, and some to shame and reproach".[3]

This subject requires clarification, as two major questions need to be answered: (1) Why is it so important to believe in the Resurrection of the Dead, to the extent that this is regarded as one of the fundamental principles of Judaism? (2) Why is it necessary for souls to descend once again from *Gan Eden* (Paradise) into a physical body in this world? The souls of the righteous such as Moshe Rabbeinu, Avraham, Yitzchak, and Yaakov, have been in *Gan Eden* for thousands of years. Our Sages add[4] that they have not idled away their time there, as "the righteous do not have any rest, neither in this world, nor in the World to Come [i.e., *Gan Eden*]."

Instead, they exist in a constant state of ascent, level after level, day after day for thousands of years now. What benefit, then, will they gain from descending once again into a physical body in this world?

A Matter of Life and Death

Before these questions can be answered, we must first understand why there is death in the first place, and from where it originates. We find in the Torah[5] that because Adam and Chava ate from the Tree of Knowledge, one of their punishments was the advent of mortality. Had they not eaten from the Tree of Knowledge, they (and we) would have lived forever. This would not have been a miracle, or something supernatural, but a natural phenomenon.[6] Thus, death is a direct result of the sin of the Tree of Knowledge. What is the inherent connection between the two?

Based on the verses, "You, who cleave to G-d your L-rd, are all alive today" (Deuteronomy 4:4); and, "For He is your life" (Deuteronomy 30:20), *Chasidus* explains that only when one is attached to G-d and G-dliness is one regarded as alive.[7] The source of all life, and in fact of all existence, is from G-d.[8] If G-d removed the life force with which He imbues all of creation, it would not be a dead creation, it would simply not be, period,[9] as discussed in the commentary on the first principle. Accordingly, by sinning in the way that they did, Adam and Chava rejected their innate connection to G-d, the Source of all life and existence, and thus incurred their own death.

Similarly, anything impure or evil is also the opposite of life,[10] and is explicitly referred to as death. When Adam and Chava sinned by eating from the Tree of Knowledge, they incurred spiritual impurity, which naturally led to physical death.[12] The two are essentially the same, except that spiritual death is becoming separated from the Source of life,[13] while physical death is becoming separated from the body's source of life, which is the soul.

This is one of the reasons why there will be no death in the World to Come. As all sin will have been rectified and purified, including the sin of the Tree of Knowledge, there will be no place for death, and life will therefore be eternal.[14] Not only will there be no death, there will be Resurrection of the Dead,[15] as will be explained further.

An additional facet of why the sin of the Tree of Knowledge incurred death is that in eating from the Tree of Knowledge, Adam and Chava became impure. If Adam and Chava had lived forever, their impurity would also have remained forever. For this reason alone, death had to be introduced, as impurity is contrary to the whole purpose of creation;[16] in this sense, death is in fact a process of purification.

Another explanation as to why there had to be death as a result of the sin of the Tree of Knowledge is because Adam and Chava's bodies were affected by their sin, and became a mix of good and evil. Knowledge, or *da'at* in Hebrew, means much more than simply knowing. It implies attachment and bonding to the point that the person and the idea become one. This is exactly what happened when Adam and Chava ate from the Tree of Knowledge. Until that moment, evil was only a potential state, removed from the person. When Adam and Chava ate from the Tree of Knowledge, evil then became an integral part of their physical being. This evil, or impurity, acquired through the sin had to be removed, which could be achieved only through death. In death, the body was recycled and cleansed of its admixture of evil.

All punishments in the Torah are a means of rectifying and purifying, and are not intended as revenge or retaliation, G-d forbid. They are for our benefit, to cleanse and remove acquired stains, as mentioned in the eleventh principle. Similarly, death is not a punishment or retribution, but a method of cleansing for the sin of the Tree of Knowledge. By way of an analogy, when clothes are placed in a washing machine, the purpose is not to keep them in the washing machine, but to wear and enjoy them following the cleaning process. So too, every punishment, including death, is intended to lead to the next step—the Resurrection of the Dead. Through death, the body becomes purified and ready for the remarkable revelations that will take place during resurrection.

The body could have lived forever, had it not been for Adam and Chava's sin. This, in fact, was G-d's original plan; if the body had remained subservient to the soul, there would have been no reason for the body to die, and man would have lived forever. Thus, once the problem created by the sin is rectified in the proper way, the body will revert to its original state of being. And just as the soul is eternal, the body, too, will be eternal, becoming a perfect vessel for the revelation of G-dliness.[17]

The Purpose of Creation

It is important to note that only the physical body was, and is, affected by sin. The soul itself remains pure and unsullied, and does not require rectification.[18] Thus, the descent of the soul from *Gan Eden* (Paradise) into a physical body was not for its own sake, as there too, the soul was aware of G-dliness. Rather, its descent was for the sake of elevating and purifying the physical body, and with it, the entire physical world. It is what Adam was intended to accomplish in the first place.[19]

As explained in the commentary on the first principle, our Sages inform us that the entire purpose of creation is for this world to become a dwelling place for G-d;[20] all of the *mitzvahs* that we perform are intended to bring this about.[21] This is why the Torah was given in a physical world[22] and why the *mitzvahs* are performed with physical objects, by a soul in a physical body. The soul descends to this world and dwells in a physical body in order to purify the body and the world through Torah and *mitzvahs,* and reveal G-dliness in the world. Each *mitzvah* corresponds to a different part of the body and its performance purifies a different aspect of the body[23]—with it, a different aspect of creation.[24] The cumulative effect of the Torah and *mitzvahs* of generations, past and present, has purified and elevated the world to unprecedented levels. (Since the very lowest levels are presently being elevated, the progress achieved so far is not readily evident.)[25]

We can now understand the importance of the Resurrection of the Dead and why it is so fundamental to Jewish belief. In the Messianic Era, the Jewish people will achieve the highest level of perfection which man is capable of, returning to the level of Adam, prior to the sin of the Tree of Knowledge[26] (see previous principle). At this stage, the physical world will become a perfect medium for the Torah. Since entering this first stage of the Messianic Era, the world in general will not yet have reached this level, and, in a sense, even the perfection of the Jewish people will not yet be complete. Consequently, all those who live during the Messianic Era will have to die prior to the Resurrection of the Dead, and be resurrected right afterward.[27]

At a later stage in the process, an even higher level will be reached when the world will be connected to the Torah the way the Torah transcends the world. Torah existed before the world was created[28] and, being the will and wisdom of G-d,[29] is eternal, transcending time and space. Torah itself is not for the sake of the world. On the contrary, the world is for the sake of the Torah.[30] There is an aspect of Torah that refines the world,[31] and then there is Torah, the way it is, in and of itself. The ultimate goal is that the world will not only be the way the Torah wants it to be—a perfect world— but become a part of a reality that is connected to Torah as Torah transcends the world.

This will take place in the era of the resurrection, when the spirit of impurity, which includes death, will have been completely removed from the earth.[32] Then, mankind as a whole will reach perfection, the purpose of creation will be completely realized, and the Essence of G-d will be revealed.[33]

Reward and the Ultimate Purpose

All of the above does not answer the second question, posed at the beginning of this section: Why is it necessary for the souls of the righteous, such as those of Moshe Rabbeinu, Avraham , Yitzchak, and Yaakov, which have been in *Gan Eden* for thousands of years, to descend once again into a physical body in this world? This clearly seems to imply that this world is actually superior to the spiritual realm known as *Gan Eden!* How is it possible that a soul within a physical body in this physical world will be worthy of a level of divine revelation that supersedes what is revealed to the soul devoid of a physical body?

Maimonides and Nachmanides disagree on this issue, as mentioned in the discussion on the eleventh principle. Both ask: where will the final reward be given? Is the

Resurrection of the Dead the final period, the final reward? Or will there be death again following the resurrection, and the soul will be given the final reward as a soul, without a body? Maimonides argues that the ultimate reward is spiritual[34] and will be bestowed upon the soul without a body. At some point after the Resurrection of the Dead, the soul will return to *Gan Eden* without the body, and will reside there forever.[35]

According to this view, since the reward is a product of the type of action that a person performed in this world, it must be granted in an appropriate manner. Hence, the body, having had a central part in fulfilling the *mitzvahs* is also deserving of a reward. The soul, which fulfilled Torah and *mitzvahs* clothed in a physical body must receive its reward in a like manner—in a physical body—which is the purpose of the Resurrection of the Dead,[36] and why the soul must descend once again into a physical body in this world. Having ensured that the body shared in its reward, the soul can return to the ultimate, spiritual reward in *Gan Eden.*

Nachmanides, on the other hand, maintains[37] that the final and ultimate reward will be granted to the soul within the body, which will then no longer experience death. This will take place during the era of the Resurrection of the Dead. Chasidic texts[38] endorse Nachmanides' view that the era of the Resurrection of the Dead will be the time when the final and ultimate reward is granted.

The question of where the final reward is granted is not just a question of priority, of which comes first and which last Rather, the argument is really about which reward is the highest one. Is the highest form of reward spiritual, given to a soul without a body (as Maimonides argues), or is the highest form of reward physical, granted to a soul in a body (as proposed by Nachmanides and endorsed by *Chasidus*). At first glance, it seems that Maimonides' opinion is the more logical, because, after all, this world is finite, limited in time and space. For a soul to be in a physical world, confined in a physical body forever should be anguish, not a reward. Therefore, Maimonides argues that the final reward is given to the soul without a body, in *Gan Eden.*

What, then, is the explanation of Nachmanides' view? The question of why the soul descends, once again, into a body poses no difficulty for this opinion. It stands to reason that the reward given to the soul for fulfilling the *mitzvahs* while in a physical body is granted to the soul also while in a physical body. Yet, it is difficult to understand why this is the ultimate reward, and not a setback for the soul—to have to leave its state of spiritual bliss in *Gan Eden* and descend once again into a physical body. Wouldn't the soul rather forgo such reward and remain in its spiritual paradise? We must, therefore, conclude that according to Nachmanides and *Chasidus,* the benefits of the soul's presence in this physical world surpass those of the spiritual world, and for this reason, the final and greater reward is granted precisely in this world and not in the spiritual ones.

Chasidus explains[39] that the physical body of a Jew is actually superior to the soul, in a certain way. While the body is a lowly, and even repulsive entity when compared with the holiness and spirituality of the G-dly soul, nevertheless, it has something that even the soul does not possess. Therefore, for the soul to receive the level of revelation that will be attained during the era of the Resurrection of the Dead, it must descend into a physical body, in this physical world.

This can be better understood by way of an analogy. When a river flows without any obstruction, it flows on in tranquility, without any great force. If the river is dammed up, and the flow of water is blocked, it appears, at first glance, that the river has dried up. However, when the weight of the dammed-up water is so great that it bursts the walls of the dam, the water gushes forth with tremendous power, sweeping along everything in its path, including the dam walls. What appears to be a barrier and obstacle to the flow of the river is precisely what causes the water to flow immeasurably, more powerfully than before.

The same is true with regard to the soul. Through the descent of the soul into this world, its power is increased immeasurably. The obstacles, conflict, resistance, and the concealment of G-dliness that the soul must face and overcome in this world awaken its latent powers and capacities. These are revealed and expressed precisely through its descent into this world.

The Equality of Spiritual and Physical

However, the above merely explains what motivates the soul to descend into this world and be clothed in a physical body. It does not explain wherein the superiority of the physical world lies over the spiritual realms. In fact, it emphasizes the deficiency of the world in that it conceals and even opposes G-dliness!

Moreover, the idea that this material world is superior to spiritual realms appears to contradict common sense and everyday experience regarding the spiritual and the material. We naturally regard the spiritual as infinitely superior to the material because the latter, by definition, is a substantial limitation and concealment of G-dliness. And yet, *Chasidus* maintains that it is specifically in this material world where souls are clothed in physical bodies that they are able to attain a revelation of G-dliness that is infinitely higher than the revelations attained by the disembodied soul in *Gan Eden!*

The questions remain: (1) How is it possible at all to compare this material world to the spiritual world of *Gan Eden?* (2) Even if we can explain how it is possible for the loftiest levels of G-dliness to be revealed in this world, we must still explain why they are revealed precisely in this world, and not in *Gan Eden.* To put these questions slightly differently: (1) How can material existence reveal G-dliness? (2) Even if it can reveal G-dliness, in what sense is it superior to spiritual existence? These questions are pertinent not only to the Resurrection of the Dead, but encompass the entire concept of the descent of the soul into a physical body in a material world.

Chasidus explains that from one point of view, the physical world is indeed the lowest world there could be.[40] In the discussion of the first principle, the various planes of reality called the four worlds, were explained. Each world comes about through the progressive concealment of G-dliness. In the physical world, G-dliness is almost completely concealed, and in this sense, it is the lowest of all worlds.[41]

However, the differences between higher worlds and lower worlds are only in terms of G-dliness that was revealed (or concealed) in the process of creation, which was only a reflection and radiance of G-d's Infinite Light.[42] In this sense, the higher spiritual worlds are more appropriate "vessels" for a greater level of revelation than this material world, which is not an appropriate "vessel" for such revelation. However, in terms of the Infinite Essence of G-d, there is no difference between the higher worlds and the lower worlds. To use an analogy,[43] it is obvious to all that the number 10 is larger than the number 1, while the number 100 is much larger than both 10 and 1. However, in relation to mathematical infinity, 1, 10 and 100 are all equal; for infinity, by definition, is equally eternally bigger than 1, 10, and 100! When limited numbers are compared with one another, there can be degrees and differences between large numbers and small ones.

But any number, large or small, is equally incomparable to infinity.

The same is true in regard to the finite revelation of G-dliness within creation. Here, there are degrees and levels; one world is regarded as higher, and another, lower. However, in regard to the infinite and uncontracted light of G-dliness which completely transcends all of creation and which will be revealed during the era of the Resurrection of the Dead, there is absolutely no difference between this material world and the supernal spiritual worlds, for none of them are appropriate "vessels" for this light. From this point of view, the spiritual worlds have no superiority over the physical world; all are equally inappropriate for this essential revelation.

In other words, the way that a higher world surpasses a lower world in qualitative and quantitative terms is not comparable to the way in which the Holy One, Blessed is He, surpasses even the highest worlds. It is inaccurate to say that the Holy One, Blessed is He, simply surpasses the very highest of all worlds in all qualitative and quantitative terms; that He is the epitome of perfection and completeness and is totally unlimited, whereas all the worlds are, in some way, limited and imperfect. Such a view simply places G-d at the top of the pyramid, because He possesses all positive qualities to the greatest degree possible. This implies that G-d is quantifiable, or at least qualifiable, and if He seems not to be, it is merely due to our human inability to comprehend His greatness and superiority over us.

However, *Chasidus* explains that the entire pyramid of values, attributes, and qualities that we could possibly ascribe to G-d, even if we had the ability to do so in infinite measure, do not really apply to Him at all, since they are all created, limited terms. In fact, any quality or attribute that we posit constitutes a limitation of His Essence. Therefore, in comparison with His Essence, all things—even the loftiest ones—are equally "distant," and the spiritual has no advantage over the physical.

The Superiority of the Material World

Having explained that in relation to the Essence of G-d, spiritual and physical are equal, we still have not answered how material existence is superior to spiritual existence in terms of revealing the infinite, the Essence of G-dliness.

Chasidus explains that precisely because this world is the lowest of all worlds, and the end point of all creation, it is superior to the highest of worlds.[44] Our Sages observed that "the beginning is wedged in the end,"[45] meaning that there is an intrinsic connection between the very highest of levels and the very lowest. Since this world is the lowest of worlds, only this world, and not any of the higher worlds is able to reveal the very highest of levels, that which is absolutely unlimited and infinite, the very Essence of G-d.

One of the explanations of this is that only G-d Himself could have created a physical world, for it could never have come about by a gradual process of contraction and descent.[46] A contraction and reduction of spirituality would merely produce something less spiritual, but never something physical, *Chasidus* explains that only G-d Himself has the power and ability to create *ex nihilo*,[47] and this supernal G-dly energy is imprinted solely on this material world. At present, this aspect is concealed, but in the future, in the World to Come and in the era of the Resurrection of the Dead, it will be revealed.[48]

It is precisely because this world and all the creatures in it were created by G-d alone that the creatures of this world feel themselves to be independent, self-sufficient entities who are even able to declare, "I made myself!"[49] On every other plane of existence, specifically in all the spiritual worlds, there is awareness that there is a Creator, and that world and the creatures in it come from a higher source. By contrast, the creatures of our world are not only unaware that they are constantly being created by G-d, they feel just the opposite' *Chasidus* explains[50] that G-d's Essence and His total independence of any other creature or existence, as explained in the first principle, is manifest in the physical world more than in any other world and on any other level.[51]

The Torah declares that King Solomon was so wise that he was able to give 3,000 parables for every concept.[52] Why does this describe his wisdom even more than the fact that he could understand the language of birds and animals? The 3,000 parables are not to be understood as simply 3,000 ways of explaining the same thing, using different analogies and terminology. Rather, with any concept, King Solomon was able to discern 3,000 levels, one lower than the other, and was able to find the appropriate analogies and terms to communicate the idea on 3,000 different levels of understanding. This means that King Solomon was 3,000 levels greater than the average person, and yet someone 3,000 levels lower than him could still understand King Solomon's wisdom. The greatness of his wisdom was that he was able to bring it down 3,000 levels. In a similar sense, the greatness of G-d is nowhere more evident than in the very lowest of levels. Thus, on the verse "Great is G-d in the city of our L-rd,"[53] *the Zohar*[54] comments that the greatness of G-d is manifest specifically in "the city of our L-rd"—referring to this world of limitation and multiplicity.[55]

Furthermore, the final and ultimate purpose of creation is revealed specifically in this world.[56] This can be better understood via another analogy. When building a home, a person makes a plan of exactly what he wants the house to look like; what windows, what fixtures, and so on. Each part, laying the foundation, putting up the walls and roof, etc. is only a step, and does not constitute the final purpose. Each room and each fixture is only a means to an end. Although the construction of the foundation, walls, and roof are far more important than painting and decorating the house and furnishing it, nevertheless, the job is regarded as complete only when the house needs no further work. Only then is the person's original intention in building the house finally achieved. In the same way, although this world is the last and the final world G-d created, and is therefore the lowest in terms of revelation, it nevertheless constitutes the completion and culmination of the entire building process; the icing on the cake, so to speak. This physical world is the culmination of the purpose of the entire creation.[57]

Body and Soul

As mentioned previously, prior to the soul's descent into this world, it resided in the spiritual realms referred to as *Gan Eden*. There, it was filled with love and awe for G-d, and in the absence of any evil inclination, it naturally cleaved to G-d and delighted in the spiritual radiance of the Divine Presence.

It is therefore self-understood that the descent of the soul into a physical body in this world is a tremendous demotion and even degradation for the soul. If so, what is the purpose of this descent, with all its inevitable difficulties and suffering? The answer is that this descent is for the purpose of an even greater ascent afterward. The ascent comes about by virtue of the soul's association with its physical body, and by fulfilling the purpose for which it descended, which is revealing the G-dliness hidden within the material world, purifying it and the physical body through Torah and *mitzvahs,* creating a "dwelling place" for G-d in the world. The

reward for this will be given to the body in the era of the Resurrection of the Dead.

Regarding the World to Come, a verse in Isaiah (11:9) states, ". . . the earth shall be full of the knowledge of G-d as the waters cover the sea." *Chasidic* texts[58] explain that this is meant to be understood literally; this physical earth and all its inhabitants, to the very lowest levels of creation will become purified, refined, and elevated, to the extent that they will achieve the very highest of levels of knowledge of G-d. Not only will this knowledge equal the knowledge of G-d attained at the highest of spiritual levels, it will even surpass it. The physical will be imbued with an awareness of the Essence of G-d which is the source of physical being, and not merely an awareness of spiritual levels, however elevated they may be which are the source of spiritual being, as previously explained.

At that point, the body will no longer need to receive its sustenance from food. It will receive its life force and energy directly from the Essence of G-d, from whence it was created; its Source will no longer be concealed, as it is at present. This is the meaning of our Sages' statement that there will be no eating or drinking in the World to Come.[59] The body will not require food and drink to stay alive; it will be nourished directly from Above.

Moreover, in the era of the Resurrection of the Dead, the body will be even greater than the soul, and instead of the soul conferring spirituality on the body, the body will confer spirituality on the soul![60] This can be inferred from several verses that refer to the revelation of G-dliness which will take place in the World to Come: Isaiah (40:5) states, "The glory of G-d shall be revealed, and all flesh shall see together that the mouth of G-d has spoken." Similarly, a verse in Joel (3:1) states, "I shall pour out My spirit upon all flesh. . ." *Chasidic* texts[61] explain that when these levels of divinity will be revealed, the "vessel" that will be able to receive these revelations will be the physical body and not the soul, since the source of the former is from the Essence of G-d, whereas the source of the soul is only associated with the radiance and reflection of G-dliness.

It is now clear that even those souls that have been in *Gan Eden* for thousands of years will once again descend into a physical body in order to receive this revelation. This is why Nachmanides maintains that the ultimate reward will be given to the soul within the body, for the revelation will transcend the source of the soul itself.[62]

Chasidus explains that all of this comes about by virtue of the *mitzvahs* which constitute the practical fulfillment of the Will of G-d. The *mitzvahs* are associated with physical objects in the physical world,[63] while the Torah remains abstract and spiritual, even though it applies to situations in this world.[64]

The superiority of the physical in this aspect explains why G-d seems overly concerned at times with the physical details of the *mitzvahs*. It might appear peculiar why G-d, Who is beyond time and space is concerned about the dimensions of a *Sukkah*, for example. A *Sukkah* can be used for the *mitzvah* only if it is of exactly the right dimensions; if it is too small or too high, it is not properly done. Similarly, one must consume a minimum amount of *matzah* on Passover in order to fulfill the *mitzvah*.

One would think that since a *mitzvah* is from G-d, its main aspect would be the spiritual facet of the *mitzvah,* with the physical either playing no role, or being of secondary importance. Yet, we find that the exact opposite is true. If a person performed the required action, even if he didn't have the right intent, he has fulfilled the *mitzvah*. However, if a person had the most beautiful, mystical thoughts but didn't actually do the *mitzvah* in a physical way, he has no *mitzvah* to his credit.

The question is answered as we reflect upon the fact that in the physical world lays the ultimate purpose of creation, and of the descent of the soul into this world. In other words, before the soul descended to this earth, when it resided in *Gan Eden,* it meditated upon G-d, attained understanding of G-d, and felt the beauty of G-d. Yet, in the physical world, through observance of the *mitzvahs,* the soul becomes one with G-d's Essence.

The Ultimate Reward

In the commentary on the eleventh principle, we explained that the word *mitzvah* comes from the word *tzavtah,* meaning attachment or bonding.[65] The greatest reward of a *mitzvah* is the connection to the Essence of G-d. Although this will be revealed only in the World to Come, the actual connection takes place now, in the physical world.[66] Our Sages interpret the verse "Do them today" (Deuteronomy 7:11) to mean, in this world, but not tomorrow;[67] "and receive their reward tomorrow" to mean in the World to Come.[68]

This is also why everyone has a share in the World to Come, as the *Mishnah*[69] explicitly states: "All Israel have a share in the World to Come." In *Gan Eden,* there are restrictions and limitations as to who can enter, and what level they can achieve.[70] *Gan Eden* is the reward given primarily for learning Torah,[71] which is chiefly a spiritual activity. Therefore, the reward for Torah is given to the soul without a body. Regarding reward in the World to Come which is the reward given primarily for the fulfillment of *mitzvahs,* it is given to a soul while in a physical body. Even a person who was wicked his entire life has hope. He will eventually be purified and rise up to cleave to his Source, G-d Himself,[72] as "all Jews, even deliberate sinners, are filled with *mitzvahs* like a pomegranate."[73]

Beyond the Torah?

Concerning the relationship of the Jewish people to the Torah, our Sages state that a Jew is even more elevated than the Torah itself.[74] *Chasidus* explains[75] that after the reward for the fulfillment of Torah and *mitzvahs* has been awarded and the G-dliness that was drawn down by their fulfillment has been revealed in the physical world, there will be an even further stage, when the Jewish people will ascend to an even higher level, transcending that which was elicited by the fulfillment of Torah and *mitzvahs*. This is the revelation of the inherent superiority of the Jewish people over the Torah, and the primary aspect of the World to Come. The revelations elicited by *the mitzvahs* will be manifested in the Messianic Era as well, but the unique revelation that will take place in the World to Come, the world of resurrection, is the revelation of the intrinsic connection between the Jewish people and the Essence of G-d.

Conclusion

Perhaps the reason that Maimonides' final principle is about the Resurrection of the Dead is connected to the maxim that "the beginning is wedged in the end, and the end in the beginning."[76] In the beginning, we explained that belief in G-d comes from G-d himself, and that G-d Himself is revealed to the soul. We conclude with the idea that the relationship of G-d to the Jewish person as a whole, to both body and soul will ultimately be revealed in the era of the Resurrection of the Dead. As explained by *Chasidus,* the Essence of G-d is connected, in every way, to the life of a Jew in this world. The final of the thirteen principles emphasizes that this intrinsic connection is everlasting, and will ultimately be revealed forever, underscoring that for G-d's essence, there never is an end point.

ENDNOTES

1 Maimonides' commentary on *Mishnah Sanhedrin* 11, thirteenth principle.

2 *Mishnah Sanhedrin* 10:1, (This *mishnah* appears in the tenth chapter of the *Mishnah* and the Jerusalem Talmud. but in the eleventh chapter of the Babylonian Talmud; Maimonides, *Code, Teshuvah* 3:6.

3 Maimonides' Essay on *Techiyat HaMeitim.*

4 *Pesikta Zuta* 7.

5 Genesis 3:19.

6 The reason for this is explained in *Or HaChaim's* commentary on the verse.

7 *Tanya,* chap. 17. *Likkutei Torah. Va'etchanan 50b; Kuntreis Ha-Hitpaalut,* chap. 1. See also *Berachot* 18b; *Midrash Bereishit* 39:7.

8 *Tanya,* chap. 48.

9 *Shaar HaYichud v'HaEmunah,* chap.1.

10 As clearly understood from the verse in Deuteronomy 30:15, "... I have placed before you life and good, and death and evil."

11 Ibid. See also Rashi's commentary, ad loc.

12 See *Or HaChaim's* commentary, Genesis 3.19.

13 Isaiah 59:2.

14 See *Bereishit Rabbah* 12:6; at length in *Avodat Hakodesh,* pt. 2, Chap. 38. See *Igrot Kodesh* of the Lubavitcher Rebbe, vol. 2, p. 65ff.; the Lubavitcher Rebbe's *Teshuvot u'Biurim* (Kehot, 5734), p. 47ff.

15 See *Sanhedrin* 92b; *Zohar,* vol. 1, p. 114a.

16 *Tanya,* chap. 37.

17 Ibid.

18 Ibid., chaps. 24, 37, 38.

19 *Pirkei d'R Elazar* 11:1.

20 *Midrash Tanchuma, Nasso* 16; quoted and explained in *Tanya, chap.* 36.

21 Ibid.

22 See *Shabbat* 88bff.

23 *Tanya,* chap. 37. See also *Sefer HaChareidim* for some of the practical implications of this idea.

24 As is understood from the *midrashic* statement *(Kohelet Rabbah* 3:16) that "the world, too, he placed in (man's) heart," meaning that man is a microcosm and affects the macrocosm.

25 *Igrot Kodesh* of the Lubavitcher Rebbe, vol. 2, p. 68.

26 See *Bereshit Rabbah* 12:6: *Avodat HaKodesh,* pt. 2, chap. 38.

27 *Igrot Kodesh* of the Lubavitcher Rebbe, vol. 2, p. 69.

28 *Tanna d'Vai Eliyahu,* chap. 12; *Midrash Tehillim* 90:12.

29 See *Tanya,* chap. 5.

30 Rashi, Genesis 1:1.

31 *See Bereishit Rabbah* 44:1.

32 *See* Zechariah 13:2.

33 *Igrot Kodesh* of the Lubavitcher Rebbe. vol. 2, p. 71. *See also Tanya,* chap. 37.

34 *Code, Teshuvah* 8:2: see also ibid., 9:1: beginning of "Preface to Chapter *Chelek."*

35 *See Sefer Halkkarim 4:31.*

36 See *Sanhedrin* 91a–b, regarding punishment of the soul and body together. The same rule applies as regards reward.

37 *Shaar Hagemul,* end. See also Raavad's comments to Rambam's Code, *Teshuvah,* 8:2.

38 *See Likkutei Torah,* Tzav, 15c: *Shir HaShirim* 65d; *Derech Mitzvotecha, Tzitzit.*

39 *Igrot Kodesh* of the Lubavitcher Rebbe, vol. 2, p. 65ff, the Lubavitcher Rebbe's *Teshuvot u'Biurim* (Kehot, 5734) p. 47ff.

40 This matter is dealt with at length in several places, among them the Tzemach Tzedek's *Derech Mitzvotecha, Mitzvat Tzitzit.* See also the references given in the footnotes following.

41 See *Tanya,* chap. 36.

42 lbid., chap. 20

43 See ibid., chap. 48

44 See ibid., chaps. 36, 37.

45 *Sefer Yetzirah* 1:7.

46 *Tanya, Iggeret HaKodesh,* chap. 20.

47 Ibid.

48 *Tanya,* chap. 37.

49 Ezekiel 29:3.

50 Rabbi Dovber of Lubavitch in *Biurei HaZohar. Beshallach,* 43c.

51 See *Tanya,* chap. 36, *Iggeret HaKodesh,* chap. 20.

52 l Kings 5:12.

53 Psalms 48:2.

54 Vol. 3, 5a; *Zohar Chadash* 44a.

55 Explained at length in the discourses ולקחתם לכם and כבוד מלכותך of the year 5661.

56 *Tanya,* chap. 36.

57 Ibid.

58 Ibid.

59 Berachot 17b; *Kallah Rabbati,* chap. 2; *Zohar Chadash Yitro* 33b, *Tikkunei Zohar Tikkun* 8. Note that Maimonides (Code, *Teshuvah* 8:2) concludes that therefore the World to Come is the world of disembodied souls.

60 See the series of discourses titled 5637 וכבה, chap. 91: *Maamarim Kuntreisim,* vol. 2. p. 413b.

61 Ibid.

62 5637 וכבה, chap. 92.

63 See *Tanya,* chap. 35.

64 See *Torah Or, Yitro* 73b: the Tzemach Tzedek's *Derech Mitzvotecha* 15b, Discourse 5679 כי ישאלך, chap. 2.

65 *Likkutei Torah, Bechukotai* 45c.

66 *Tanya,* chap. 37.

67 Eruvin 22a; Avodah Zarah 50a.

68 As explained in *Tanya,* chap. 17.

69 Sanhedrin 10:1 (or 11:1).

70 Discourse 5700 כי ישאלך, chap. 1; *Igrot Kodesh* of the Lubavitcher Rebbe, vol. 30, p. 141: *Teshuvot u'Biurim,* p. 28. See *Torah Or,* Yitro 73b: the Tzemach Tzedek's *Derech Mitzvotecha* 15b. Discourse 5679 כי ישאלך, chap. 2.

71 *Igrot Kodesh* and *Teshuvot u'Biurim,* ad loc. The Rebbe explains this at length in several ways, citing numerous sources.

[72] *Eruvin* 19a, *Chagiga* 27a. This explanation is given in *Maama-rim Melukat,* vol. 3. p. 34.

[73] *Tanna d'Vei Eliyahu*, chaps. 14, 31; *Bereishit Rabbah* 1:4.

[74] *Maamarim Melukat,* vol. 3, p. 34ff.

[75] Ibid., Discourses 5666, p. 507.

[76] Sefer Yetzirah 1:7.

The Thirteen Principles of Faith: A Chasidic Viewpoint (New York: Menachem Education Foundation, 2017)

Reprinted with permission of Rabbi Noson Gurary

What's So Great About Failure? Rewriting Your Own Script

By Rabbi Tzvi Freeman

RABBI TZVI FREEMAN
1955–

Rabbi, computer scientist, and writer. A published expert, consultant, and lecturer in the field of educational technology, Rabbi Freeman has held posts at the University of British Columbia and the Digipen School of Computer Gaming. Rabbi Freeman's books include *Bringing Heaven Down to Earth* and *Men, Women and Kabbalah*. He is a senior editor at Chabad.org.

We need failure. The world is designed in such a way that people can fail—and fail so often. So often that at times it seems there is more failure than success.

We all need failure. Failure, you see, is the only way you can fall out of the script.

Yes, that is frightening. Your very essence is intrinsically bound with this script. The script is the primordial thought of G-d, of a breath of Himself descending into the constrictions of a physical body with earthly drives, of that breath reaching back up to its origin and carrying all the world along with it—it was within this script that your soul was originally conceived.

And now, instead of reaching up to Him, what if you decide to reach downward into the darkness? What if, instead of repairing His world, you bring it into yet further confusion? What if, instead of rescuing divine sparks, you bury them yet further?

That is not what your soul is about, or what it came here for. That is not in the script—not for your soul, not for the world in which it was invested. What now?

Now, even if you go back to do all the right things, back to fixing and connecting, you will still be left with a gaping hole, an absence of light where light should have been, a gaping wound festering with chaos where tikkun was meant to come, and nothing in the script to address that hole—since that emptiness, that chaos was never meant to be.

So now G-d looks down, shakes His head, and says, "Well, I guess now you're going to have to write your own script."

Which you do. You take your life in your hands and turn it around. You say, "I don't like what I did. I'm not going to be that person anymore." And you carry that plan into action.

Just Do It

The word for this in Hebrew is *teshuvah* תשובה, which means "return." It also means taking ownership of your own life.

Distraught and wearied by his journeys, the young man finally came to the *tzaddik* Rabbi Menachem Mendel of Kotzk, and cried bitterly, "Rabbi, I sinned! The worst sins! How do I do *teshuvah*? I went to many rabbis, but none could help me!"

"And before you sinned," the rabbi asked, "did you ask anyone for advice how to do that?"

"No," he confessed, "I just sinned."

"So just do *teshuvah*," the rabbi replied, "the same way you just sinned."

Meaning: Just as your failure was not scripted for you, but was purely from you alone, so too your *teshuvah* can come only from you alone.

No one returns because they were told to do so. At the point of return, you revolve by your power alone.

Out of Nowhere

From where did that script come? From where did you get that power? When G-d thought of your soul, He did not see it there. Which means it wasn't anywhere else in the whole of creation, or in the Creator's concept of creation. Where was it? It never was. It never emerged from the nothingness into being.

Which means that when you go ahead after doing this crazy mess-up and write your own script, you are reaching back deeper than the place from whence your soul was breathed, reaching deeper and pulling something out from there that never was. From that place we call *ha'atzmut*, the core essence of G-d.

The term for this place is *he'elem ha'atzmi*, which means "the intrinsically hidden." Call it, if you will, G-d's subconscious. After all, consciousness is not G-d. G-d exists before there is anything at all, including consciousness. If we would call it that, then we would say that by getting it right you can reach into G-d's consciousness, but no further. But when failure befalls you, then by picking yourself back up, you reach to a place the perfectly righteous could never know.

Which explains the statement of the rabbis, "In the place where stands the one who has failed and returned, the perfectly righteous are incapable of standing." Of course they can't stand there. For them, it doesn't even exist.

The Good, the Bad and the Very Good

How is the soul capable of reaching there through *teshuvah*? Because that is truly its place.

For ultimately, this soul, this breath of G-d, begins before the script begins, before existence begins, in the utter darkness and mystery we called G-d's subconscious. Now to that place it returns, back to its ultimate origin, before it crossed the threshold of being to become a conscious thought.

What about the repair of the world you were supposed to make? What happens to those lost sparks your soul was meant to find?

With your return, they return along with you. The past is transformed as well since you have reached to a place beyond time. And yet deeper, sparks that could never have been reached directly, those that were tied down and bound by the forces of darkness, and therefore prohibited—you have reached to them and now carry them upwards.

Yet even that is not enough. Writing a new script means you need to accomplish something entirely new. And you do. Because now not only the spark is redeemed; even the darkness it generated is transformed to light.

"And G-d saw all that He had made, and behold, it was very good."

"Good," say the sages, refers to the capacity to do good. "Very good" includes the capacity to fail. To fail and then to do good. And that is "very good"—beyond anything the script could have contained.

www.chabad.org/2127058

5

MAN BLOWING SHOFAR
January 2015, Aliza Marton, oil on canvas,
private collection in Los Angeles

OUT OF THE BLUES

*So, will we wake up one day in a glorious wonderland?
Or is the Redemption more of a gradual process? Let's
study the sources on the actual transition from our
reality today into a world of revelation. On the way,
we will also get to know the special human being who
will usher in the Redemption.*

I. "I WILL HASTEN IT IN ITS TIME"

This course has explored the centrality of the Redemption to Judaism and our incredible proximity to that much-anticipated reality. Our study has so far focused heavily on the Redemption's *why, what*, and *when*. The journey now shifts gears to focus on *how* and *who*; the current lesson examines (a) the manner in which the Redemption will unfold, and (b) the identity of the individual tasked with the role of Mashiach.

EXERCISE 5.1

Imagine yourself as an active journalist. Mashiach arrives, and your bosses in the media scramble you for the task of rapidly producing a news article that will professionally inform the public of the astounding development. Based on all that you know to date about Mashiach, what might your article look like?

Fill in the basic components of your news item:

HEADLINE

Large, bold text above an article, indicating the topic. It must be geared to catch the reader's attention.

LEAD (OR "LEDE")

An article's introductory paragraph that briefly captures the story's most important facts and answers the questions: *who, what, where, when, why*, and *how.*

BODY

The main text of the news story, presenting the details and elaborating on the lead.

QUOTE

Quotes are added to the main story to increase interest and to supply corroborating support or viewpoints.

EXERCISE 5.2

The following texts (1–5) appear to offer two dissimilar portrayals of Mashiach's arrival. Read the texts and then group them accordingly in the chart on p. 201.

TEXT 1

A Sudden Appearance

Malachi 3:1

הִנְנִי שֹׁלֵחַ מַלְאָכִי וּפִנָּה דֶרֶךְ לְפָנָי וּפִתְאֹם יָבוֹא
אֶל הֵיכָלוֹ הָאָדוֹן אֲשֶׁר אַתֶּם מְבַקְשִׁים.

Behold!—I will send My angel and he will clear a way before Me. And suddenly, the G-d Whom you seek will come to His Temple.

MALACHI

Biblical book. The book of Malachi contains the prophecies delivered by Malachi in the 4th century BCE, at the beginning of the period of the Second Temple. Malachi was the last of the biblical prophets, and his prophecies include rebuke of the priests for their failures of leadership, as well as speaking of G-d's great love for the Jewish people.

TEXT 2

Unlike a Terrestrial Royal Visit

Rabbi Yosef Caro, *Magid Meisharim*, *Parshat Tsav*

**RABBI YOSEF CARO
(MARAN, *BEIT YOSEF*)
1488–1575**

Halachic
authority and
author. Rabbi Caro was
born in Spain but was
forced to flee during
the Expulsion in 1492
and eventually settled in
Safed, Israel. He authored
many works, including
the *Beit Yosef, Kesef
Mishneh*, and a mystical
work, *Magid Meisharim*.
Rabbi Caro's magnum
opus, the Shulchan Aruch
(Code of Jewish Law),
has been universally
accepted as the basis
for modern Jewish law.

דְּאוֹרְחָא דְעָלְמָא כַּד אָתָא מַלְכָּא לְמֵיהַדַר לְבֵיתֵיהּ,
מְבַשְׂרִין לְבַשְׂרָא. וּמְבַשְׂרָא קַדְמָאָה קָאָמַר,
הָא עֲשָׂרָה יוֹמִין הוּא. וּמְבַשְׂרָא תִּנְיָנָא קָאָמַר חֲמִשָׁה,
וּתְלִיתָאָה אָמַר ד'. וְכֵן עַד דְּבַתְרָאָה, סָמִיךְ לְקַרְתָּא.

קָאָמַר נְבִיאָה, דְּבִגְאוּלַת יִשְׂרָאֵל לֹא יְהֵא בְּכִי הַאי. תְּהֵא
כְּהֶרֶף עָיִן. וּמְבַשְׂרָא קַדְמָאָה דְּיַיתֵי הֵנָה הֵנָה שִׁבְטַיָּא דְּאָתוּ
סְמִיכִין לֹא יַרְגִּישׁוּ בְּהוֹן בְּנֵי קַרְתָּא וְכָל כָּךְ בְּפֶתַע פִּתְאוֹם
יְהֵא דְּאַף עַל גַּב דְּאִינּוּן סְמִיכִין לֹא יַרְגִּישׁוּ בְּהוֹן בְּנֵי קַרְתָּא
עַד דַּהֲוָא לְבַשְׂרָא בְּהֵיכָלָא דְּמַלְכָּא דְּאִיהוּ צִיּוֹן בָּתַר דְּיַיפֵּק
מִלְבַשְׂרָא לְצִיּוֹן בִּירוּשָׁלַיִם וִיהִי לְהוֹן בְּשׂוֹרָה וּמִילְתָא חַדְתָּא
דְּלָא אַרְגִּישׁוּ בָּהּ עַד שֶׁאָמַר עַד וְלִירוּשָׁלַיִם מְבַשֵׂר אֶתֵּן.

When a mortal monarch plans to return to his
home, it is typical protocol for his arrival to be
announced in advance. An initial announcement
may give notice that he will arrive in ten days,
followed perhaps by a second advisory five days
in advance, and then four days, until the final
proclamation, "The king is approaching the capital!"

The prophet Isaiah informed us that the Jewish
Redemption will *not* unfold in this manner. Rather,
it will arrive in the blink of an eye. As he foretold,
"The first one to Zion, behold, here they are, and for

Jerusalem I will give a herald" (ISAIAH 41:27). In other words, Jerusalem's residents will not notice that all the tribes of Israel are converging on their city before the initial announcement is made by the first individual to reach Jerusalem, who will call out, "Look—here they all are, about to enter the city!" It will be so sudden that the city's residents will not notice a thing before the reality materializes. . . . The announcement and the event will come as one, hence the initial notice—"For Jerusalem I will give a herald"—will be, "Behold, here they are!"

MASHIACH
Yehoshua Wiseman,
Israel

TEXT 3

Opening the Gate of Redemption

Zohar 1, p. 170a

ZOHAR

The seminal work of kabbalah, Jewish mysticism. The *Zohar* is a mystical commentary on the Torah, written in Aramaic and Hebrew. According to the Arizal, the *Zohar* contains the teachings of Rabbi Shimon bar Yocha'i, who lived in the Land of Israel during the 2nd century. The *Zohar* has become one of the indispensable texts of traditional Judaism, alongside and nearly equal in stature to the Mishnah and Talmud.

בְּזִמְנָא דְקוּדְשָׁא בְּרִיךְ הוּא יוֹקִים לוֹן לְיִשְׂרָאֵל וְיָפִיק לוֹן מִן גָּלוּתָא הָדֵין יִפְתַּח לוֹן פִּתְחָא דִּנְהוֹרָא דַּקִּיק זָעִיר, וּלְבָתַר פִּתְחָא אַחֲרִינָא דְּאִיהוּ רַב מִינֵיהּ, עַד דְּקוּדְשָׁא בְּרִיךְ הוּא יִפְתַּח לוֹן תַּרְעִין עִלָּאִין פְּתִיחָן לְאַרְבַּע רוּחֵי עָלְמָא.

When G-d will raise up the people of Israel and redeem them from this exile, He will open a small, thin ray of light for them. Thereafter, He will open another, far wider aperture. Finally, G-d will throw open the supernal gates that open to all four corners of the universe.

TEXT 4

Can He Really Be Coming Now?

Midrash, *Pirkei Heichalot Rabati*, ch. 36

שֶׁיִּשְׂרָאֵל שֶׁבְּאוֹתוֹ הַדּוֹר אוֹמְרִים,

"אֶפְשָׁר עוֹלָם כְּמִנְהָגוֹ נוֹהֵג וְיֵשׁ גְּאוּלָה בְּשָׁנָה זוֹ?"

וְהֵם אֵינָם יוֹדְעִים שֶׁפִּתְאוֹם יָבֹא.

The Jewish people of that generation will say,
"Is it possible that the world functions as usual and
nevertheless the Redemption will arrive this year?"

However, they do not realize that
Mashiach's arrival will be sudden.

PIRKEI HEICHALOT RABATI

Pirkei Heichalot Rabati
is a Talmudic-era work of
Jewish mysticism, part of
the *Heichalot* literature.
The *Heichalot* literature
describes the structure of
the spiritual worlds and
the process of Creation.

THE JOY OF REDEMPTION
2014, Baruch Nachshon,
acrylic on canvas, Hebron,
The artist's archive,
nachshonart.com

TEXT 5

Like the Crack of Dawn

Jerusalem Talmud, Berachot 1:1

רַבִּי חִיָּא בַּר אַבָּא וְרַבִּי שִׁמְעוֹן בֶּן חֲלַפְתָּא
הָיוּ מְהַלְּכִין בְּבִקְעַת אַרְבֵּל וְרָאוּ אַיֶּלֶת הַשַּׁחַר.

אָמַר לוֹ רַבִּי חִיָּא: "כָּךְ הִיא גְּאוּלָתָן שֶׁל יִשְׂרָאֵל, בַּתְּחִלָּה
קִמְעָא קִמְעָא, כָּל מָה שֶׁהִיא הוֹלֶכֶת, הִיא רַבָּה וְהוֹלֶכֶת.
כְּמוֹ שֶׁכָּתוּב: 'כִּי אֵשֵׁב בַּחֹשֶׁךְ ה' אוֹר לִי' (מִיכָה ז, ח)".

Rabbi Chiya bar Aba and Rabbi Shimon ben Chalafta once walked through the Arbel Valley and watched the break of dawn.

Whereupon, Rabbi Chiya told Rabbi Shimon, "So will be the Jewish Redemption! It will begin with small steps, as it is stated, 'Although I will sit in darkness, G-d will be a light to me' (MICAH 7:8). Then, as it progresses, it will greatly swell and expand."

JERUSALEM TALMUD

A commentary to the Mishnah, compiled during the 4th and 5th centuries. The Jerusalem Talmud predates its Babylonian counterpart by 100 years and is written in both Hebrew and Aramaic. While the Babylonian Talmud is the most authoritative source for Jewish law, the Jerusalem Talmud remains an invaluable source for the spiritual, intellectual, ethical, historical, and legal traditions of Judaism.

SUDDEN	GRADUAL

Hastening Its Time

Isaiah 60:22

הַקָּטֹן יִהְיֶה לָאֶלֶף, וְהַצָּעִיר לְגוֹי עָצוּם;
אֲנִי ה', בְּעִתָּהּ אֲחִישֶׁנָּה.

The smallest will become a thousand, and the least a mighty nation. I am G-d; I will hasten it, in its time.

ISAIAH

Biblical book. The book of Isaiah contains the prophecies of Isaiah, who lived in the 6–7th centuries BCE. Isaiah's prophecies contain stern rebukes for the personal failings of the contemporary people of Judea and the corruption of its government. The bulk of the prophecies, however, are stirring consolations and poetic visions of the future Redemption.

The Merit Factor

Talmud, Sanhedrin 98a

כְּתִיב "בְּעִתָּהּ" וּכְתִיב "אֲחִישֶׁנָּה"?
זָכוּ אֲחִישֶׁנָּה; לֹא זָכוּ בְּעִתָּהּ

The same verse that states [that the Redemption will arrive] "in its time" also states, "I will *hasten* it"! [Is there a set time for the Redemption, or not?]

[The Talmud resolves this seeming contradiction:] If they merit—"I will hasten it." If they do not merit, [it will occur only when] "its time" [arrives].

BABYLONIAN TALMUD

A literary work of monumental proportions that draws upon the legal, spiritual, intellectual, ethical, and historical traditions of Judaism. The 37 tractates of the Babylonian Talmud contain the teachings of the Jewish sages from the period after the destruction of the 2nd Temple through the 5th century CE. It has served as the primary vehicle for the transmission of the Oral Law and the education of Jews over the centuries; it is the entry point for all subsequent legal, ethical, and theological Jewish scholarship.

II. ELIJAH THE PROPHET

The redemption process, like all universal Jewish liberations of the past, will be ushered in through the agency of a human leader. In this case, the role will be filled by an individual whom Judaism refers to simply as the Mashiach ("anointed," i.e., divinely appointed). However, before analyzing the leader of the Redemption, it will prove instructive to first discuss the role in the Redemption played by another human—a prophet of ancient times who will make a reappearance.

The Announcer

TEXT 7   Malachi 3:23

הִנֵּה אָנֹכִי שֹׁלֵחַ לָכֶם אֵת אֵלִיָּה הַנָּבִיא לִפְנֵי בּוֹא יוֹם ה'.

I will send Elijah the Prophet to you
before the arrival of the day of G-d.

**CIRCUMCISION, CHAIR
OF PROPHET ELIJAH**
illustration from *mohel's*
book, early 18th cent., vellum,
Jewish Theological Seminary
of America Library, N.Y.

Who was Elijah and why is he
so much a part of our Jewish
observances? "Understanding
Elijah the Prophet," a fascinating
lecture by **Rabbi Chaim Block**:
myjli.com/canhappen

FIGURE 5.1   Elijah will . . .

 1. Announce Mashiach's imminent arrival

 2. Inspire Israel to better their ways and prepare their hearts for the Redemption

 3. Restore prophecy to the Jewish people

 4. Answer unresolved halachic queries

 5. Restore the Sanhedrin

FIGURE 5.2

Elijah Blowing the Shofar of Redemption

Passover *Haggadah*, Mantua 1560, Braginsky Collection

III. MASHIACH'S PROFILE

The center around which the entire process of redemption revolves is a mortal who will activate its features. Regardless of how developments unfold, whether as a gradual process or as an instantaneous event, one point is clear: all the pieces will be put in place by a physical human, the Mashiach.

To accomplish this, G-d will bless Mashiach with a range of impressive abilities. This section outlines a sampling of Mashiach's primary qualities, as described in Jewish and kabbalistic sources.

TEXT 8

Flesh and Blood

Rabbi Chaim Vital, *Arba Me'ot Shekel Kesef,* p. 241

מֶלֶךְ הַמָּשִׁיחַ יִהְיֶה וַדַּאי אָדָם צַדִּיק נוֹלַד מֵאִישׁ וְאִשָּׁה.

King Mashiach will certainly be a righteous human, born of a man and a woman.

**RABBI CHAIM VITAL
C. 1542–1620**

Lurianic kabbalist. Rabbi Vital was born in Israel, lived in Safed and Jerusalem, and later lived in Damascus. He was authorized by his teacher, Rabbi Yitschak Luria, the Arizal, to record his teachings. Acting on this mandate, Vital began arranging his master's teachings in written form, and his many works constitute the foundation of the Lurianic school of Jewish mysticism. His most famous work is *Ets Chaim.*

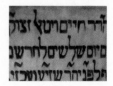

TEXT 9

At the Pinnacle

Midrash, *Yalkut Shimoni*, Isaiah, *remez* 476

YALKUT SHIMONI

A Midrash that covers the entire biblical text. Its material is collected from all over rabbinic literature, including the Babylonian and Jerusalem Talmuds and various ancient Midrashic texts. It contains several passages from *Midrashim* that have been lost, as well as different versions of existing *Midrashim*. It is unclear when and by whom this Midrash was redacted.

" הִנֵּה יַשְׂכִּיל עַבְדִּי", זֶה מֶלֶךְ הַמָּשִׁיחַ,
"יָרוּם וְנִשָּׂא וְגָבַהּ מְאֹד" (יְשַׁעְיָהוּ נב, יג).
"יָרוּם" מִן אַבְרָהָם . . . "וְנִשָּׂא" מִמֹּשֶׁה . . .
"וְגָבַהּ" מִמַּלְאֲכֵי הַשָּׁרֵת.

"Behold My servant will succeed; he will be exalted and elevated, and he will reach tremendous heights" (ISAIAH 52:13)—this is a reference to the King Mashiach who will be "exalted" over Abraham . . . "elevated" higher than Moses . . . "and he will reach tremendous heights," greater than the angels.

ABUNDANCE
Yaeli Vogel, acrylic on canvas,
Cedarhurst, N.Y.

TEXT 10

Greater than the Great

Maimonides, *Mishneh Torah*, Laws of *Teshuvah* 9:2

אוֹתוֹ הַמֶּלֶךְ שֶׁיַּעֲמֹד מִזֶּרַע דָּוִד, בַּעַל חָכְמָה יִהְיֶה יֶתֶר מִשְּׁלֹמֹה, וְנָבִיא גָּדוֹל הוּא קָרוֹב לְמֹשֶׁה רַבֵּנוּ. וּלְפִיכָךְ יְלַמֵּד כָּל הָעָם וְיוֹרֶה אוֹתָם דֶּרֶךְ ה' וְיָבוֹאוּ כָּל הַגּוֹיִם לְשׁוֹמְעוֹ.

The king Mashiach who will arise from David's descendants will be wiser than Solomon, and a great prophet, close to the level of Moses. He will therefore teach the entire nation and instruct them in the path of G-d, and all the nations will come to hear his words.

RABBI MOSHE BEN MAIMON (MAIMONIDES, RAMBAM) 1135–1204

Halachist, philosopher, author, and physician. Maimonides was born in Córdoba, Spain. After the conquest of Córdoba by the Almohads, he fled Spain and eventually settled in Cairo, Egypt. There, he became the leader of the Jewish community and served as court physician to the vizier of Egypt. He is most noted for authoring the *Mishneh Torah*, an encyclopedic arrangement of Jewish law; and for his philosophical work, *Guide for the Perplexed*. His rulings on Jewish law are integral to the formation of halachic consensus.

TEXT 11

And Humble Too!

Rabbi Yosef Yitschak Schneersohn,
cited in *Hayom Yom*, 1 Menachem Av

מַעֲלַת הַמָּשִׁיחַ שֶׁיִּהְיֶה עָנָיו, דְּהַגַּם שֶׁיִּהְיֶה בְּתַכְלִית
הַגַּדְלוּת, וִילַמֵּד תּוֹרָה עִם הָאָבוֹת וּמֹשֶׁה רַבֵּנוּ
עָלָיו הַשָּׁלוֹם, בְּכָל זֶה יִהְיֶה בְּתַכְלִית הָעֲנָוָה
וְהַבִּטּוּל לְלַמֵּד גַּם עִם אֲנָשִׁים פְּשׁוּטִים.

Mashiach's uniqueness will be his humility:
despite reaching the pinnacle of greatness, due
to which he will teach Torah to the Patriarchs
and to Moses, he will nevertheless achieve the
ultimate in humility and self-nullification, due
to which he will also teach the simplest folk.

RABBI YOSEF YITSCHAK SCHNEERSOHN (RAYATS, FRIERDIKER REBBE, PREVIOUS REBBE) 1880–1950

Chasidic rebbe, prolific writer, and Jewish activist. Rabbi Yosef Yitschak, the sixth leader of the Chabad movement, actively promoted Jewish religious practice in Soviet Russia and was arrested for these activities. After his release from prison and exile, he settled in Warsaw, Poland, from where he fled Nazi occupâtion and arrived in New York in 1940. Settling in Brooklyn, Rabbi Schneersohn worked to revitalize American Jewish life. His son-in-law Rabbi Menachem Mendel Schneerson succeeded him as the leader of the Chabad movement.

**DAVID BEHATZOT
(KING DAVID AT ABOUT MIDNIGHT)**
Yehoshua Wiseman, Israel

FIGURE 5.3

The Five Levels of the Soul

LEVEL	ENGLISH TRANSLATION	PRIMARY FACULTY
נֶפֶשׁ *Nefesh*	**VITALITY**	Biological life
רוּחַ *Ru'ach*	**SPIRIT**	Emotions
נְשָׁמָה *Neshamah*	SOUL	Intellect
חַיָּה *Chayah*	**LIFE**	Faith
יְחִידָה *Yechidah*	**UNITY; SINGULARITY**	Essence

TEXT 12

The General *Yechidah*

The Rebbe, Rabbi Menachem Mendel Schneerson,
Kuntres Inyanah Shel Torat Hachasidut, ch. 5

עִנְיָנוֹ הָעִקָּרִי שֶׁל מָשִׁיחַ הוּא - יְחִידָה. כַּיָדוּעַ, שֶׁדָּוִד
זָכָה לִבְחִינַת נֶפֶשׁ, אֵלִיָּהוּ - לְרוּחַ, מֹשֶׁה - לִנְשָׁמָה,
אָדָם הָרִאשׁוֹן - לְחַיָּה וּמָשִׁיחַ יִזְכֶּה לִיחִידָה.

מַעֲלַת הַיְחִידָה עַל ד' הַבְּחִינוֹת נֶפֶשׁ רוּחַ נְשָׁמָה חַיָּה
[בַּחֲמִשָּׁה הַמַּדְרֵגוֹת שֶׁל כָּל נְשָׁמָה]: ד' הַבְּחִינוֹת נֶפֶשׁ
רוּחַ נְשָׁמָה חַיָּה הֵם מַדְרֵגוֹת פְּרָטִיּוֹת, וּבְחִינַת יְחִידָה
הִיא עֶצֶם הַנְּשָׁמָה שֶׁלְּמַעְלָה מִגֶּדֶר פְּרָטִים, כְּשֵׁמָהּ . . .

וּכְמוֹ שֶׁבְּכָל נְשָׁמָה פְּרָטִית, בְּחִינַת הַיְחִידָה הִיא
נְקֻדָּה הָעַצְמִית שֶׁל הַנְּשָׁמָה, כֵּן הוּא בְּ(הַחַיּוּת וְ)
הַנְּשָׁמָה שֶׁל כְּלָלוּת הַהִשְׁתַּלְשְׁלוּת, שֶׁבְּחִינַת הַיְחִידָה
שֶׁבָּהּ (בְּחִינָתוֹ שֶׁל מָשִׁיחַ) הִיא - עֶצֶם נְקֻדַּת הַחַיּוּת
שֶׁלְּמַעְלָה מִגֶּדֶר צִיּוּר. וּמִנְּקֻדָּה זוֹ, מִסְתַּעֲפוֹת כָּל
מַעֲלוֹת הַפְּרָטִיּוֹת, נֶפֶשׁ רוּחַ נְשָׁמָה חַיָּה דִכְלָלוּת,

כִּי עֶצֶם הַחַיּוּת הוּא בִּלְתִּי מֻגְבָּל . . . גַּם בְּעִנְיַן הָאֵיכוּת
וְהַמַּעֲלָה, שֶׁשָּׁלֵם הוּא בְּתַכְלִית הַשְּׁלֵמוּת. וְלָכֵן,
כְּשֶׁתִּמְשַׁךְ בָּעוֹלָמוֹת בְּחִינַת הַיְחִידָה וְיִהְיוּ בְּחַיּוּת
עַצְמִי, יִהְיוּ בְּמֵילָא בְּתַכְלִית הַמַּעֲלָה וְהַשְּׁלֵמוּת.

Mashiach's fundamental quality is that he is the
[collective] *Yechidah* [of the Jewish nation. For
the mystics reveal that King] David merited the
[collective soul dimension of] *Nefesh*; Elijah

RABBI MENACHEM
MENDEL SCHNEERSON
1902–1994

The towering
Jewish leader of
the 20th century, known
as "the Lubavitcher
Rebbe," or simply as "the
Rebbe." Born in southern
Ukraine, the Rebbe
escaped Nazi-occupied
Europe, arriving in
the U.S. in June 1941.
The Rebbe inspired
and guided the revival
of traditional Judaism
after the European
devastation, impacting
virtually every Jewish
community the world
over. The Rebbe often
emphasized that the
performance of just
one additional good
deed could usher in
the era of Mashiach.
The Rebbe's scholarly
talks and writings have
been printed in more
than 200 volumes.

merited the *Ru'ach*; Moses, the *Neshamah*; Adam, the *Chayah*; and Mashiach will merit the *Yechidah*.

Of the five dimensions that each soul possesses, the lower four—*Nefesh, Ru'ach, Neshamah*, and *Chayah*—are individualized rungs [with particular features and functions]. By contrast, the *Yechidah* is the soul's singular, indivisible core. . . .

Just as this is true regarding each individual soul—its very essence is the *Yechidah*—the same is true of the life force of all of Creation. That life force itself has a *Yechidah*: that is the *very essence* of the divine energy that causes it to exist. And this *Yechidah* is abstract, defying every qualification or form. From this *Yechidah,* all the individualized branches of divine energy [necessary for Creation] emerge. Now the Mashiach is associated with this collective *Yechidah* [of all of Creation].

This essential core energy is unlimited . . . not only in quantity, but in quality as well. It is entirely perfect and complete. Therefore, when this energy manifests in this world [through Mashiach], everything will function at the highest and most perfect level.

TEXT 13

Following in Moses's Path

Rabbi Moshe Sofer, *Chatam Sofer*, Collected Responsa #98

**RABBI MOSHE SOFER
(*CHATAM SOFER*)
1762–1839**

A leading
rabbinical
authority of the 19th
century. Born in
Frankfurt am Main,
Chatam Sofer ultimately
accepted the rabbinate
of Pressburg (now
Bratislava), Slovakia.
Serving as rabbi and
head of the yeshiva that
he established, Rabbi
Sofer maintained a
strong traditionalist
perspective, opposing
deviation from Jewish
tradition. *Chatam Sofer* is
the title of his collection
of halachic responsa
and his commentary
to the Talmud.

כְּמוֹ מֹשֶׁה רַבֵּנוּ הַגּוֹאֵל הָרִאשׁוֹן, שֶׁנִּזְדַּקֵּן שְׁמוֹנִים
שָׁנָה וְלֹא יָדַע וְלֹא הִרְגִּישׁ בְּעַצְמוֹ שֶׁהוּא יִהְיֶה גּוֹאֵל
יִשְׂרָאֵל . . . כֵּן יִהְיֶה, אִם יִרְצֶה ה', הַגּוֹאֵל הָאַחֲרוֹן . . .

וְלִכְשֶׁיַּגִּיעַ הַזְּמַן, יִתְגַּלֶּה אֵלָיו ה' יִתְבָּרַךְ, וְאָז יֵעָרֶה רוּחוֹ שֶׁל
מָשִׁיחַ הַטָּמוּן וְגָנוּז לְמַעְלָה עַד בּוֹאוֹ . . . כְּמוֹ לְמֹשֶׁה בַּסְּנֶה.

Moses, the first redeemer, reached the age of eighty
years with no knowledge or intuition about his
eventual role as the redeemer of Israel. . . . So will
it be, G-d willing, with the future redeemer. . . .

When the time comes, G-d will appear to
him, and then the spirit of Mashiach—that
until that moment was hidden on High—
will descend upon him . . . similar to the
experience of Moses at the [burning] bush.

IV. IDENTIFYING MASHIACH

All of the above information regarding Mashiach's impressive persona is fascinating, but does not necessarily assist us in identifying the individual who will serve as the redeemer. In practical terms, is there a formal method to positively identify this person?

TEXT 14

Identifying Features

Maimonides, *Mishneh Torah*, Laws of Kings 11:4

וְאִם יַעֲמֹד מֶלֶךְ מִבֵּית דָּוִד, הוֹגֶה בַּתּוֹרָה וְעוֹסֵק בְּמִצְוֹת כְּדָוִד אָבִיו כְּפִי תּוֹרָה שֶׁבִּכְתָב וְשֶׁבְּעַל פֶּה, וְיָכוֹף כָּל יִשְׂרָאֵל לֵילֵךְ בָּהּ וּלְחַזֵּק בִּדְקָהּ, וְיִלָּחֵם מִלְחֲמוֹת ה', הֲרֵי זֶה בְּחֶזְקַת שֶׁהוּא מָשִׁיחַ.

אִם עָשָׂה וְהִצְלִיחַ וּבָנָה מִקְדָּשׁ בִּמְקוֹמוֹ וְקִבֵּץ נִדְחֵי יִשְׂרָאֵל, הֲרֵי זֶה מָשִׁיחַ בְּוַדַאי.

When a king from the House of David will arise who, like his ancestor David, diligently studies the Torah and observes its *mitzvot* as prescribed by the Written Law and the Oral Law, influences all of Israel to walk in [the way of the Torah], rectifies the breaches in its observance, and wages G-d's battles—this person is presumed to the Mashiach.

If he succeeds in the above, and he builds the Temple in its place and gathers the dispersed of Israel—he is certainly the Mashiach.

FIGURE 5.4

Presumed and Proven Mashiach

THE PRESUMED MASHIACH MUST:

A.   Be a descendant of King David

B.   Be supremely pious and well versed in Torah

C.   Influence the Jewish nation to follow the ways of the Torah

D.   Wage G-d's battles

THE CONFIRMED MASHIACH MUST:

A.   Ingather the Jewish People

B.   Build the Third Holy Temple

V. MASHIACH IN EVERY GENERATION

We have clarified the process of identifying the legitimate Mashiach: when an individual demonstrates the qualities delineated above and successfully executes the aforementioned tasks, we know that he is Mashiach.

However, there is an earlier stage—before the full-fledged realization of the Redemption—at which point the same individual is merely considered a "potential Mashiach." A specific person can be pointed at as being *available for and worthy of* being Mashiach, but that individual is forced to wait for the people and for the world at large to be ready for the Redemption.

TEXT 15

The Birth of Mashiach

Jerusalem Talmud, Berachot 2:4

עוֹבְדָא הֲוָה בְּחַד בַּר נַשׁ דַּהֲוָה קָא רָדֵי, גָּעַת חֲדָא
תּוֹרְתֵיהּ. עֲבַר עֲלוֹי חַד עַרְבִי, אֲמַר לֵיהּ, "מָה אַתְּ?"

אֲמַר לֵיהּ, "יְהוּדָאי אֲנָא".

אֲמַר לֵיהּ, "שָׁרֵי תּוֹרָךְ וְשָׁרֵי פַּדְנָךְ".

אֲמַר לֵיהּ, "לָמָה?"

אֲמַר לֵיהּ, "דְּבֵית מִקְדָּשׁוֹן דִּיהוּדָאֵי חָרֵב".

אֲמַר לֵיהּ, "מְנָא יָדַעַתְּ?"

אֲמַר לֵיהּ, "יַדְעִית מִן גְּעָיָתָא דְתוֹרָךְ".

עַד דְּהֲוָה עָסִיק עִמֵיהּ גָּעַת זִמְנָא אַחֲרִיתִי. אָמַר לוֹ,
"אָסַר תּוֹרָךְ אָסַר פַּדָּנָךְ, דְּאִתְיַלִיד פְּרִיקְהוֹן דִּיהוּדָאֵי".

A man was plowing his field when his ox suddenly lowed. An Arab passerby inquired, "What is your nationality?"

"I am a Jew," the plowman replied.

"Untie your ox," the Arab advised, "and unharness your plow." [This was considered a sign of mourning.]

"Why?"

"Because the Jewish Holy Temple has just been destroyed."

"What is your source for this information?" the Jew demanded.

"I deciphered that from your ox's low," replied the Arab.

As they were talking, the ox suddenly lowed once more.

"Harness your ox and retie the plow!" the Arab exclaimed. "The Jewish redeemer has just been born!"

The birth of the Messiah was a centerpiece of a religious disputation in 1263. **Rabbi Mordechai Dinerman** discusses this infamous event in "Judaism on Trial": *myjli.com/canhappen*

TEXT 16

A Candidate in Every Generation

Rabbi Ovadiah of Bartenura, Commentary to Ruth 4:6

בְּכָל דּוֹר וָדוֹר נוֹלַד אֶחָד מִזֶּרַע יְהוּדָה
שֶׁהוּא רָאוּי לִהְיוֹת מָשִׁיחַ לְיִשְׂרָאֵל.

In every generation, a descendant of
Judah is born who is a befitting candidate
to be the Jewish Mashiach.

RABBI OVADIAH OF BARTENURA C. 1445–1524

Scholar and author. Born in Italy, Rabbi Ovadiah is commonly known as "the Bartenura," after the city in which he held the rabbinate. Arriving in Jerusalem in 1488, he quickly became an effective leader of the oppressed Jewish community, especially focusing his energies on the influx of Sephardic Jews to Jerusalem following the Spanish expulsion. His highly-acclaimed commentary on the Mishnah appears in almost every printed edition.

TEXT 17

The Name Game

Talmud, Sanhedrin 98b

מָה שְׁמוֹ?

דְּבֵי רַבִּי שֵׁילָא אָמְרֵי: שִׁילֹה שְׁמוֹ. שֶׁנֶּאֱמַר,
"עַד כִּי יָבֹא שִׁילֹה" (בְּרֵאשִׁית מט, י).

דְּבֵי רַבִּי יַנַּאי אָמְרֵי: יִנּוֹן שְׁמוֹ. שֶׁנֶּאֱמַר,
"יְהִי שְׁמוֹ לְעוֹלָם לִפְנֵי שֶׁמֶשׁ יִנּוֹן שְׁמוֹ" (תְּהִלִּים עב, יז).

דְּבֵי רַבִּי חֲנִינָה אָמְרֵי: חֲנִינָה שְׁמוֹ. שֶׁנֶּאֱמַר,
"אֲשֶׁר לֹא אֶתֵּן לָכֶם חֲנִינָה" (יִרְמְיָהוּ טז, יג).

וְיֵשׁ אוֹמְרִים, מְנַחֵם בֶּן חִזְקִיָּה שְׁמוֹ. שֶׁנֶּאֱמַר,
"כִּי רָחַק מִמֶּנִּי מְנַחֵם מֵשִׁיב נַפְשִׁי" (אֵיכָה א, טז).

אָמַר רַב נַחְמָן, אִי מִן חַיָּיא הוּא, כְּגוֹן אֲנָא. שֶׁנֶּאֱמַר,
"וְהָיָה אַדִּירוֹ מִמֶּנּוּ וּמֹשְׁלוֹ מִקִּרְבּוֹ יֵצֵא" (יִרְמְיָהוּ ל, כא).

אָמַר רַב, אִי מִן חַיָּיא הוּא, כְּגוֹן רַבֵּנוּ הַקָּדוֹשׁ.
אִי מִן מֵתַיָּיא הוּא, כְּגוֹן דָּנִיֵּאל אִישׁ חֲמוּדוֹת.

What is Mashiach's name?

The scholars of Rabbi Shila's academy would say,
"His name is *Shiloh*, as it is stated, '[The scepter shall
not depart from Judah . . .] until Shiloh comes [and
all the nations will rally to him]' (GENESIS 49:10)."

The scholars of Rabbi Yanai's academy would say, "His name is *Yinon*, as it is stated, 'May his name endure forever—for as long as the sun, may his name continue [*yinon*]' (PSALMS 72:17)."

The scholars of Rabbi Chaninah's academy would say, "His name is *Chaninah*, as it is stated, 'For [during your exile] I will show you no favor [*chaninah*]' (JEREMIAH 16:13)."

Some scholars insist that his name is Menachem the son of Chizkiyah, as it is stated, "Because [at the time of the Destruction,] the comforter [*menachem*] that should relieve my soul is far from me" (LAMENTATIONS 1:16). . . .

Rabbi Nachman stated, "If the Messiah is among the living, he is a person [who already occupies a government position] such as me. As it is stated, 'Their prince shall be of themselves, and their governor shall proceed from their midst' (JEREMIAH 30:21)."

Rav stated, "If the Messiah is among those currently alive, he is the holy Rabbi Yehudah [the Prince]. If the Messiah is among the dead, he is Daniel the Beloved."

TEXT 18

Identifying the Mashiach of the Generation

Rabbi Chaim Chizkiyahu Medini, *Sedei Chemed,*
Pe'at Hasadeh, Maarechet Ha'alef, Klal 70

**RABBI CHAIM
CHIZKIYAHU MEDINI
1833-1905**

Scholar and
prolific author.
A Jerusalem native,
Rabbi Medini was born
into a distinguished
Sephardic family. He
served as the rabbi of
Constantinople and
later in the Crimea,
during which time he
authored many volumes
of Torah scholarship.
His most famous
work is the 18-volume
Sedei Chemed, a
comprehensive
encyclopedia of the
Talmud. He eventually
returned to Israel, where
he passed away in 1905.

הָיָה מְשַׁעֵר אֶצְלָם בְּכָל דּוֹר מִי הוּא . . . רַבֵּנוּ הַקָּדוֹשׁ . . .
בְּדוֹרוֹ אָמְרוּ וְיָדְעוּ שֶׁהוּא הַמּוּכָן . . . וְעַל פִּי זֶה כָּתְבוּ גַם כֵּן
תַּלְמִידֵי הָאֲרִיזַ"ל שֶׁבְּיָמָיו הָיָה הָאֲרִיזַ"ל. וְכָל זֶה הוּא פָּשׁוּט.

In each generation, people would assume that a
particular individual was the Mashiach [if the
Redemption were to occur at that time]. . . . In
his generation, it was declared and accepted
that Rabbi Judah the Prince was the suitable
candidate [to serve as the Mashiach]. . . . Similarly,
the students of Rabbi Yitschak Luria, the
Arizal, wrote that he was the Mashiach of that
generation. All this is a straightforward matter.

**JEWISH VILLAGES
GREETING THE MESSIAH**
1937, J. D. Kirszenbaum,
oil on cardboard, Israel
Museum, Jerusalem

Bar Kochba's Arms Bearer

Maimonides, *Mishneh Torah*, Laws of Kings 11:3

TEXT 19

רַבִּי עֲקִיבָא חָכָם גָּדוֹל מֵחַכְמֵי מִשְׁנָה הָיָה. וְהוּא הָיָה נוֹשֵׂא כֵּלָיו שֶׁל בֶּן כּוֹזִיבָא הַמֶּלֶךְ. וְהוּא הָיָה אוֹמֵר עָלָיו שֶׁהוּא הַמֶּלֶךְ הַמָּשִׁיחַ. וְדִמָּה הוּא וְכָל חַכְמֵי דוֹרוֹ שֶׁהוּא הַמֶּלֶךְ הַמָּשִׁיחַ. עַד שֶׁנֶּהֱרַג בַּעֲוֹנוֹת. כֵּיוָן שֶׁנֶּהֱרַג נוֹדַע לָהֶם שֶׁאֵינוֹ.

Rabbi Akiva was a phenomenal sage among the [great] sages of the Mishnaic era; he personally served as King Bar Koziba's arms bearer and would proclaim that [Bar Koziba] was the King Messiah. Along with all the sages of his generation, he considered Bar Koziba to be the King Messiah— until [Bar Koziba] was killed because of sins.

Dr. Henry Abramson
explores "Bar Kokhba"—his
era, his personality, his impact:
myjli.com/canhappen

TEXT 20

Mashiach's Evolution

The Rebbe, Rabbi Menachem Mendel Schneerson,
Likutei Sichot 35, p. 210

הַצֹּרֶךְ בְּעִנְיַן הַמְּלוּכָה הוּא (כַּנִּזְכָּר לְעֵיל מֵרַמְבַּ"ם)
"כְּדֵי לְהָרִים דַּת הָאֱמֶת וּלְמַלֹּאות הָעוֹלָם צֶדֶק
וְלִשְׁבֹּר זְרוֹעַ הָרְשָׁעִים וּלְהִלָּחֵם מִלְחֲמוֹת ה'",

וּמִזֶּה מוּבָן, דְּלְאַחֲרֵי שֶׁמָּשִׁיחַ "יְתַקֵּן אֶת הָעוֹלָם
כֻּלּוֹ לַעֲבֹד אֶת ה' בְּיַחַד", "וְלֹא יִהְיֶה עֵסֶק כָּל
הָעוֹלָם אֶלָּא לָדַעַת אֶת ה' בִּלְבַד", הֲרֵי אֵין
צֹרֶךְ (כָּל כָּךְ) בִּפְעֻלַּת מָשִׁיחַ בְּתוֹר מֶלֶךְ, וְעִקַּר
תַּפְקִידוֹ שֶׁל מֶלֶךְ הַמָּשִׁיחַ יִהְיֶה לְלַמֵּד אֶת הָעָם
וּלְהוֹרוֹתָם דֶּרֶךְ ה' . . . הַשְׁפָּעָתוֹ בְּתוֹר נָשִׂיא.

The need for Mashiach to serve as a monarch
is, as defined by Maimonides, "To elevate
the true faith, fill the world with justice,
destroy the power of the wicked, and
wage the campaigns of G-d" (*MISHNEH
TORAH*, LAWS OF KINGS 4:10).

Accordingly, once Mashiach has successfully
influenced all humanity to serve G-d in unison,
and the entire world will be exclusively engaged
in divine pursuits, Mashiach's role as a monarch
will no longer be necessary (to the same degree).
At that stage, his primary role will be to teach
the people and direct them on the divine path . . .
influencing them as a *nasi* [leader and teacher].

Belief in an "executive
world spiritual leader"—the
Mashiach—is a central tenet
of Judaism. Why is such a
person needed? Eavesdrop
on a conversation on this topic
between **Dr. Michael Chighel**
and **Rabbi Manis Friedman**:
myjli.com/canhappen

For even more . . .

For a deeper plunge into the need for a messianic *king*, see this lesson's
Appendix (p. 227).

MASHIACH
1991, Zalman Kleinman, USA, oil on canvas

KEY POINTS

1   Isaiah describes two options for the Redemption: "in its time" and "hastily." If we are meritorious, the Redemption will arrive earlier, and in a sudden and abrupt manner. If not, the Redemption will come in its default time, and it will unfold as a gradual process.

2   Malachi prophesied that Elijah the Prophet will return "before the arrival of the day of G-d"—before the coming of Mashiach. Chief among his duties will be to announce the imminence of Mashiach's arrival.

3   Mashiach will be a mortal who will possess incredible qualities and will achieve tremendous spiritual heights. On top of that, he will be exceedingly humble. The kabbalists reveal that Mashiach's soul will embody the essence of the collective soul—the *Yechidah*—of all of creation.

4   Maimonides outlines two stages in identifying Mashiach: (a) Presumed Mashiach, and (b) Confirmed Mashiach. A descendant of King David who is pious and versed in Torah, influences the Jewish nation to follow the Torah's ways, and wages G-d's battles is presumed to be Mashiach. If he gathers the Jews to the Land of Israel and builds the third Holy Temple, he is the Confirmed Mashiach.

5　Each generation has a Potential Mashiach. Throughout history, students of various influential Jewish spiritual leaders have pointed to their leader as the potential Mashiach. However, the Redemption has not begun until Mashiach successfully completes the tasks of the Confirmed Mashiach.

6　There have been various historical attempts at actual messianic campaigns. Two particularly famous attempts are Bar Kochba and Shabbetai Tzvi—with the distinction that Bar Kochba was a *failed* (Potential) Mashiach, whereas Shabbetai Tzvi was a *false* Mashiach.

7　At a certain point, Mashiach's role will transition, or mature, from king to primarily that of an inspiring teacher and religious mentor.

APPENDIX

This lesson has made it abundantly clear that Mashiach will be a physical, human king. Understandably, many are uncomfortable with this notion. Why would we want to return to monarchy, a system of government that is so prone to corruption and abuse, has failed time and again, and which almost all of enlightened civilization has moved away from? What's more, the fact that we need a human being rather than G-d taking care of it on His own is undesirable to many.

TEXT 21

The Mitzvah to Crown a King

Deuteronomy 17:14–20

כִּי תָבֹא אֶל הָאָרֶץ אֲשֶׁר ה' אֱלֹקֶיךָ נֹתֵן לָךְ, וִירִשְׁתָּהּ וְיָשַׁבְתָּה בָּהּ, וְאָמַרְתָּ, "אָשִׂימָה עָלַי מֶלֶךְ כְּכָל הַגּוֹיִם אֲשֶׁר סְבִיבֹתָי". שׂוֹם תָּשִׂים עָלֶיךָ מֶלֶךְ, אֲשֶׁר יִבְחַר ה' אֱלֹקֶיךָ בּוֹ . . .

וְהָיָה כְשִׁבְתּוֹ עַל כִּסֵּא מַמְלַכְתּוֹ, וְכָתַב לוֹ אֶת מִשְׁנֵה הַתּוֹרָה הַזֹּאת עַל סֵפֶר מִלִּפְנֵי הַכֹּהֲנִים הַלְוִיִּם.

וְהָיְתָה עִמּוֹ, וְקָרָא בוֹ כָּל יְמֵי חַיָּיו. לְמַעַן יִלְמַד לְיִרְאָה אֶת ה' אֱלֹקָיו, לִשְׁמֹר אֶת כָּל דִּבְרֵי הַתּוֹרָה הַזֹּאת וְאֶת הַחֻקִּים הָאֵלֶּה לַעֲשֹׂתָם. לְבִלְתִּי רוּם לְבָבוֹ מֵאֶחָיו וּלְבִלְתִּי סוּר מִן הַמִּצְוָה יָמִין וּשְׂמֹאול, לְמַעַן יַאֲרִיךְ יָמִים עַל מַמְלַכְתּוֹ הוּא וּבָנָיו בְּקֶרֶב יִשְׂרָאֵל.

When you come to the land that your G-d shall give you, and you possess and settle it, you will say, "We wish to appoint a king over ourselves, as is the practice of all our surrounding nations." Indeed, appoint a king over yourselves, the individual whom your G-d will choose. . . .

When the monarch assumes his royal throne, he shall write for himself on parchment scrolls two copies of this Torah. [These scrolls should be directly copied from the Torah that is housed in the Temple,] before the priests, the Levites.

This Torah scroll shall always be with the king, and he shall read from it all the days of his life, so that he will learn to fear his G-d and keep and perform all the words of this Torah and these statutes. Then his heart will not be haughty over his brothers, and he will not turn away from the commandments, neither to the right nor to the left. He and his descendants will then have a prolonged reign over Israel.

QUESTION

Winston Churchill famously said, "Democracy is the worst form of government, except for all the others." Why might that be so? What is bad about democracy?

TEXT 22

Requesting a Monarch = Rejecting G-d
I Samuel 8:4–9

וַיִּתְקַבְּצוּ כֹּל זִקְנֵי יִשְׂרָאֵל וַיָּבֹאוּ אֶל שְׁמוּאֵל הָרָמָתָה. וַיֹּאמְרוּ אֵלָיו, "הִנֵּה אַתָּה זָקַנְתָּ, וּבָנֶיךָ לֹא הָלְכוּ בִּדְרָכֶיךָ. עַתָּה, שִׂימָה לָּנוּ מֶלֶךְ לְשָׁפְטֵנוּ כְּכָל הַגּוֹיִם". וַיֵּרַע הַדָּבָר בְּעֵינֵי שְׁמוּאֵל כַּאֲשֶׁר אָמְרוּ, "תְּנָה לָּנוּ מֶלֶךְ לְשָׁפְטֵנוּ". וַיִּתְפַּלֵּל שְׁמוּאֵל אֶל ה'.

וַיֹּאמֶר ה' אֶל שְׁמוּאֵל, "שְׁמַע בְּקוֹל הָעָם לְכֹל אֲשֶׁר יֹאמְרוּ אֵלֶיךָ. כִּי לֹא אֹתְךָ מָאָסוּ, כִּי אֹתִי מָאֲסוּ מִמְּלֹךְ עֲלֵיהֶם. כְּכָל הַמַּעֲשִׂים אֲשֶׁר עָשׂוּ מִיּוֹם הַעֲלֹתִי אוֹתָם מִמִּצְרַיִם וְעַד הַיּוֹם הַזֶּה, וַיַּעַזְבֻנִי וַיַּעַבְדוּ אֱלֹהִים אֲחֵרִים, כֵּן הֵמָּה עֹשִׂים גַּם לָךְ.

"וְעַתָּה, שְׁמַע בְּקוֹלָם. אַךְ, כִּי הָעֵד תָּעִיד בָּהֶם וְהִגַּדְתָּ לָהֶם מִשְׁפַּט הַמֶּלֶךְ אֲשֶׁר יִמְלֹךְ עֲלֵיהֶם".

SAMUEL

Biblical book. The book of Samuel relates the history of the Jewish people during the lifetime of the prophet Samuel and the reigns of the first Jewish kings, Saul and David, in the 9th and 10th centuries BCE. Samuel wrote the descriptions of the events of his lifetime, and the book was completed by the prophets Gad and Nathan. The book has been artificially divided into I Samuel and II Samuel, but it is essentially one book.

All the elders of Israel gathered and came to Samuel in Ramah. They said to Samuel, "You have grown old, and your sons do not walk in your ways. Therefore, appoint a king for us, to govern us like all the nations." Samuel was very displeased with their request for a king to govern them, and he prayed to G-d.

G-d said to Samuel, "Heed the demand of the people in everything that they say to you. For it is not you that they have rejected; it is My sovereignty that they have rejected. Like everything else they have done ever since I brought them up out of Egypt and to this day—forsaking Me and serving other gods—so they are [now] doing to you.

"Heed their demand. But warn them solemnly and tell them about the practices of any king that will rule over them."

TEXT 23

A Vehicle for Subservience to G-d

Rabbi Menachem Mendel of Lubavitch, *Derech Mitsvotecha* 108a

הַמְכַוָן בְּמִנּוּי הַמֶּלֶךְ הוּא שֶׁבּוֹ וְעַל יָדוֹ יִהְיוּ הֵיִשְׂרָאֵל בְּטֵלִים לַה'. כִּי כָּל יִשְׂרָאֵל צְרִיכִים לִהְיוֹת בְּטֵלִים לַמֶּלֶךְ וְסָרִים לְמִשְׁמַעְתּוֹ בְּכָל אֲשֶׁר יִגְזֹר . . . וְהִנֵּה הַמֶּלֶךְ בְּעַצְמוֹ בָּטֵל לָאֱלֹקוּת . . . וּמֵאַחַר שֶׁהַמֶּלֶךְ הוּא בָּטֵל לְמַלְכוּת שָׁמַיִם וְיִשְׂרָאֵל בְּטֵלִים לַמֶּלֶךְ הֲרֵי נִמְצָא בּוֹ וְעַל יָדוֹ הֵיִשְׂרָאֵל בְּטֵלִים לֶאֱלֹקוּתוֹ יִתְבָּרֵךְ.

The purpose of appointing a king is so that through him, the nation is subservient to G-d. For the nation, by law, is subservient to the king and must obey all his decrees . . . and the king himself is subservient to G-d. . . . By extension, the people are subservient to G-d.

The National Unifier

The Rebbe, Rabbi Menachem Mendel Schneerson,
Likutei Sichot 25, p. 114

דֶער גְמַר אוּן שְׁלֵמוּת פוּן אַן עַם אִיז דַוְקָא בְּשְׁעַת עֶר וֶוערְט
אַן עַם **אֶחָד** בְּיַחַד, נִיט וֶוען יֶעדֶער אֵיינֶער אִיז בִּפְנֵי עַצְמוֹ.

אוּן דָאס וֶוערְט אוֹיפְגֶעטָאן עַל יְדֵי הַמֶּלֶךְ, וּבִלְשׁוֹן
הָרַמְבַּ"ם וֶועגְן דֶער מִצְוָה פוּן מִנוּי מֶלֶךְ: שֶׁצִוָּנוּ לְמַנּוֹת
עָלֵינוּ מֶלֶךְ יְקַבֵּץ כָּל אֻמָתֵנוּ וְיַנְהִיגֵנוּ. אוּן דֶעריבֶּער
דְרִיקְט זִיךְ אוֹיס דִי בְּחִירָה פוּן כְּלָלוּת עַם יִשְׂרָאֵל
אַלְס אֵיין עַם אִין דֶעם וָואס דֶער אוֹיבֶּערְשְׁטֶער הָאט
בּוֹחֵר גֶעוֶוען אַ מֶלֶךְ עַל יִשְׂרָאֵל **לְעוֹלָם**, דִי בְּחִירָה
בְּדָוִד וּבִשְׁלֹמֹה - "מַלְכֵי בֵּית דָוִד . . הָעוֹמְדִים לְעוֹלָם",
וָואס עַל יָדָם קוּמְט דִי "מַלְכוּת ה' עַל יִשְׂרָאֵל".

The nation reaches perfection when they are
a single unit, not individually fragmented.

And this is accomplished by the king. As
Maimonides states regarding the mitzvah of
appointing a king, "We are commanded to appoint
a king to *rally together* our nation and *lead us*"
(*SEFER HAMITZVOT*, MITZVAH 173). The
fact that G-d chose that there be one dynasty to
rule the Jewish people—the Davidic dynasty—
demonstrates this sort of cohesion, for these kings
represent G-d's sovereignty over the people.

TEXT 25

Imitating the Nations

Rashi, I Samuel 8:6

RABBI SHLOMO YITSCHAKI (RASHI)
1040–1105

Most noted biblical and Talmudic commentator. Born in Troyes, France, Rashi studied in the famed *yeshivot* of Mainz and Worms. His commentaries on the Pentateuch and the Talmud, which focus on the straightforward meaning of the text, appear in virtually every edition of the Talmud and Bible.

וַיֵּרַע הַדָּבָר: לְפִי שֶׁאָמְרוּ לְשָׁפְטֵנוּ כְּכָל הַגּוֹיִם.

Samuel was displeased—because they requested a king who would "govern us like all the nations."

ADDITIONAL READINGS

The Personality of Mashiach

by Rabbi J. Immanuel Schochet

RABBI JACOB IMMANUEL SCHOCHET, PHD 1935–2013

Torah scholar and philosopher. Rabbi Schochet was born in Switzerland. Rabbi Schochet was a renowned authority on kabbalah and Jewish law and authored more than 30 books on Jewish philosophy and mysticism. He also served as professor of philosophy at Humber College in Toronto, Canada. Rabbi Schochet was a member of the executive committee of the Rabbinical Alliance of America and of the Central Committee of Chabad-Lubavitch Rabbis, and served as the halachic guide for the Rohr Jewish Learning Institute.

A. Mashiach Human

Mashiach and the Messianic age are the ultimate end for the world, preconceived from the very beginning, for which the world was created.[1] Mashiach, therefore, is one of the things that precede the creation.[2] This refers, however, to the principle and soul of Mashiach. On the actual level of the physical world's reality, Mashiach is a human being:

Mashiach is a human being, born in normal fashion of human parents.[3] The only qualification about his origins is that he is a descendant of King David,[4] through the lineage of his son Solomon.[5] From his birth onwards his righteousness will increase continually, and by virtue of his deeds he will merit sublime levels of spiritual perfection.[6]

B. Mashiach in Every Generation

Any time is a potential time for the coming of Mashiach.[7] This does not mean, however, that at the appropriate time he will suddenly emerge from Heaven to appear on earth.[8] On the contrary: Mashiach is already on earth, a human being of great saintly status (a *tzadik*) appearing and existing in every generation. "In every generation is born a progeny of Judah fit to be Israel's Mashiach!"[9]

On the particular day that marks the end of the *galut*, when Mashiach will redeem Israel, the unique pre-existing soul of Mashiach 'stored' in Gan Eden from aforetimes will

descend and be bestowed upon that *tzadik*.[10] R. Mosheh Sofer summarizes this principle in his responsa:[11]

"As for the coming of the scion of David, I need to posit the following premise: Moses the first redeemer of Israel, reached the age of eighty years and did not know or sense that he would redeem Israel. Even when the Holy One, blessed be He, said to him, 'Come and I will send you to Pharao. . . .' (Exodus 3:10), he declined and did not want to accept that mission. So it will be with the final redeemer.

"The very day that the *Bet Hamikdash* was destroyed, was born one who, by virtue of his righteousness, is fit to be the redeemer.[12] At the proper time G-d will reveal Himself to him and send him, and then will dwell upon him the spirit of Mashiach which is hidden and concealed above until his coming.

"Thus we find also with Saul that the spirit of royalty and the Holy Spirit which he had not sensed at all within himself came upon him after he was anointed. . . .

"The *tzadik* himself does not realize this potential. Because of our sins many such *tzadikim* passed away already. We did not merit that the Messianic spirit was conferred upon them. They were fit and appropriate for this, but their generations were not fit. . . ."[13]

This explains why R. Akiva would consider Bar Kochba to be Mashiach

(*Yerushalmi*, Ta'anit 4:5; see *Hilchot Melachim* 11:3; and cf. *Yeshu'ot Meshicho, Iyun Harishon*: ch. 4). Furthermore, it explains a discussion in Sanhedrin 98b about the name of Mashiach, with different authorities suggesting Shiloh, Yinon, Chaninah and Menachem (cf. *Yeshu'ot Meshicho, Iyun Hasheni*, ch. 3, that the term Mashiach is an acronym of these four names): each school picked the name of its own master (Rashi). The implication is clear: each school regarded its own master as the most likely potential Mashiach of that generation by virtue of his saintliness and perfection; see R. Tzadok Hakohen, *Peri Tzadik*, Devarim: 13. In later generations, too, we find the same attitude among the disciples of R. Isaac Luria, the Baal Shem Tov, the Vilna Gaon, R. Chaim David Azulay, and many other extraordinary personalities, as stated explicitly in their writings.

C. The Character and Qualities of Mashiach

"The spirit of G-d will rest upon him, a spirit of wisdom and understanding, a spirit of counsel and might, a spirit of knowledge and of the fear of G-d. He shall be inspired with fear of G-d, and he shall not judge with the sight of his eyes nor decide according to the hearing of his ears. He shall judge the poor with righteousness and decide with equity for the humble of the earth; he shall smite the earth with the rod of his mouth and slay the wicked with the breath of his lips. Righteousness shall be the girdle of his loins, and faith the girdle of his reins." (Isaiah 11:2–5)[14] "Through his knowledge My servant shall justify the righteous to the many. . . ." (Isaiah 53:11)

"Behold, My servant shall be wise, he shall be exalted and lofty, and shall be very high." (Isaiah 52:13). His wisdom shall exceed even that of King Solomon;[15] he shall be greater than the patriarchs, greater than all the prophets after Moses, and in many respects even more exalted than Moses.[16] His stature and honor shall exceed that of all kings before him.[17] He will be an extraordinary prophet, second only to Moses,[18] with all the spiritual and mental qualities that are prerequisites to be endowed with the gift of prophecy.[19]

As a faithful shepherd he already cares so much about his people that he volunteered to suffer all kinds of agonies to assure that not a single Jew of all times will be lost.[20]

Mashiach shall meditate on the Torah[21] and be preoccupied with *mitzvot*. He shall teach all the Jewish people and instruct them in the way of G-d. He will prevail upon Israel to follow and observe the Torah, repair its breaches, and fight the battles of G-d.[22]

Mashiach will reveal altogether new insights, making manifest the hidden mysteries of the Torah,[23] to the point that "all the Torah learned in the present world will be vain compared to the Torah of Mashiach."[24]

Though Mashiach comes first and foremost to Israel, all the nations will recognize his wisdom and sublimity and submit to his rule.[25] He will guide and instruct them as well.[26]

There is no need for Mashiach to perform signs and wonders to prove himself.[27] Nonetheless, he will do so.[28]

ENDNOTES

[1] Sanhedrin 98b; *Pesikta Rabaty* 34:6 (ed. Friedmann, ch. 33). See also *Bereishit Rabba* 2:4; and cf. R. Bachaya on Genesis 1:2; and *Netzach Yisrael*, ch. 43.

[2] Pesachim 54a; *Pirkei deR. Eliezer* ch. 3 (see there *Bi'ur Haradal* note 14); *Bereishit Rabba* 1:4 (and see there *Minchat Yehudah*). Cf. *Yeshu'ot Meshicho, Iyun Hasheni*: ch. 3.

[3] *Or Hachamah* on *Zohar* II: 7b; R. Chaim Vital, *Arba Me'ot Shekel Kessef*, ed. Tel Aviv 5724, p. 241a–b. See also *Yeshu'ot Meshicho, Iyun Hashelishi*: ch. 3ff.

[4] See Isaiah 11:1; Jeremiah 23:5–6 and 33:14ff. See also II Samuel 7:12–16, and Psalms 89. In this context, Mashiach is often referred to as (and identified with) David see Hosea 3:5; Jeremiah 30:9; Ezekiel 34:23–24 and 37:24–25 (cf. below. note 51).

[5] *Tanchuma*, Toldot: 14, and in ed. Buber, par. 20 (and see there note 139); *Agadat Bereishit* ch. 44. (See *Emek Hamelech, Hakdamah*, ch. 12, p. 14d, and *Sha'ar Kiryat Arba*, ch. 112, p. 108d). Rambam, *Principles*, Article 12, and *Igeret Teyman*, ch. 3. (Cf. also his *Sefer Hamitzvot* II: 262). Cf. *Zohar* I: 110b and III:188a, and commentaries there.

[6] Sources in notes 4 and 5.

[7] See below, ch. V.

[8] A superficial glance at *Zohar* II:7b would seem to suggest this; but see the commentaries cited in note 45.

9 R. Ovadiah of Bartenura, Commentary on Ruth (appended to *Mikra'ot Gedolot-Bamidbar*, p. 479), see there.

10 Ibid. Cf. *Igeret Teyman*, ch. 4: "With respect to his arising, he will not be known beforehand until it is declared to him . . . a man, unknown prior to his manifestation, shall rise, and the signs and wonders that will come about through him will be the proof for the authenticity of his claim and pedigree . . ." Note that this concept of the 'bestowal and infusion' of Mashiach's soul unto a living *tzadik* (related to the Kabbalistic concepts of *gilgul* and *ibbur* reincarnation and 'impregnation') explains the identification of Mashiach with King David himself (see *Yeshu'ot Meshicho, Iyun Harishon*, ch. 5:*hakdamah* 6; and see also R. Ya'akov Emden's commentary on the hymns of *Hoshana Rabba*, end, s.v. *hu David atzmo*). Likewise, it explains the identification of Mashiach with Moses, when he is called "the first redeemer and the last redeemer" (see *Shemot Rabba* 2:4, and *Devarim Rabba* 9:9); and as noted in *Zohar* I:25b and 253a that the numerical equivalent of Mosheh is the same as that of Shiloh (the term in Genesis 49:10 denoting Mashiach): the soul of Mashiach is the "soul-of-the-soul" of Moses, so that in effect Moses will be the final redeemer (and there is no problem with the seeming discrepancy of Mashiach being a descendant of David of the tribe of Judah while Moses is a descendent of the tribe of Levi). See R. Chaim Vital's *Likutei Torah*, and *Sha'ar Hapesukim*, on Genesis 49:10. Note also *Or Hachayimon*, Genesis 49:11!

11 *Responsa Chatam Sofer* VI: 98. See also *Chatam Sofer al Hatorah*, ed. Stern, vol. II: p. 18a, on Exodus 4:26, and note 9 there.

12 See *Agadat Bereishit*, ch. 67 (68). See also *Yerushalmi*, Berachot 2:4, and *Eichah Rabba* 1:51.

13 See also *Sdei Chemed, Pe'at Hasadeh: Kelalim*, s.v. *aleph*: sect. 70.

14 See *Likkutei Diburim*, vol. II, p. 628ff.

15 *Hilchot Teshuvah* 9:25.

16 *Tanchuma*, and *Agadat Bereishit*, cited above, note 47. Cf. *Yeshu'ot Meshicho, Iyun Hashlishi*: ch. 1. See also *Or Hatorah-Na"ch*, vol. I, p. 265f.

17 Rambam, *Introduction to Sanhedrin X*; *Principles*, Article 12 (in popular versions, though not in ed. Kapach); and *Igeret Teyman*, ch. 4.

18 *Hilchot Teshuvah* 9:2; *Igeret Teyman*, ch. 4.

19 See *Igeret Teyman*, ch. 4.

20 *Pesikta Rabaty* 37:1 (ed. Friedmann, ch. 36).

21 See *Midrash Tehilim* 2:9 and 110:4.

22 *Hilchot Teshuvah* 9:2; *Hilchot Melachim* 11:4. Note also *Yalkut Shimoni*, Pinchas: par. 776, that Mashiach will have the unique gift of understanding and persuading each individual despite the wide diversity in people's minds and attitudes.

23 *Eliyahu Zutta* ch. 20; *Oti'ot deR. Akiva*, s.v. *zayin*. See Rashi (and other commentaries) on Song 1:2. Cf. *Zohar* III: 23a; and *Vayikra Rabba* 13:3. See also *Tanchuma* , ed. Buber, Chukat:24, and *Pesikta deR. Kahana*, ed. Buber, ch. IV (p. 39af.), and the editor's notes there.

24 *Kohelet Rabba* 11:12. For a comprehensive analysis of the concept of the new manifestations of Torah in the Messianic era, discussing the various Halachic and philosophical issues involved, see R. Menachem M. Schneerson *shalita, Kuntres Be'inyan "Torah*

Chadashah Me'iti Tetze." Cf. also the commentaries on *Zohar* III: 23a; and R. Abraham Azulay, *Chessed Le'Avraham, Mayan* II: 11 and 27, and ibid. *Mayan* V: 36.

25 *Midrash Tehilim* 2:3 and 87:6–7.

26 *Bereishit Rabba* 98:9 (see there *Minchat Yehudah*); *Midrash Tehilim* 21:1. Cf. above II-E.

27 *Hilchot Melachim* 11:2.

28 See *Midrash Pirkei Mashiach*; and end of *Perek R. Yoshiyahu*.

Note *Or Hachayim* on Exodus 21:11; and cf. above, note 23.

Mashiach: The Principle of Mashiach and the Messianic Era in Jewish Law and Tradition (Brooklyn, N.Y.: SIE, 2004), ch. 3, pp. 37–44

Reprinted with permission from Sichos in English

The Idealistic Realism of Jewish Messianism:

The real deal on Chabad's apocalyptic calculations, and why Jews have always predicted elusive ends

By Eli Rubin

RABBI ELI RUBIN

Researcher, writer. Rubin studied Chasidic literature and Jewish Law at the Rabbinical College of America and at *yeshivot* in the U.K., the U.S., and Australia. He has been a research writer and editor at Chabad.org since 2011, focusing on the social and intellectual history of Chabad Chasidism. His work has also appeared in *Hakirah* and *Mosaic Magazine*.

A Dialectical Tradition of Prediction

The suspicion with which Jewish messianism is often regarded may well stem from the apparent contradiction it embodies. To await the Messiah is to live a life marked by optimistic anticipation for an unimaginably brighter future. But to live as a Jew requires full immersion in the demands of the present moment. The false-messiahs that litter the history of Jewish exile are nothing other than the failure of real events to live up to idealistic hopes. And yet a Judaism stripped of messianic inspiration is inconceivable. It is precisely such inspiration that has continued to sustain us despite all the trying upheavals of the ages.

For messianism to be authentically Jewish, and for it to inspire an authentically Jewish future, it must somehow bridge the gap between idealism and realism. As the writer, philosopher and critic Leon Wieseltier has put it, "Messianism is commonly interpreted as a variety of idealism. But if idealism is only a part of Judaism's attitude towards the world, messianism must stand in a relationship also to realism."[1]

The paradoxical nature of Jewish messianism is well illustrated by the phenomenon known as *hishuv ha-ketz,* "calculating the end." Even before the children of Jacob became a nation, even before they were enslaved by the Pharaohs, the Bible records the first attempt to reveal the date when the Messiah would appear. As the patriarch Jacob lay on his death bed, his sons gathered to witness his last pronouncement, "And Jacob called his sons and said, 'Gather and I will tell you that which will occur at the end of days.'" In the next verse the tension builds, "Gather and listen to the words of Jacob, and listen to Israel your father." (Genesis, 49:1-2.) Then Jacob / Israel changes the subject. He blesses each of his sons in turn, but nothing more is said about the end of days. Following various Talmudic and Midrashic texts, the great commentator Rashi explains, "He wished to reveal the end, and the divine presence departed from him, so he began to say other things." Jews have ever sought to predict the end. The end has ever remained elusive.

Since Talmudic times it seems that almost no generation has gone by without a rabbinic authority who practiced such calculations and another who condemned them. Maimonides famously stood on both sides of the fence. In his great legal code, *Mishneh Torah,* he rules that it is forbidden to calculate end dates (*Hilchot Melachim,* 12:1). In his *Epistle to Yemen* he also warns against such predictions, but goes on to note "an extraordinary tradition which I received from my father" that the Messianic era would begin in the Hebrew year 4970 (1210 according to the secular calendar) with the renewal of prophecy.

"Today—If You Listen"

Closer to our own time, two great scholars usually perceived in direct opposition to one another were both inspired to calculate end dates. Both were well versed in Jewish law and in the mystical tradition known as Kabbalah. But while one was the most authoritative opponent of the Chassidic movement, the other was one of Chassidism's most abidingly influential leaders. The former was Rabbi Eliyahu, the famed Gaon of Vilna, the latter was Rabbi Schneur Zalman of Liadi, the founding rebbe of Chabad-Lubavitch.

Several scholars have argued that it was the calculation of 1781 as an end date that inspired the Gaon's unrealized attempt to travel to the Holy Land. This end date was grounded in the rabbinic notion that history is divided into six millennia, corresponding to the six days of creation, and that the seventh millennium, corresponding to Shabbat, will be the era of the Messiah. (See Nachmanides commentary to Genesis 2:3.) The year 1740 coincided with the Hebrew year 5500, the midpoint ("midday") of the sixth millennium. While some Kabbalists had predicted that this milestone would mark the onset of the Messianic era, Jews have ever sought to predict the end. The end has ever remained elusive. others fixed the decisive date a "half hour" later, which in millennial terms translated to 1781.[2]

Explicit evidence of the Gaon's attempt to divine the precise date of the end of exile, as well as his reluctance to reveal it, is found in his commentary to the Zoharic text, *Sifra di-Tsni'uta,* "Know that all these days hint to the six millennia, which are the six days . . . and from this you can know the end date of redemption, which will be in its time if we are not meritorious . . . And I make the reader swear by G-d, the L-rd of Israel, not to reveal this." This citation includes an important caveat. We need only await the predicted date if we are not meritorious. If our conduct as human beings is sufficiently worthy, the final redemption will transpire in an instant.[3]

The notion that the Messiah's arrival can be hastened through positive human behaviour is rooted in the Talmudic account of yet another attempt to find out when the exile would end. Rabbi Joshua ben Levi once met the prophet Elijah at the entrance to Rabbi Shimon ben Yohai's tomb, and asked him, "When will the Messiah come?" Elijah directed him to put this question to the Messiah himself, saying that he could be found amongst the lepers at the city gate, and could be identified by the distinct manner in which he untied and retied his bandages. The Messiah, the Talmud tells us, replied to Rabbi Joshua's question with a single word, "Today." When the day passed without the Messiah's promised revelation, Rabbi Joshua complained to Elijah. Said Elijah, "This is what the Messiah said to you, 'I will come today—*if you listen to G-d's voice.*'" The Talmudic sage Rav put it slightly differently, "All end dates have passed. The matter is dependent on nothing other than repentance and good deeds."[4]

Collapsing the Interval of Time

The Talmudic narrative implies that by listening to the voice of G-d in the present, we bring about the arrival of the Messiah in the future. Simply speaking, this suggests that the realistic present and the idealistic future are separated by the interval of time. But a passage in Rabbi Schneur Zalman of Liadi's *Tanya* suggests that the fulfillment of G-d's commandments during the time of exile actually has a much more immediate result. In Rabbi Schneur Zalman's conception, the commandments are not simply rituals, and the Messiah's coming is not simply a reward for our obedience. The commandments are intimate expressions of divine wisdom and will, and as such they are synonymous with the messianic ideal. By listening to G-d's voice and acting upon G-d's commandments as revealed in the Torah, we are drawing divine enlightenment into the environment that we inhabit, and actualizing the messianic ideal in real time.

In Rabbi Schneur Zalman's own words: "The ultimate completion of the Messianic era . . . , which is the revelation of the light of the infinite, is dependent on our work and toil throughout the era of exile . . . because in practicing the commandment the individual draws forth the revelation of the light of the infinite."[5] According to this formulation, it is specifically in the present that the messianic ideal is to be realized. But this realization is a cumulative process. With By listening to G-d's voice and acting upon G-d's commandments . . . we are actualizing the messianic ideal in real time. The fulfillment of each additional commandment another element of the messianic revelation is actualized.

Echoing Maimonides, Rabbi Schneur Zalman and later leaders of Chabad displayed some ambivalence when it came to end date calculations. His grandson, Rabbi Menachem Mendel of Lubavitch, known in Chabad as the Tzemach Tzedek, chastised anyone brazen enough to predict a date that even the patriarch Jacob had been unable to reveal.[6] And yet there is irrefutable evidence that Rabbi Schneur Zalman himself made such a calculation. This reckoning does not appear in any of his written works or letters, but in the transcript of an orally delivered discourse that has reached us in several manuscript copies.[7] One of these manuscripts even includes notes appended by the aforementioned Tzemach Tzedek.[8]

Rabbi Schneur Zalman's reckoning is framed as an interpretation of a Biblical verse describing details of the temporary sanctuary built in the desert. Specifically, it records that Moses used one thousand seven hundred and seventy-five silver shekels to make hooks upon which to hang the curtains from the pillars (Exodus, 38:28). In Zoharic literature this passage, along with its masoretic cantillation marks, is obscurely connected to the time span of the exile. Taking various other allusions into account, Rabbi Schneur Zalman explains this to mean that there will be 1,775 years between the destruction of the second temple and the onset of the Messianic era. Considering that the temple was destroyed in the Hebrew year 3828, the addition of 1,775 years brings us to the year 5603, which began in September 1842 on the secular calendar.[9] Recent reports claiming that the prediction was made for 5775, whose start coincides with September 2014, do not appear to have any basis in original Chabad sources.

Messianic Wellsprings

To make things even more complicated, several corroboratory traditions agree that although this calculation points to the Hebrew year 5603 (corresponding to 1842–3), which is the year recorded in the manuscripts, Rabbi Schneur Zalman actually mentioned a different date, causing some confusion among his listeners. There are contradictory accounts about what he actually said, but the consensus seems to be that instead of saying 5603 he said 5608 (corresponding to 1847–8).[10]

Be this as it may, both years passed by without the foretold event actually transpiring.

Rabbi Schneur Zalman's grandson, the Tzemach Tzedek, had by then succeeded his predecessors as the third Chabad rebbe. When asked what had become of the projected messianic revelation, he pointed out that in the year 5608 a collection of Rabbi Schneur Zalman's oral discourses, titled *Likkutei Torah,* had been published for the first time. In some versions of this story it is recorded that the questioner was not satisfied with this response, "We need the Messiah, "To have access to a new font of learning and spiritual illumination . . . is to be exposed to a new degree of messianic revelation. he insisted, "in the most literal sense."[11]

The underlying assumption reflected in the Tzemach Tzedek's response is that the onset of the Messianic era is a relative notion as well as an absolute one. To have access to a new font of learning and spiritual illumination, such as that embodied by *Likkutei Torah,* is to be exposed to a new degree of messianic revelation. And yet the questioner's unanswered comeback, demanding the literal arrival of the Messiah, stands as a hard reminder that small victories can never be cause for complacency. Only if we vigorously fan the flame of spiritual enlightenment will it expand into the all-embracing fire of the ultimate messianic revelation. Like other predicted end dates, the opportunity foreseen by R. Schneur Zalman was realized partially, but not completely.

The idea that the spiritual insight provided by Chassidic teachings carries a distinctly messianic quality is rooted in the famous letter penned by Rabbi Yisrael Baal Shem Tov, the movement's founding figure, in which he described his heavenly visit to the chamber of the Messiah. The Baal Shem Tov asked, "When will sir come?" And the Messiah replied, "When your wellsprings spread to the outside."[12]

In Chabad thought this linkage between the Messianic advent and Chassidic teachings (the Baal Shem Tov's wellsprings) is understood to be far more than cause and effect. The seventh Rebbe, Rabbi Menachem Mendel Schneerson, explained that at their core both the Messiah and Chassidism embody the quintessential purpose of all existence.[13] The function of Chassidism, and especially the intellectually inclined Chabad school, is to cumulatively draw the Messianic ideal closer to its cognitive and practical apprehension. In the words of Rabbi Yoel Kahn, contemporary Chabad's preeminent scholar, "Chassidism and the Messiah are one and the same."[14]

"Not Like My Fools"

On Simchat Torah of the year 1919, Rabbi Shalom DovBer Schneersohn, the fifth rebbe of Chabad-Lubavitch, discussed the end date set by Rabbi Schneur Zalman and shared another related anecdote: It once happened that Rabbi Schneur Zalman sent two emissaries to Rabbi Nachum of Chernobyl, a contemporary Chassidic leader, regarding a certain matter. They arrived late on the day before Rosh Hashanah, and on the eve following Rosh Hashanah they sat together in the fashion of Chassidim, sharing inspiration and schnapps. At one point, R. Nachum turned to his guests and said, "This year the messiah will come." The response of Rabbi Schneur Zalman's emissaries was both affirmative and reserved, "If the messiah will come," they said, "all will be well." Said R. Nachum, "You are not like my fools, they would already be packing their travel chests."[15]

As recounted by Rabbi Shalom DovBer, this episode sheds light on the balance of realism that Chabad's messianic idealism attempts to strike. We must always expect the Messiah to appear at a moment's notice. But that expectancy must never distract us from the realities of the present moment. So long as the Messiah has not arrived in actuality, we can never allow ourselves the luxuries of over-optimism and over-satisfaction. To truly perceive the end is to see beyond the various forms of messianic hype that so easily proliferate.

The messianic revelation is most essentially characterized by the implementation of our loftiest ideals in real life. Accordingly, messianic opportunity always lies within our immediate grasp, but we must never turn a blind eye to truly perceive the end is to see beyond the various forms of messianic hype that so easily proliferate. to the dark realities of the exile. The reality of exile is that we are simply unable to fulfill all of the Torah's precepts in actuality. And it is the Torah's vision of a world where we will fully live in accord with G-d's commandments that enshrines the ultimate arrival of the Messiah an eternal certitude.[16] It is only by living the Torah's precepts as fully as we can in the here and now that we can hope to live them fully in the future. To live messianically is not to abandon the present moment, but to live the present moment so completely that it transcends its own limitations.[17]

There are end date predictions that incite speculation and hysteria, hype and sensationalism. And there are end date predictions that bring the ultimate destiny of humankind into palpable relation with the here and now. According to Leon Wieseltier, "It was not knowledge that these dates furnished, it was hope. When the predictions were valued, it was not for the historical illumination that they provided, but for the spiritual fortification."[18] In this he is only partially correct. These end dates cannot be reduced to an attempt to inspire hope. The foresight of a true visionary stands as a lasting testimony that the Torah's concrete idealism can and will be successfully implemented, if only the messianic moment is properly embraced.

The seventh Rebbe, Rabbi Menachem Mendel, often emphasized that each end date predicted by the spiritual giants of bygone generations actually embodied a real opportunity for the realization of the complete redemption. But in every case so far society has failed to rise to the occasion. End date calculations express an authentic vision of the ultimate power that can be unleashed in a single moment.[19] Missed opportunities should only intensify our resolve not to let the next messianic moment pass us by.[20] In the words of Maimonides: "Every individual should the entire year see themselves as if they are half meritorious and half guilty, and similarly the entire world . . . one mitzvah turns themselves and the entire world to the side of good."[21]

Moshiach Now!

Messianism is so essential to the Jewish experience that there has not been a generation of Jews, nor any significant Jewish movement, which did not have a messianic self-perception. As has recently been demonstrated by scholars Moshe Idel and Israel Bartel, even purportedly secular Jewish movements could not escape their inherent messianism. According to Idel, most of the formative leaders of Israel's intellectual culture, including David Ben Gurion, overtly conceived of their Zionism in messianic terms; Gershom Scholem was the notable exception.[22] Bartel argues that Zionism as messianism actually had its roots in the end date widely predicted for the Hebrew year 5600 (1840), a year that is alluded to in the Zohar.[23]

According to Leon Wieseltier, Scholem's attempt to distance himself from messianic idealism was rooted in a misconception. To embrace a messianic vision, Scholem thought, is to embrace "a life lived in deferment." To live in hope, Scholem wrote, "diminishes the singular worth of the individual . . . he can never fulfill himself . . . nothing can be done definitively, nothing can be irrevocably accomplished." If you are always looking towards a future ideal, must not the realities of the present be dismissed as inadequate? Wieseltier rejects Scholem's characterization of Jewish messianism as "spectacularly wrong." The absolute opposite, he asserts, is true: "It was the objective of halacha . . . to ensure that something can be done definitively, that something can be irrevocably accomplished, and this objective was achieved annually, monthly,If we abandon our sense of history or our vision for the future, then the present too will lose its significance. weekly, daily, and hourly."[24]

Scholem's conception places messianism in direct opposition to existentialism. The present moment is seen as nothing more than a deficient steppingstone towards the future ideal. But as Elliot Wolfson has pointed out, Chabad messianism is intimately tied to a unique conception of time. We normally think of time as a linear sequence of distinct events; the past precedes the present, which is followed by the future. G-d, however, transcends the limitations that distinguish one moment of time from another. From the divine perspective, which is more real than our own, the past is never lost and the future has already come. Likewise, no single moment can be divorced from its context in the greater expanse of history. Time is not a succession of isolated events, but the unfolding of a united singularity.[25]

It is this more essential notion of time that Scholem failed to grasp. As we have already seen, Rabbi Schneur Zalman does not perceive the messianic revelation as something that will only be attained at some future date. On the contrary, messianic revelation can only be drawn forth via our actions in the present. To arrive in the Messianic era is not to lose the inadequate past, but to bring the incremental permanence of history to its ultimate culmination. It is the Torah's prescription of repentance and good deeds throughout the era of exile that gradually uncovers the full spectrum of divine manifestation. Every thought, speech or action for the good carries the infinite potency of the messianic ideal.[26]

In order to understand what is demanded of us in the present moment, we must look both backwards and forwards. Real life is raised beyond mundane drudgery by messianic hope and inspiration. If we abandon our sense of history or our vision for the future, then the present too will lose its significance. The ideal of Jewish messianism can only be realized through our actions in the here and now.

The Maimonidean declaration of messianic anticipation and hope, "though he tarries . . . I await his coming every day," unequivocally anchors Jewish idealism in the concrete present.[27] A contemporary slogan puts it even more succinctly: "Moshiach now!"

ENDNOTES

[1] Leon Wieseltier, *A Passion for Waiting: Messianism, History and the Jews,* delivered on October 24, 2012 at the University of California, Berkeley.

[2] For a full overview see Arie Morgenstern, *The Gaon of Vilna and His Messianic Vision* (Gefen Publishing 2012).

[3] *Sifra di-Tsni'uta Im Biur Ha-gra* (Vilna and Horodno, 1820), 54b.

[4] Talmud Bavli, Sanhedrin 97b and 98a.

[5] *Likutei Amarim Tanya,* Chapter 37.

[6] *Ohr Ha-torah – Tanach* Vol. 1, page 183.

[7] For a full overview of the extant manuscripts and a discussion of related sources see Yehoshua Mondshine, *Hishuvei Kitzin* in *Migdal Oz,* pp. 483. See also *Sefer Maamarei Admur Ha-zaken – Parshiyot,* pp. 419.

[8] *Sefer Maamarei Admur Ha-zaken* – Parshiyot, page 423.

[9] See also Rabbi DovBer Schneuri of Lubavitch, *Imrei Binah,* folio 193a (Part 3, Section 152).

[10] See sources cited by Yehoshua Mondshine, Ibid.

[11] See Rabbi Shalom DovBer Schneersohn, *Torat Shalom,* pp. 237. See additional sources cited by Yehoshua Mondshine, Ibid.

[12] See Yehoshua Mondshine, *Nusach Kadum Shel Igeret Aliyat Ha-neshamah Le-ha-besht,* Ibid., pp. 119. See also Naftali Loewenthal, *The Baal Shem Tov's Iggeret Ha-Kodesh and Contemporary HaBaD "Outreach",* in *Let the Old Make Way for the New,* Vol. 1 (Edited by David Assaf and Ada Rapoport-Albert, Zalman Shazar Center for Jewish History, 2009), pp. 69.

[13] Rabbi Menachem Mendel Schneerson, *Inyaanah Shel Torat Ha-chassidut,* sections 5-6.

[14] Rabbi Yoel Kahn, *Chassidut U-mashiach Hai'nu Hach* in *Kovetz Mashiach U-ge'ulah,* Vol. 2, pp. 3.

[15] *Torat Shalom,* Ibid. It should be noted too that R. Shalom DovBer himself singled out the year 5666 as an end date. See Rabbi Menachem Mendel Schneerson, *Sichot Kodesh* 5713, page 370.

[16] See Maimonides, *Sefer Shoftim – Hilchot Melachim U-milchamotaihem,* 11:1-2. See also the analysis of these passages by Rabbi Menachem Mendel Schneerson, *Likutei Sichot* Vol. 34, pp. 114, and Ibid., Vol 18, pp. 276.

[17] Rabbi Menachem Mendel Schneerson, *Torat Menachem - Hitvaduyot* 5745 Vol. 5. pages 2622-2623.

[18] Leon Wieseltier, Ibid.

[19] See for example *Sichot Kodesh 5725* Vol. 1, pages 323-324.

[20] *Torat Menachem,* Ibid.

[21] *Sefer Ha-madah – Hilchot Teshuvah,* 3:4.

[22] Moshe Idel, *Messianic Scholars: On Early Israeli Scholarship, Politics and Messianism in Modern Judaism* (2012) 32 (1), pages 22–53.

[23] Israel Bartel, *Messianism and nationalism: Liberal Optimism vs. Orthodox Anxiety in Jewish History* (2006) 20, pages 5–17.

[24] Leon Wieseltier, Ibid.

[25] Elliot R. Wolfson, *Open Secret: Postmessianic Messianism and the Mystical Revision of Menahem Mendel Schneerson* (Columbia University Press, 2009), pages 284–289. See also pages 22-24.

[26] *Likutei Amarim Tanya,* Chapter 37.

[27] The quote is from the twelfth of Maimonides' thirteen articles of faith as formulated in many versions of the traditional prayer liturgy. The liturgical formulation was not authored by Maimonides himself but is based on the principles he laid down in his *Introduction to Perek Chelek.*

Why Must Moshiach Be a Person?

By Rabbi Yanki Tauber

RABBI YANKI TAUBER
1965–

Chasidic scholar and author. A native of Brooklyn, N.Y., Rabbi Tauber is an internationally renowned author who specializes in adapting the teachings of the Lubavitcher Rebbe. He is a member of the JLI curriculum development team and has written numerous articles and books, including *Once Upon a Chassid* and *Beyond the Letter of the Law*.

Skeptic: Do you mind if I ask a rather simplistic question?

Believer: Those are usually the most difficult to address.

Skeptic: Why?

Believer: Because a simple question usually has a simple answer. And a simple answer is the most difficult answer to accept.

Skeptic: Anyway, here's my question. Why are you always speaking of a future perfect world in terms of Moshiach, the person? If humanity has a destiny and goal, if history is the evolution toward a state of harmony and perfection, why the need for the individual human being you call Moshiach?

Believer: Look at the last 5,000 years of human experience: every major movement and instrument of change, positive or negative, beneficial or destructive, centered upon an individual. The religions which deeply affected the lives of hundreds of millions, the infamous wars and carnages which swept the earth, the movements on behalf of oppressed peoples, the great revolutions in philosophy, art and technology—all are identified with a specific individual. There was always a leader who inspired and motivated his followers and whose influence ultimately extended beyond his community and his generation.

Skeptic: What you're saying is that that's the way we are, that this is an inescapable fact of human nature. But why are we this way? Is this the way we ought to be? Is it not a weakness on our part that we cannot do anything on our own, that we must be led by the hand like small children?

Believer: That we are inspired by leaders does not mean that "we cannot do anything on our own." No leader can move us to something that we do not already desire on some level, or enable us to do things which we do not already possess the aptitude and ability for. It is we who are doing these things, things which we already wanted to do and were already capable of doing.

The role of the leader is that of a lamplighter. When the lamplighter approaches the lamp, all necessary elements to produce light are already present: the oil, the wick, the vessel designed to contain them and to keep the flame going. The lamplighter adds nothing of substance. He merely touches his flame to the wick, stimulating the release of the latent energy and luminary potential which the lamp contains.

Moshiach does not come to do the work of humanity. What he is is the spark that ignites the soul of every man and woman on earth. Moshiach is an individual who will kindle the potential good within each and every one of us into glowing reality.

Skeptic: So we need a white knight on a white donkey to jump-start our souls. That's how G-d made us. But Why? Why must we be dependent on someone else? Could we not have been given the tools to "ignite our potential" on our own?

Believer: Life is created by the means of the relationship between man and woman. Now, let us take the nature of existence back to the drawing board: Why the need for male and female? Surely all creatures could have been created with the capacity to reproduce on their own!

Skeptic: Well thank G-d it wasn't designed that way. We would have been deprived of one of the most beautiful and fulfilling aspects of our lives.

Believer: It's far more than one of life's aspects: relationships—that is to say, the concept of a giver-recipient partnership—are the very essence of life itself. The most obvious and basic of these is the creation of life through the union between the giver and initiator, man, and the recipient and nurturer, woman. But it extends to all areas of life. At the heart of a functioning society is the flow of resources and goods between individuals: commerce, trade and credit are indispensable to life as we know it. Charity and generosity are deeply ingrained in the human soul: every right-thinking individual believes in the responsibility of the haves toward the have-nots. Again, G-d could certainly have created us as self-sufficient entities. But then, as you said, life would be quite empty and unfulfilled.

The same is true on the intellectual and moral level. We are not self-contained worlds — we give and take, teach and learn, influence and are influenced. Every individual is a teacher, with the ability to bestow upon others insights and qualities that are unique to him alone. But the richness of life's relationships is that they also include a passive, receiving element, as well. So every man is also a student, a recipient who awaits a stimulating "spark" to ignite his latent potentials.

Skeptic: Still I ask: Why must this "igniting spark" come from a human being? You say that the Torah is G-d's blueprint for life. So why can't we realize the "recipient" aspect of our lives by opening the books and learning directly from them?

Believer: Why do you prefer a book to an individual?

Skeptic: Because every person has his or her own axe to grind. Who can you trust nowadays? What is to be gained by a mortal Moshiach?

Believer: Any parent will tell you that, ultimately, the only way to educate a child is by example. You can employ all sorts of inventive ways to impart an idea or a value but, more than anything else, the child will learn from your character and behavior. Books and other media may stimulate and inspire us but only rarely do they move us to take action—especially action that demands much of us. Moshiach is a "book" authored by G-d—only not one of paper and ink but of flesh and blood. He is an individual who personifies, in the most absolute and unequivocal manner, what it is that man was created to be. As a living, breathing Torah, he is the optimal (and, ultimately, the only possible) instrument to bring to light the goodness and perfection that is intrinsic to the soul of man.

"The Skeptic and the Believer, Conversation X," www.chabad.org/63564

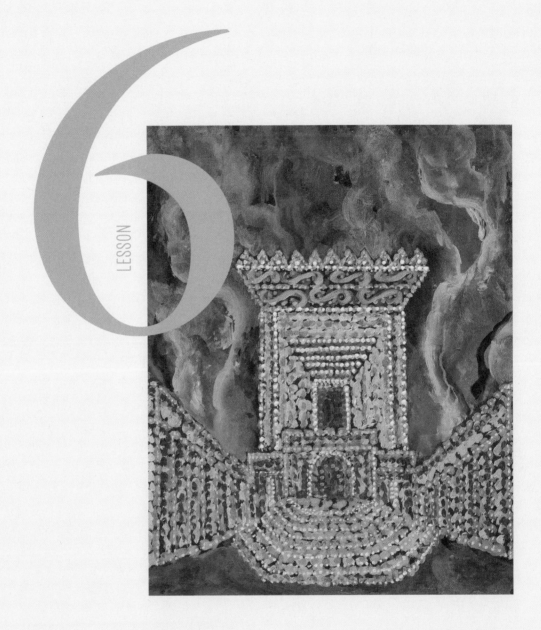

THE POINTS OF LIGHT OF THE TEMPLE
Yehoshua Wiseman, acrylic on canvas, Israel

AND THEN . . .

We've seen why the Redemption needs to happen and the human role in making it happen. Now let us peek into that perfect—and perfectly possible—world as the prophets and sages vividly describe it.

I. A NATURAL REDEMPTION

The final lesson of *This Can Happen* examines Judaism's revelations and scholarly observations regarding the nature of the messianic era. Maimonides (1135–1204) serves as a primary source of scholarly insight into the Redemption. He offers a general principle: we should not presume that nature will change by the Redemption's arrival. At the same time, we will certainly experience drastic positive transformations that allow the Redemption's purpose to be served.

QUESTION

Have you heard of any teachings about events or changes associated with the messianic era? What are they?

"Mashiach: What Will Happen Before and After His Arrival?" **Mrs. Fruma Schapiro** provides the answers provided by Jewish sages of yore: *myjli.com/canhappen*

TEXT 1A

Sameness

Maimonides, *Mishneh Torah*, Laws of Kings 12:1

אַל יַעֲלֶה עַל הַלֵּב שֶׁבִּימוֹת הַמָּשִׁיחַ יִבָּטֵל דָּבָר
מִמִּנְהָגוֹ שֶׁל עוֹלָם. אוֹ יִהְיֶה שָׁם חִדּוּשׁ בְּמַעֲשֵׂה
בְרֵאשִׁית. אֶלָּא עוֹלָם כְּמִנְהָגוֹ נוֹהֵג.

Do not presume that in the messianic age any facet of the world's nature will change or that there will be innovations in the work of creation. The world will continue according to its pattern.

MISHNEH TORAH ILLUMINATION
Nehemiah (artist), Master of the Barbo Missal (illuminator), c. 1457, tempera and gold leaf on parchment, N. Italy. Metropolitan Museum of Art, N.Y.

RABBI MOSHE BEN MAIMON (MAIMONIDES, RAMBAM) 1135–1204

Halachist, philosopher, author, and physician. Maimonides was born in Córdoba, Spain. After the conquest of Córdoba by the Almohads, he fled Spain and eventually settled in Cairo, Egypt. There, he became the leader of the Jewish community and served as court physician to the vizier of Egypt. He is most noted for authoring the *Mishneh Torah*, an encyclopedic arrangement of Jewish law; and for his philosophical work, *Guide for the Perplexed*. His rulings on Jewish law are integral to the formation of halachic consensus.

Rabbi Pinchas Taylor delivers a "Crash Course on Resurrection": *myjli.com/canhappen*

TEXT 1B

Difference

Isaiah 11:6

ISAIAH

Biblical book. The book of Isaiah contains the prophecies of Isaiah, who lived in the 6–7th centuries BCE. Isaiah's prophecies contain stern rebukes for the personal failings of the contemporary people of Judea and the corruption of its government. The bulk of the prophecies, however, are stirring consolations and poetic visions of the future Redemption.

וְגָ֤ר זְאֵב֙ עִם־כֶּ֔בֶשׂ וְנָמֵ֖ר עִם־גְּדִ֣י יִרְבָּ֑ץ וְעֵ֥גֶל
וּכְפִ֛יר וּמְרִ֥יא יַחְדָּ֖ו וְנַ֥עַר קָטֹ֖ן נֹהֵ֥ג בָּֽם׃

The wolf will dwell with the lamb; the leopard will lie down with the young goat. The calf and the yearling will be with the lion, and a little child will lead them all.

QUESTION

Can you reconcile Texts 1a and 1b?

TEXT 1C

Metaphoric Meaning

Maimonides, *Mishneh Torah*, Laws of Kings 12:1

וְזֶה שֶׁנֶּאֱמַר בִּישַׁעְיָה "וְגָר זְאֵב עִם כֶּבֶשׂ וְנָמֵר עִם גְּדִי יִרְבָּץ"
מָשָׁל וְחִידָה. עִנְיַן הַדָּבָר שֶׁיִּהְיוּ יִשְׂרָאֵל יוֹשְׁבִין לָבֶטַח עִם
רִשְׁעֵי עַכּוּ"ם הַמְּשׁוּלִים כִּזְאֵב וְנָמֵר . . . וְלֹא יִגְזְלוּ וְלֹא
יַשְׁחִיתוּ אֶלָּא יֹאכְלוּ דָּבָר הַמֻּתָּר בְּנַחַת עִם יִשְׂרָאֵל . . .

וְכֵן כָּל כַּיּוֹצֵא בְּאֵלּוּ הַדְּבָרִים בְּעִנְיַן הַמָּשִׁיחַ הֵם
מְשָׁלִים. וּבִימוֹת הַמֶּלֶךְ הַמָּשִׁיחַ יִוָּדַע לַכֹּל לְאֵי
זֶה דָּבָר הָיָה מָשָׁל. וּמָה עִנְיָן רָמְזוּ בָּהֶן.

"The wolf will dwell with the lamb; the leopard will lie down with the young goat." These words are an allegory and parable. The interpretation of the prophecy is that the Jews will dwell at peace together with those wicked gentiles who had sought to devour them like a wolf and a leopard. . . . They will no longer steal or destroy but live at peace with Israel. . . .

Similarly, other messianic prophecies of this kind are allegories. Only in the messianic era will we understand their true meaning.

TEXT 2

End of Subjugation

Maimonides, ibid., 12:2

אָמְרוּ חֲכָמִים: אֵין בֵּין הָעוֹלָם הַזֶּה לִימוֹת
הַמָּשִׁיחַ אֶלָּא שֶׁעִבּוּד מַלְכֻיּוֹת בִּלְבַד.

Our Sages taught (TALMUD, SANHEDRIN 99A):
"There will be no difference between the current age
and the messianic era except the emancipation from
our subjugation to the gentile governments."

**HALLEL: KING DAVID
PLAYING HIS HARP**

Haggadah, Hijman (Hayyim
ben Mordecai) Binger, 1796
Braginsky Collection

II. SPURRED BY MASHIACH

Proceeding with Maimonides's description of the Redemption, we encounter the rebuilding of the Jerusalem Temple, the ingathering of the Jewish exiles, and the restoration of the Jewish legal system.

TEXT 3

Mashiach's Doing

Maimonides, ibid., 11:1

הַמֶּלֶךְ הַמָּשִׁיחַ עָתִיד לַעֲמֹד וּלְהַחֲזִיר מַלְכוּת דָּוִד לְיָשְׁנָהּ לַמֶּמְשָׁלָה הָרִאשׁוֹנָה. וּבוֹנֶה הַמִּקְדָּשׁ וּמְקַבֵּץ נִדְחֵי יִשְׂרָאֵל. וְחוֹזְרִין כָּל הַמִּשְׁפָּטִים בְּיָמָיו כְּשֶׁהָיוּ מִקֶּדֶם.

The messianic king will arise and renew the Davidic dynasty, restoring it to its initial sovereignty. He will build the Temple and gather the dispersed of Israel. In his days, the observance of all the statutes will return to their previous state.

In "Maimonides on Mashiach,"
Rabbi Shmuel Kaplan
discusses Maimonides's view on how the messianic era will unfold: *myjli.com/canhappen*

FIGURE 6.1

The Jerusalem Temple

Passover *Haggadah*, Aaron Wolf Herlingen,
Vienna 1730, Braginsky Collection

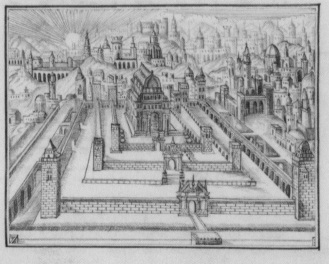

Mrs. Etty Bogomilsky
provides a
comprehensive
description of the
Third Holy Temple
and who will build it:
myjli.com/canhappen

TEXT 4

International Protection

Midrash, *Bamidbar Rabah* 1:3

אִלּוּ הָיוּ אֻמּוֹת הָעוֹלָם יוֹדְעִים מָה הָיָה הַמִּקְדָּשׁ יָפֶה לָהֶם,
קַסְטְרִיּוֹת הָיוּ מַקִּיפִים אוֹתוֹ כְּדֵי לְשָׁמְרוֹ.

If the nations of the world knew how beneficial
the Holy Temple was for them, they would have
surrounded it with fortifications in order to guard it.

BAMIDBAR RABAH

An exegetical
commentary on the first
seven chapters of the
book of Numbers and a
homiletic commentary
on the rest of the
book. The first part
of *Bamidbar Rabah* is
notable for its inclusion
of esoteric material;
the second half is
essentially identical to
Midrash Tanchuma on
the book of Numbers.
It was first printed in
Constantinople in 1512,
together with four other
midrashic works on
the other four books
of the Pentateuch.

A tour of "The Temple
Mount" with **Rabbi
Cheski Edelman:**
myjli.com/canhappen

House for All Nations

Isaiah 2:1–3

הַדָּבָר אֲשֶׁר חָזָה יְשַׁעְיָהוּ בֶּן אָמוֹץ עַל יְהוּדָה וִירוּשָׁלָיִם. וְהָיָה בְּאַחֲרִית הַיָּמִים נָכוֹן יִהְיֶה הַר בֵּית ה׳ בְּראשׁ הֶהָרִים, וְנִשָּׂא מִגְּבָעוֹת, וְנָהֲרוּ אֵלָיו כָּל הַגּוֹיִם. וְהָלְכוּ עַמִּים רַבִּים וְאָמְרוּ לְכוּ וְנַעֲלֶה אֶל הַר ה׳ אֶל בֵּית אֱלֹקֵי יַעֲקֹב, וְיוֹרֵנוּ מִדְּרָכָיו וְנֵלְכָה בְּאֹרְחֹתָיו.

The word that Isaiah, son of Amoz, prophesied concerning Judah and Jerusalem:

It shall be at the end of the days that the mountain of G-d's home shall be firmly established at the top of the mountains. It shall be raised above the hills, and all the nations shall stream to it.

Many peoples shall go, and they shall say, "Come, let us go up to G-d's mountain, to the house of the G-d of Jacob, and let Him teach us of His ways, and we will go in His paths."

TEXT 6

Two Meanings of Day

Mishnah, Sanhedrin 10:3

עֲשֶׂרֶת הַשְּׁבָטִים אֵינָן עֲתִידִין לַחֲזֹר, שֶׁנֶּאֱמַר "וַיַּשְׁלִכֵם אֶל אֶרֶץ אַחֶרֶת כַּיּוֹם הַזֶּה": מַה הַיּוֹם הַזֶּה הוֹלֵךְ וְאֵינוֹ חוֹזֵר, אַף הֵם הוֹלְכִים וְאֵינָם חוֹזְרִים. דִּבְרֵי רַבִּי עֲקִיבָא.

רַבִּי אֱלִיעֶזֶר אוֹמֵר: "כַּיּוֹם הַזֶּה" - מַה הַיּוֹם הַזֶּה מַאֲפִיל וּמֵאִיר, אַף עֲשֶׂרֶת הַשְּׁבָטִים שֶׁאָפֵל לָהֶן, כָּךְ עָתִיד לְהָאִיר לָהֶן.

The ten tribes are not destined to return, as it is stated, "G-d cast them into another land, like this day" (DEUTERONOMY 29:27). Just as the day passes, never to return, so have they gone into exile, never to return. This is the view of Rabbi Akiva.

Rabbi Eliezer stated, "Like this day"—just as the day darkens and then brightens, so the ten tribes who experience darkness will in the future experience light.

MISHNAH

The first authoritative work of Jewish law that was codified in writing. The Mishnah contains the oral traditions that were passed down from teacher to student; it supplements, clarifies, and systematizes the commandments of the Torah. Due to the continual persecution of the Jewish people, it became increasingly difficult to guarantee that these traditions would not be forgotten. Rabbi Yehudah Hanasi therefore redacted the Mishnah at the end of the 2nd century. It serves as the foundation for the Talmud.

FIGURE 6.2

Israel Divided by Tribes

Passover *Haggadah*, Amsterdam 1695,
Library of Agudas Chasidei Chabad

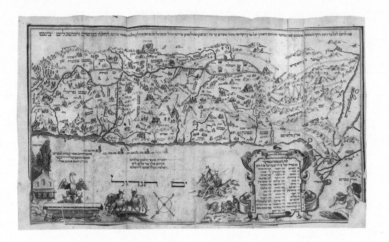

TEXT 7

Judicial Restoration

Isaiah 1:26

וְאָשִׁיבָה שֹׁפְטַיִךְ כְּבָרִאשֹׁנָה וְיֹעֲצַיִךְ כְּבַתְּחִלָּה,
אַחֲרֵי כֵן יִקָּרֵא לָךְ עִיר הַצֶּדֶק קִרְיָה נֶאֱמָנָה.

I will restore your judges as in the days
of old, and your counselors as in the
beginning. Afterward you shall be called
the City of Righteousness, Faithful City.

In "Woman of the World—The
Feminine Era," **Mrs. Rochel
Goldman** provides a
perspective-altering lecture
on the spiritual evolution of
the world and the key role
of the woman in bringing
the universe to completion:
myjli.com/canhappen

TEXT 8

Tiberias First

Maimonides, *Mishneh Torah,* Laws of Sanhedrin 14:12

בַּתְּחִלָּה כְּשֶׁנִּבְנְבָה בֵּית הַמִּקְדָּשׁ הָיוּ בֵּית דִּין הַגָּדוֹל יוֹשְׁבִין בְּלִשְׁכַּת הַגָּזִית . . . וּכְשֶׁנִּתְקַלְקְלָה הַשּׁוּרָה גָּלוּ מִמָּקוֹם לְמָקוֹם. וְלַעֲשָׂרָה מְקוֹמוֹת גָּלוּ, וְסוֹפָן לִטְבֶרְיָא, וּמִשָּׁם לֹא עָמַד בֵּית דִּין גָּדוֹל עַד עַתָּה. וְקַבָּלָה הִיא שֶׁבִּטְבֶרְיָא עֲתִידִין לַחֲזֹר תְּחִלָּה וּמִשָּׁם נֶעֶתָקִין לַמִּקְדָּשׁ.

Originally, when the Holy Temple was built, the Supreme Sanhedrin would hold session in its Chamber of Hewn Stone. . . . When things went awry, the Sanhedrin went into exile, convening in various locations—ten in total—the last being Tiberias. Since then, the Sanhedrin has not reconvened. We have a tradition that the Sanhedrin will be restored in Tiberias first, and from there it will relocate to the Temple.

III. ARMAGEDDON?

One of the more curious Redemption topics is a great war that apparently will then occur, as described in several prophecies. Surprisingly at first, Maimonides offers little information on this subject. It is left to us to uncover why that is, and also to probe the reasoning of the ancient Jewish sage, Rabbi Shimon (2nd century CE), who believed that there is not much reason for concern.

**G-D'S JUDGMENT
UPON GOG**
c. 1851–1852, Asher Brown Durand,
oil on canvas, Chrysler Museum
of Art, Norfolk, Va.

TEXT 9

The Unknown

Maimonides, *Mishneh Torah,* Laws of Kings 12:2

יֵרָאֶה מִפְּשׁוּטָן שֶׁל דִּבְרֵי הַנְּבִיאִים. שֶׁבִּתְחִלַּת יְמוֹת הַמָּשִׁיחַ
תִּהְיֶה מִלְחֶמֶת גּוֹג וּמָגוֹג. וְשֶׁקֹּדֶם מִלְחֶמֶת גּוֹג וּמָגוֹג
יַעֲמֹד נָבִיא לְיַשֵּׁר יִשְׂרָאֵל וּלְהָכִין לִבָּם. שֶׁנֶּאֱמַר (מַלְאָכִי
ג, כג), "הִנֵּה אָנֹכִי שֹׁלֵחַ לָכֶם אֵת אֵלִיָּה" וְגוֹ' . . . וְיֵשׁ מִן
הַחֲכָמִים שֶׁאוֹמְרִים שֶׁקֹּדֶם בִּיאַת הַמָּשִׁיחַ יָבוֹא אֵלִיָּהוּ.

וְכָל אֵלּוּ הַדְּבָרִים וְכַיּוֹצֵא בָּהֶן לֹא יֵדַע אָדָם אֵיךְ יִהְיוּ
עַד שֶׁיִּהְיוּ. שֶׁדְּבָרִים סְתוּמִין הֵן אֵצֶל הַנְּבִיאִים.

A straightforward interpretation of the prophets'
words appears to imply that the war of Gog and
Magog will occur at the beginning of the messianic
age. Before this war, a prophet will arise to inspire
Israel to be upright and to prepare their hearts, as it
is stated (MALACHI 3:23), "Behold, I am sending
you Elijah." . . . Some sages stated that Elijah's
coming will precede the coming of Mashiach.

All these and similar matters cannot be definitely
known until they occur, for these matters
are not clarified in the prophets' words.

TEXT 10

Priorities

Talmud, Berachot 7b

BABYLONIAN TALMUD

A literary work of monumental proportions that draws upon the legal, spiritual, intellectual, ethical, and historical traditions of Judaism. The 37 tractates of the Babylonian Talmud contain the teachings of the Jewish sages from the period after the destruction of the 2nd Temple through the 5th century CE. It has served as the primary vehicle for the transmission of the Oral Law and the education of Jews over the centuries; it is the entry point for all subsequent legal, ethical, and theological Jewish scholarship.

וְאָמַר רַבִּי יוֹחָנָן מִשׁוּם רַבִּי שִׁמְעוֹן בֶּן יוֹחַי: קָשָׁה תַּרְבּוּת רָעָה בְּתוֹךְ בֵּיתוֹ שֶׁל אָדָם יוֹתֵר מִמִּלְחֶמֶת גּוֹג וּמָגוֹג, שֶׁנֶּאֱמַר (תְּהִלִּים ג, א): מִזְמוֹר לְדָוִד בְּבָרְחוֹ מִפְּנֵי אַבְשָׁלוֹם בְּנוֹ, וּכְתִיב בַּתְרֵיה (ג, ב) "ה' מָה רַבּוּ צָרָי רַבִּים קָמִים עָלָי". וְאִלּוּ גַּבֵּי מִלְחֶמֶת גּוֹג וּמָגוֹג כְּתִיב (תְּהִלִּים ב, א): "לָמָּה רָגְשׁוּ גוֹיִם וּלְאֻמִּים יֶהְגּוּ רִיק", וְאִלּוּ "מָה רַבּוּ צָרָי" לֹא כְּתִיב.

Rabbi Yochanan taught in the name of Rabbi Shimon bar Yochai:

Suffering a wayward child at home is more difficult than the war of Gog and Magog.

For it is stated, "A Psalm of David, when he fled from his son, Absalom" (PSALMS 3:1). And the next verse reads: "G-d! How numerous are my enemies! Many have risen against me!" (PSALMS 3:2).

By contrast, regarding the war of Gog and Magog it is stated (PSALMS 2:1), "Why are the nations in an uproar? Why do the peoples speak emptiness?" It does not state, "How numerous are my enemies!"

QUESTION

What is Rabbi Shimon trying to convey in this text?

**ON THE THEME OF
THE LAST JUDGMENT**
1913, Wassily Kandinsky,
oil on canvas

IV. PHYSICAL BLESSINGS

Many of the headline biblical Redemption prophecies pertain to material blessings—such as health and abundance—that will prevail in messianic times. We revisit Maimonides for insight as to why material blessings are critical for the Redemption's purpose.

FIGURE 6.3

Messianic Prophecies

THERE WILL BE NO MORE . . .	BIBLICAL SOURCE
WAR	Isaiah 2:4; Micah 4:3
CRIME	Isaiah 60:18
POVERTY	Zechariah 14:21
SCARCITY	Isaiah 30:23
DISABILITY	Isaiah 35:5-6

TEXT 11

Physical Blessings

Maimonides, Mishnah, Sanhedrin, Chapter 10, Introduction

אֲבָל יְמוֹת הַמָּשִׁיחַ הוּא זְמַן שֶׁבּוֹ תַּחֲזֹר הַמַּלְכוּת
לְיִשְׂרָאֵל, וְיַחְזְרוּ לְאֶרֶץ יִשְׂרָאֵל . . . אֶלָּא שֶׁבְּאוֹתָם
הַיָּמִים תּוּקַל עַל בְּנֵי אָדָם פַּרְנָסָתָם מְאֹד, עַד שֶׁכְּשֶׁיַּעֲבֹד
הָאָדָם אֵיזֶה עֲבוֹדָה מוּעֶטֶת שֶׁתִּהְיֶה יַשִּׂיג תּוֹעֶלֶת
גְּדוֹלָה. וְזֶהוּ עִנְיָן אָמְרָם "עֲתִידָה אֶרֶץ יִשְׂרָאֵל לְהוֹצִיא
גְּלוּסְקָאוֹת וּכְלֵי מֵילַת" (תַּלְמוּד בַּבְלִי, שַׁבָּת ל, ב) . . .

וְהַתּוֹעֶלֶת הַגְּדוֹלָה בְּאוֹתוֹ הַזְּמַן הִיא שֶׁנָּנוּחַ מִשִּׁעְבּוּד
מַלְכוּת הָרְשָׁעָה הָעוֹצֶרֶת בַּעֲדֵנוּ מִלַּעֲשׂוֹת הַטּוֹב, וְתִרְבֶּה
הַדַּעַת כְּמוֹ שֶׁאָמַר "כִּי מָלְאָה הָאָרֶץ דֵּעָה אֶת ה'" (יְשַׁעְיָהוּ
יא, ט). וְיִפָּסְקוּ הַקְּרָבוֹת וְהַמִּלְחָמוֹת כְּמוֹ שֶׁאָמַר "וְלֹא
יִשְׂאוּ גוֹי אֶל גוֹי חֶרֶב" (מִיכָה ד, ב) . . . וְגַם יַאַרְכוּ חַיֵּי בְּנֵי
אָדָם, כִּי בְּהֶעְדֵּר הַדְּאָגוֹת וְהַצָּרוֹת יֶאֶרְכוּ הַחַיִּים . . .

וְאֵין אָנוּ מִתְאַוִּים לִימוֹת הַמָּשִׁיחַ לֹא כְּדֵי שֶׁיִּרְבּוּ
הַתְּבוּאוֹת וְהַנְּכָסִים, לֹא כְּדֵי שֶׁנִּרְכַּב עַל סוּסִים וְנִשְׁתֶּה
בִּכְלֵי זֶמֶר כְּמוֹ שֶׁחוֹשְׁבִים מְבֻלְבְּלֵי הַדֵּעוֹת, אֶלָּא נִתְאַוּוּ
לָהֶם הַנְּבִיאִים וְנִשְׁתּוֹקְקוּ לָהֶם הַחֲסִידִים בִּגְלַל מָה
שֶׁיִּהְיֶה שָׁם מִקִּבּוּץ הַצַּדִּיקִים, וְהַהִתְנַהֲגוּת הַטּוֹבָה
וְהַחָכְמָה . . . וְקִיּוּם כָּל תּוֹרַת מֹשֶׁה בְּלִי דְאָגוֹת וְלֹא פַּחַד.

The messianic era is defined as the time in which
sovereignty will revert to Israel, and the Jewish
people will return to the Land of Israel. . . . In
those days, it will be extremely easy for people to

make a living; a minimum of labor will produce tremendous benefits. This is the meaning of our sages' statement that, "in the future, the Land of Israel will bring forth ready baked rolls and fine woolen garments" (TALMUD, SHABBAT 30B). . . .

The great benefit of that era is that we will experience respite from the oppression that prevents us from doing good. There will be a widespread increase of wisdom, as it is stated, "For the earth will be filled with the knowledge of G-d" (ISAIAH 11:9). War and battle will cease, as it is stated, "Nation will not lift up sword against nation" (MICHA 4:12). . . . The human lifespan will be lengthened as a result of the absence of stress and suffering. . . .

We do not long and hope for the messianic era simply because we desire an abundance of produce and property, or because we wish to ride horses, or drink wine to the accompaniment of music, as some confused people think. Rather, our prophets and pious yearned for that era because then the righteous will assemble, and good conduct and wisdom will prevail. . . . It will be possible then to observe the entire Torah without worry or fear.

V. RESURRECTION

The biblical prophecies and Talmudic teachings regarding the revival of the dead apparently contradict Maimonides's model of the Redemption. To address this concern, Maimonides authored an epistle that expresses a more nuanced approach concerning Redemption era miracles.

This course was heavily influenced by Maimonides's writings. It is therefore appropriate to lend Maimonides the honor of concluding this course on the Redemption with his oft-quoted motivational teaching regarding our efforts to bring global redemption into actuality.

TEXT 12

We'll Know Then

Maimonides, *Epistle on Resurrection*

וְדַע, שֶׁאֵלּוּ הַיִּעוּדִים וְכַיּוֹצֵא בָּהֶם אֲשֶׁר נֹאמַר שֶׁהֵם מָשָׁל
אֵין דְּבָרֵינוּ זֶה גְּזֵרָה, שֶׁהֲרֵי לֹא בָּאַתְנוּ מֵהַשֵּׁם נְבוּאָה
שֶׁהוֹדִיעָתְנוּ שֶׁהוּא מָשָׁל, וְלֹא מָצָאנוּ קַבָּלָה לַחֲכָמִים
מֵהַנְּבִיאִים שֶׁיְּבָאֲרוּ בָּהּ בְּחֶלְקֵי אֵלּוּ הַדְּבָרִים שֶׁהֵם מָשָׁל.

וְאָמְנָם הֱבִיאָנוּ אֶל זֶה הָעִנְיָן אֲבָאֲרֵהוּ לָךְ, וְהוּא הִשְׁתַּדְלוּתֵנוּ . . .
לְקַבֵּץ בֵּין הַתּוֹרָה וְהַמֻּשְׂכָּל, וְנַנְהִיג הַדְּבָרִים עַל סֵדֶר טִבְעִי
אֶפְשָׁר בְּכָל זֶה. אֶלָּא מָה שֶׁהִתְבָּאֵר בּוֹ שֶׁהוּא מוֹפֵת וְלֹא
יִתָּכֵן לְפָרֵשׁ כְּלָל, אָז נִצְטָרֵךְ לוֹמַר שֶׁהוּא מוֹפֵת . . .

סוֹף דָּבָר, כָּל אֵלֶּה הֵם דְּבָרִים שֶׁאֵינָם פִּנּוֹת הַתּוֹרָה,
וְאֵין לְהַקְפִּיד אֵיךְ יַאֲמִינוּ בָּהֶם, וְצָרִיךְ שֶׁיַּמְתִּין הָאָדָם
לְגוּף הָאֱמוּנָה בְּאֵלּוּ הַדְּבָרִים, עַד אֲשֶׁר יֵרָאוּ בִּמְהֵרָה
בְיָמֵינוּ, וְאָז יִתְבָּאֵר אִם הֵם מָשָׁל אוֹ מוֹפֵת.

It is important to realize that when I stated that certain prophecies are to be understood allegorically, this is not absolute. No prophetic communication informed me that they are allegorical, nor did I receive a tradition from the sages and prophets that these particular matters are parables.

Let me explain what brought me to the allegorical approach. . . . I strive to bring harmony between the Torah and human intellect, which is why I explain things in a natural way whenever possible. However, when it is self-evident that the connotation is miraculous indeed, and it is not possible to interpret otherwise, I say that it is a miracle. . . .

The bottom line is that regarding specific prophecies about the Redemption that do not involve the fundamentals of our Jewish faith, it matters not whether one believes that they are literal or allegorical. We will have to wait for their realization—may it occur speedily in our days!—to discover whether these statements refer to actual miracles or are simply allegories for natural changes.

TEXT 13

Two Premises

Maimonides, *Epistle on Resurrection*

שֶׁזֹּאת תְּחִיַּת הַמֵּתִים אָמְנָם תִּנְהַג מִנְהַג הַמּוֹפֵת כְּמוֹ
שֶׁבֵּאַרְנוּ, וְהָאֱמָנַת מָה שֶׁזֶּה דַרְכּוֹ לֹא תִּהְיֶה רַק בְּסִפּוּר הַנָּבִיא.

וְהָיוּ בְּנֵי אָדָם כֻּלָּם בַּזְּמַן הַהוּא . . . הַמַּכְזִיבִים הַגִּיעַ הַנְּבוּאָה
מֵאֵת הַשֵּׁם לִבְנֵי אָדָם. וְכֵן תִּתְחַיֵּב לָהֶם לְפִי אֱמוּנָתָם הַכְזָבַת
הַמּוֹפְתִים, וְיִחֲסוּ אוֹתָם לְכִשּׁוּף וּלְתַחְבּוּלָה. הֲלֹא תִרְאֶה
אוֹתָם מִשְׁתַּדְּלִים לַחֲלֹק עַל מוֹפֵת מֹשֶׁה רַבֵּנוּ עָלָיו הַשָּׁלוֹם
בְּלַהֲטֵיהֶם "וַיַּשְׁלִיכוּ אִישׁ (אֶת) מַטֵּהוּ" (שְׁמוֹת ז, יב), וַהֲלֹא
תִרְאֶה אֵיךְ אָמְרוּ מַתְמִיהִים (דְּבָרִים ה, כא) "הַיּוֹם הַזֶּה רָאִינוּ
כִּי יְדַבֵּר אֱלֹקִים אֶת הָאָדָם וָחָי", הוֹרָה שֶׁהָיְתָה הַנְּבוּאָה
אֶצְלָם מִכַּת הַנִּמְנָע, וְאֵיךְ יְסֻפַּר לְמִי שֶׁלֹּא הִתְבָּאֲרָה אֶצְלוֹ
הַנְּבוּאָה בְּדָבָר שֶׁאֵין רָאוּי עָלָיו אֶלָּא הַאֲמָנַת הַנָּבִיא, וְהוּא גַם
כֵּן נִמְנָע אֶצְלָם לְגַמְרֵי לְפִי אֱמוּנָתָם בְּקַדְמוּת הָעוֹלָם, כִּי לוּלֵי
הַמּוֹפְתִים לֹא הָיְתָה אֶצְלֵנוּ תְּחִיַּת הַמֵּתִים מִכַּת הָאֶפְשָׁר.

וְכַאֲשֶׁר רָצָה הַשֵּׁם יִתְעַלֶּה לָתֵת תּוֹרָה לִבְנֵי אָדָם . . . חִדֵּשׁ
הַמּוֹפְתִים הַגְּדוֹלִים הַכְּתוּבִים בְּכָל הַתּוֹרָה, עַד שֶׁהִתְאַמְּתוּ
בָּהֶם נְבוּאַת הַנְּבִיאִים וְחִדּוּשׁ הָעוֹלָם . . . וְלֹא הוֹצִיאָם
מֵעִנְיְנֵי הָעוֹלָם הַזֶּה בַּגְּמוּל וּבָעֹנֶשׁ וּמֵהָעִנְיָן אֲשֶׁר הוּא
בַּטֶּבַע . . . וְלֹא נִכְנַס לְזוּלַת זֶה מֵעִנְיַן הַתְּחִיָּה. וְהִתְמִיד
הָעִנְיָן כֵּן עַד שֶׁנִּתְחַזְּקוּ אֵלּוּ הַפִּנּוֹת וְהִתְאַמְּתוּ בְּהֶמְשֵׁךְ
הַדּוֹרוֹת, וְלֹא נִשְׁאַר סָפֵק בִּנְבוּאוֹת הַנְּבִיאִים וּבְחִדּוּשׁ
הַמּוֹפְתִים. וְאַחֲרֵי כֵן סִפְּרוּ לָנוּ הַנְּבִיאִים מָה שֶׁהוֹדִיעָם
ה' יִתְעַלֶּה מֵעִנְיַן תְּחִיַּת הַמֵּתִים וְהָיָה קַל לְקַבְּלוֹ.

The Resurrection of the Dead will occur as
a miraculous event, as we have explained.
However, the credibility of such an event can
only be based on the words of a prophet.

Now, at the time of the giving of the Torah, nearly
all of humankind . . . denied the transmission of
prophecy from G-d to humans. They also denied
that G-d could perform miracles, considering
them instead acts of magic or trickery. Indeed, the
Egyptians denied that Moses performed G-dly
miracles and tried to show that they could turn
sticks into snakes by other means (EXODUS
7:12). The Jews themselves were influenced by
this worldview, evidenced by their expressing
astonishment that G-d revealed Himself to them at
Mount Sinai (DEUTERONOMY 5:21)—indicating
that they had considered prophecy impossible.
How then could such a miraculous event that relies
exclusively on belief in prophecy be conveyed to
those who were not ready to accept the concept
of prophecy or the concept of a miracle?

When G-d wished to give us the Torah . . . He
first had to produce the great miracles recorded
throughout the Torah to authenticate thereby
the prophecy of the prophets and the possibility
of miracles. . . . For that reason, at this stage

G-d only divulged the concept of reward and punishment that occurs within the scope of nature. . . . G-d did not mention anything about resurrection. This continued until, after the passage of generations, the belief in prophecy and miracles became verified and there remained no doubt about their truth. At that point, the prophets shared with us that which G-d had informed them regarding the Resurrection of the Dead. By that time, it was easy to accept this belief.

TEXT 14

One Act

Maimonides, *Mishneh Torah*, Laws of Repentance 3:4

צָרִיךְ כָּל אָדָם שֶׁיִּרְאֶה עַצְמוֹ כָּל הַשָּׁנָה כֻּלָּהּ כְּאִלּוּ
חֶצְיוֹ זַכַּאי וְחֶצְיוֹ חַיָּב, וְכֵן כָּל הָעוֹלָם חֶצְיוֹ זַכַּאי וְחֶצְיוֹ
חַיָּב . . . עָשָׂה מִצְוָה אַחַת הֲרֵי הִכְרִיעַ אֶת עַצְמוֹ וְאֶת כָּל
הָעוֹלָם כֻּלּוֹ לְכַף זְכוּת וְגָרַם לוֹ וְלָהֶם תְּשׁוּעָה וְהַצָּלָה.

You should view yourself at all times as equally balanced
with merits and faults, and view the world similarly—
equally balanced with merits and faults. . . . Therefore,
if you perform one mitzvah, you tip the balance—
your own, and that of all humankind—and effect
personal and global deliverance and salvation.

**WOMAN HOLDING
A BALANCE** (DETAIL)
c. 1664, Johannes Vermeer,
oil and mixed media on canvas,
National Gallery of Art,
Washington, D.C.

KEY POINTS

1   In his halachic code, Maimonides states that we should not presume that the world's nature will change in the messianic era. Prophecies implying otherwise are to be understood as allegories. That said, this era *will* be marked by huge changes.

2   One radical change: a complete end to antisemitism and total independence for the Jewish people.

3   Mashiach will rebuild the Jerusalem Temple to the applause of all nations, who will recognize the benefit that G-d's sacred home offers the entire world.

4   Non-Jews will also experience the Redemption. The Jewish Redemption is a universal concept.

5   Building the Temple will cause the global ingathering of all Jews, who will recognize its great sanctity and desire a share in its environs.

6   The return of the Ten Lost Tribes is a matter of Talmudic dispute. Some attribute the uncertainty to the tribes' assumed assimilation. Regardless, it is undisputed that all twelve tribes will be represented in the Land of Israel.

7   The possibility of observing all of the Torah's laws will return, due to the existence of the Jewish monarch and Temple, and the reality of Jews living securely on their land.

8   The Sanhedrin, forced to disband centuries ago, will return. One resultant change will be that the Jewish calendar will revert to a system of observation.

9   The Jewish prophets mention a great war associated with the messianic era, but the prophecies are difficult to interpret with any certainty. Rabbi Shimon demonstrates (by applying Psalms 2 to this war) that the threat and tumult will amount to nothing.

10 The cessation of war, crime, poverty, scarcity, and disability will enable us to fully fulfill the purpose for which G-d created us without pain or worry.

11 In his *Epistle on Resurrection*, Maimonides clarified that nature-altering miracles may indeed occur in the messianic era. We are aware of one—the Resurrection of the Dead—but others are possible as well.

12 The Resurrection is important because it will enable all who participated in making this world into a home for G-d to share in the magnificent outcome. It will also demonstrate the complete spiritual transformation of the body and, by extension, the entire physical world.

ADDITIONAL READINGS

The Messianic Era

by Rabbi J. Immanuel Schochet

**RABBI JACOB IMMANUEL
SCHOCHET, PHD
1935–2013**

Torah scholar and philosopher. Rabbi
Schochet was born in Switzerland.
Rabbi Schochet was a renowned
authority on kabbalah and Jewish law
and authored more than 30 books
on Jewish philosophy and mysticism.
He also served as professor of
philosophy at Humber College in
Toronto, Canada. Rabbi Schochet was
a member of the executive committee
of the Rabbinical Alliance of America
and of the Central Committee of
Chabad-Lubavitch Rabbis, and
served as the halachic guide for the
Rohr Jewish Learning Institute.

A. Restoration of the *Bet Hamikdash*

Mashiach shall restore the *Bet Hamikdash* in Jerusalem.[1] This refers to the third *Bet Hamikdash* that will stand forever, in fulfillment of the Divine prophecy of Ezekiel 37:26-28: "I shall give My Sanctuary in their midst forever. My dwelling-place shall be over them. . . . The nations shall know that I am G-d who sanctifies Israel, when My Sanctuary shall be in the midst of them forever."[2]

B. Ingathering of the Exiles of Israel

Through Mashiach shall be effected the ingathering of all the exiles of Israel:[3]

Deuteronomy 30:3–4: "G-d, your G-d, shall bring back your captivity . . . and He will return and gather you from all the nations whither G-d, your G-d, has scattered you. If your banished shall be at the utmost end of the heavens, G-d, your G-d, shall gather you from there, and He shall take you from there."

Isaiah 11:11–12,16: "It shall be on that day that G-d shall again set His hand for a second time to acquire the remnant of His people that shall remain from Assyria and from Egypt, from Pathros and from Cush and from Elam, from Shinar and from Chamat and from the islands of the sea. . . .

There shall be a highway for the remnant of His people that shall remain from Assyria, as there was for Israel on the day they went up from the land of Egypt."

Isaiah 43:5-6: "Fear not, for I am with you; I will bring your seed from the east and gather you from the west. I shall say to the north, 'Give up,' and to the south, 'Do not hold back, bring My sons from far and My daughters from the end of the earth.'"

Amos 9:14-15: "I shall return the captivity of My people Israel and they shall build the waste cities and settle. . . . I shall plant them upon their land, and they shall no more be plucked out of their land that I have given them, says G-d, your G-d."

Jeremiah 23:7-8: "Therefore behold, days shall come, says G-d, that they shall no longer say, 'As G-d lives who has taken up the children of Israel from the land of Egypt;' but 'As G-d lives who has taken up and brought the seed of the House of Israel from the North Country and from all the countries where He had banished them,' and they shall dwell in their land."

Ezekiel 39:25, 27–29: ". . . Now I shall bring back the captivity of Jacob and I shall have compassion on the whole House of Israel, and I shall be zealous for My holy Name . . . When I shall have returned them from the nations and gathered them from the lands of their ene-mies . . . They shall know that I am G-d, their G-d, in that I exiled them to the nations and gathered them unto their land, and I will not leave any one of them there. I will no more hide My face from them, as I will pour out My spirit upon the House of Israel. . . ."[4]

The Ten Tribes of the Northern Kingdom of Israel, exiled by the Assyrians before the destruction of the first *Bet Hamikdash* (II Kings, ch. 17), and dispersed beyond the river Sambation and the 'Mountains of Darkness,' will also return.[5]

This Divine promise of the return and restoration of Israel is unconditional. It will occur even if the people should not want to return:

"That which arises in your mind shall not come to pass, namely that which you say, 'We shall be like the nations, like the families of the countries, to serve wood and stone.' As I live, says the L-rd G-d, I shall surely rule over them with a mighty hand and with an outstretched arm and with fury poured out. I shall take you out from the nations and gather you from the lands in which you were scattered, with a mighty hand, an outstretched arm and with fury poured out . . . I shall pass you under the rod and bring you into the covenant . . . For on My holy mountain, on the mountain of the height of Israel, says the L-rd G-d, there shall all of the whole House of Israel serve Me . . . when I bring you out from the nations and gather you from the lands where you were scattered, and I shall be sanctified in you in the eyes of the nations. You shall know that I am G-d when I bring you to the earth of Israel, to the land about which I raised My hand to give it to your fathers." (Ezekiel 20:32–37, 40–42)

"Therefore say to the House of Israel, Thus said the L-rd G-d: I am not doing (this) for your sake, House of Israel, but for My holy Name which you profaned among the nations wither you came. I shall sanctify My great Name that was profaned among the nations, that you profaned in their midst, and the nations shall know that I am G-d, says the L-rd G-d, when I shall be sanctified in you before their eyes. I shall take you from the nations, and I shall gather you from all the lands, and I shall bring you to your land. I shall sprinkle pure waters upon you and you shall be purified from all your sins, and I will purify you from all your idols. . . ." (Ezekiel 36:22–25)

C. End to Evil and Sin

The Messianic era will mark the end of evil and sin:

Ezekiel 37:23: "They shall not defile themselves anymore with their idols and with their abominations and with all their transgressions. . . ."

Zephaniah 3:13: "The remnant of Israel will not do any wrong, and they will not speak lies nor shall a deceitful tongue be found in their mouth."

Zechariah 13:2: "It shall be in that day . . . that I shall cut off the names of the idols from the earth and they shall no longer be remembered; and I shall also remove from the earth the [false] prophets and the spirit of impurity."

Malachi 3:19: "For behold the day comes burning like a furnace, and all the wanton sinners and everyone that does wickedness shall be stubble . . . that to them shall not be left root and branch."

Isaiah 60:21: "Your people shall all be righteous, they shall inherit the land forever . . ."

Jeremiah 50:20: "In those days and in that time, says G-d, the iniquity of Israel shall be searched for but it will not be, and the sins of Judah but they shall not be found . . ."[6]

D. Awareness and Knowledge of G-d

The Messianic era will be a time of universal awareness, per-ception and knowledge of G-d:

Isaiah 11:9: (cf. Habakuk 2:14): ". . . the earth shall be full of knowledge of G-d as the waters cover the sea."

Isaiah 40:5: "The glory of G-d shall be revealed, and all flesh shall see together that the mouth of G-d has spoken."[7]

Isaiah 52:8: ". . . for eye to eye they shall see as G-d returns to Zion."

Jeremiah 31:32–33: ". . . I shall put My teaching in their inward parts and write it in their heart, and I shall be to them for G-d and they shall be to Me for a people. They shall no longer teach one another, and a man his brother, saying 'Know G-d,' for they shall all know Me from the least of them to the greatest of them . . ."

The Divine spirit will be upon the people, endowing them with the power of prophecy and vision:

Joel 3:1–2: ". . . I shall pour out My spirit upon all flesh, and your sons and your daughters shall prophesy, your elders shall dream dreams, your young shall see visions. In those days I shall pour out My spirit also upon the servants and handmaids."[8]

E. Universal Worship of G-d

Mashiach shall mend the whole world so that all shall serve G-d in unity:[9]

Zephaniah 3:9: "For then I shall turn to the peoples a pure tongue that all shall call upon the Name of G-d to serve Him with one consent."

Isaiah 2:2–3 and Michah 4:1–2: ". . . The mountain of G-d's House shall be established at the top of the mountains and it shall be raised above the hills, and all the nations shall stream to it. Many peoples shall go and say, 'Come, let us go up to the mountain of G-d, to the House of the G-d of Jacob, and let him [Mashiach] teach us of His ways and we shall go in His paths;' for from Zion shall go forth Torah, and the word of G-d from Jerusalem."[10]

Zechariah 9:16: ". . . every one that is left of all the nations that came against Jerusalem shall go up from year to year to bow before the King, G-d. . . ."

Zechariah 14:9: "G-d shall be King over the entire earth. In that day G-d shall be One and His Name One."

F. Universal Peace and Harmony

The awareness and knowledge of G-d will remove the narrow-minded dispositions that lead to strife and war. It will be an era of peace and harmony in the Holy Land[11] and throughout the world:

Isaiah 2:4 and Michah 4:3: ". . . they shall beat their swords into plowshares and their spears into pruning-hooks. Nation shall not lift a sword against nation, nor shall they learn war any more." [Michah 4:4 continues: "Each man shall sit under his vine and under his fig-tree, and none shall make them afraid. . . ."]

Hosea 2:20: ". . . I shall break from the earth the bow, the sword and warfare, and I shall make them lie down securely."

Zechariah 9:10: ". . . the bow of war shall be cut off, and [Mashiach] shall speak peace unto the nations. . . ."

This new attitude of mankind will also be reflected in the animal world:

Isaiah 11:6–9: "The wolf shall dwell with the lamb and the leopard shall lie with the kid, and a calf with a lion's cub and a fatling together, and a small child shall lead them. The cow and the bear shall graze, their young ones shall lie down together, and the lion shall eat straw like cattle. An infant shall play over the hole of an asp, and the weaned child shall put out his hand over the eyeball of an adder. They will not harm or destroy on all My holy mountain, for the earth shall be full of the knowledge of G-d as the waters cover the sea."

Isaiah 65:25: "The wolf and the lamb shall feed together, and the lion shall eat straw like cattle, dust shall be the serpent's food. They shall not harm nor destroy in all My holy mountain, says G-d."[12]

G. Resurrection of the Dead

"Your dead shall be revived, my corpses shall arise; awaken and sing you who dwell in the dust, for a dew of lights is your dew. . . ." (Isaiah 26:19)

"Behold I will open your graves and raise you from your graves, My people; and I will bring you into the Land of Israel. You shall know that I am G-d when I open your graves and when I revive you from your graves, My people. I shall put My spirit into you and you will live, and I will place you upon your land, and you will know that I, G-d, have spoken and done, says G-d." (Ezekiel 37:12–14)

"Many of them that sleep in the land of dust shall awake. . . ." (Daniel 12:2)[13]

H. Blissful Utopia: End to Disease and Death

The Messianic era will witness ultimate physical and spiritual bliss. All will be healed.[14] The blind, the deaf and the dumb, the lame, whosoever has any blemish or disability, shall be healed from all their disabilities: "The eyes of the blind shall be clearsighted, and the ears of the deaf shall be opened. . . . the lame shall leap as a hart and the tongue of the dumb shall sing. . . ." (Isaiah 35:5–6).[15] Death itself shall cease, as it is said, "Death shall be swallowed up forever and G-d shall wipe the tears from every face. . . ." (Isaiah 25:8)[16]

There will be a life of ease.[17] Our physical needs will be taken care of by others, as it is said, "Strangers shall stand and feed your flocks and aliens shall be your plowmen and your vinedressers." (Isaiah 61:5)[18]

The earth will manifest extraordinary fertility, yielding an overabundance of every kind of produce, and trees growing ripe fruits every day.[19] Zion's wilderness will be made "to be like Eden, and her desert like the garden of G-d" (Isaiah 51:3). "I will call for the grain and increase it. . . . and I will increase the fruit of the tree and the produce of the field. . . ." (Ezekiel 36:29–30) ". . . The plowman shall overtake the reaper, and the treader of grapes him who sows seed; and the mountains shall drip sweet wine, and all the hills shall melt." (Amos 9:13)[20]

"At that time there will be neither famine nor war, neither envy nor strife. All good things will be bestowed in abundance, and all delicacies will be accessible like dust."[21]

The wondrous events and conditions of the Messianic era will completely overshadow all and any miracles that happened before then, even those associated with the exodus from Egypt.[22]

Even so, these Divine blessings are not an end in themselves. They are but a means towards a higher goal:

Our longing for the Messianic era is not for the sake of dominating the world, to rule over the heathens, or to be exalted by the nations. Nor is it that we might eat, drink and rejoice,[23] "have much produce and wealth, ride horses and indulge in wine and song, as thought by some confused people."[24]

It is, rather, to have relief from the powers that presently do not allow us to be preoccupied with Torah and *mitzvot* properly.[25] Our aspirations are to be free to devote ourselves to Torah and its wisdom, with no one to oppress and disturb us. We long for that time because there will be an assembly of the righteous, an era dominated by goodness, wisdom, knowledge and truth. It will be a time when the commandments of the Torah shall be observed without inertia, laziness or compulsion (other version: "worries, fear or compulsion").[26]

The sole preoccupation of the whole world will be to know G-d. The Israelites will be great sages: they will know things that are presently concealed, and will achieve knowledge of their Creator to the utmost capacity of human beings, as it is said, "The earth shall be full of the knowledge of G-d as the waters cover the sea." (Isaiah 11:9)[27]

ENDNOTES

[1] From some sources it appears that Mashiach will build the third *Bet Hamikdash* (*Vayikra Rabba* 9:6; *Bamidbar Rabba* 13:2; *Shir Rabba* end of ch. 4, etc.; followed by Rambam, *Hilchot Melachim* 11:1 and 4). From other sources it follows that the third *Bet Hamikdash* is built by the Almighty Himself (*Zohar* I:28a, 114a, 183b and III:221a etc. [and cf. *Zohar* II:240b!]; followed by Rashi and Tossafot on Sukah 41a, Rosh Hashanah 30a, and Shevu'ot 15b). Cf. *Torah Shelemah*, Beshalach 15:17 (especially note 211); and *Sha'arei Zohar* on Sukah 41a (see there; and R. Menachem M. Schneerson *shalita*, *Likkutei Sichot* Vol. XI, p. 98 note 61; Vol. XVII, p. 418; and Vol. XXVII, p. 204f.; for ways to reconcile the two views).

[2] See also Ezekiel ch. 40ff.; and cf. Isaiah 2:2f. cited below ch. II-E.

[3] See *Bereishit Rabba* 98:9; *Midrash Hagadol* on Genesis 49:11.

[4] Additional sources for the ingathering of the exiles are: Isaiah 27:12, 49:8–9, and 60:4; Jeremiah 30:2 and 31:7; Ezekiel 34:11–13 and 37:21; Zechariah 8:7–8; etc.

[5] Sanhedrin 110b; *Bamidbar Rabba* 16:25; *Tanchuma*, ed. Buber, *Shlach-Tossafot*:6 (and see the editor's notes there); *Pesikta Rabaty* 32:10 (ed. Friedmann, ch. 31). Cf. Ramban, *Sefer Hage'ulah*, *sha'ar* I.

[6] For further details on the eradication of evil, the evil inclination and Satan, see Sukah 52a; *Eliyahu Rabba* ch. 4; *Bereishit Rabba* 48:11; *Pesikta Rabaty* 33:4; and *Yalkut Shimoni*, I:133, on Genesis 33:13, p. 42a.

[7] "In the present world, the *Shechinah* manifests Itself only to certain individuals [prophets]; in the time to come, however, 'the glory of G-d shall be revealed and all flesh shall see together . . .';" *Vayikra Rabba* 1:14. The Messianic era will thus witness an empirical manifestation of Divinity even as occurred with the revelation at Sinai; see *Tanchuma*, Bamidbar: end of par. 17; and *Tanya*, ch. 36. Cf. *Sha'ar Ha'emunah*, ch. 25; and see note following.

[8] "The Holy One, blessed is He, said: 'In the present world [only] certain individuals prophesied; in the world to come, however, all Israel will be made prophets, as it is said, 'It shall come to pass afterwards that I shall pour out My spirit upon all flesh, and your sons and your daughters shall prophesy . . .';'" *Tanchuma*, Beha'alotecha: end of par. 16. Cf. *Tikunei Zohar* 18:36b; and above, in the previous note. Note *Igeret Teyman*, end of ch. 3, that there will be a restoration of prophecy even before the actual manifestation of Mashiach. Cf. *Likkutei Sichot*, vol. II: Balak, p. 588f.

[9] *Hilchot Melachim* 11:4

[10] See also Isaiah 60:14; and Zechariah 8:23.

[11] See Leviticus 25:18-19 and 26:5; Jeremiah 23:6 and 33:16; Ezekiel 28:26 and 34:25-28; Joel 4:17.

[12] See also Hosea 2:20.

[13] Resurrection of the Dead is another of the 13 fundamental Principles of the Faith (Rambam, Article 13), distinct from that of the Messianic redemption. It will occur after the redemption, the very last event of the Messianic era (see *Zohar* I:139a), thus in a way distinct from it. Even so, there are various stages in the process of resurrection itself, with some individuals rising before all others. Moses and Aaron, for example, will be present already in the very early period, when the *Bet Hamikdash* will be re-established, in order to guide the order and procedures of the Temple-service (see *Tossafot* on Pesachim 114b; and cf. *Devarim Rabba* 3:17 and similar passages). A number of other saints, too, will be revived at various stages prior to the general Resurrection of the Dead (see R. Joseph Albo, *Ikkarim* IV:35; R. David ibn Zimra, *Teshuvot Radvaz* III:no. 644; R. Daniel Tirani, *Ikrei Hadat* (*Ikrei Dinim*), vol. II: *Yoreh De'ah* 36:66; *Sdei Chemed*, *Kuntres Hakelalim*, s.v. *mem:klal* 218; and the sources cited there).For the whole subject of the resurrection, see especially Sanhedrin 90a-92b; Pirkei deR. Eliezer ch. 33–34; R. Saadiah Gaon, *Emunot Vede'ot*, sect. VII; Rambam, *Ma'amar Techiyat Hametim*; Ramban, *Sha'ar Hagemul*; R. Chasdai Crescas, *Or Hashem* III:4, ch. 1-4; and R. Menachem M. Schneerson *shalita*, *Teshuvot Ubi'urim*, ch. 8 and 11 (offering a comprehensive and systematic analysis of this subject).

[14] *Bereishit Rabba* 20:56

[15] *Bereishit Rabba* 95:1; *Tanchuma*, Vayigash:8 and Metzora:2 (and see ed. Buber, Vayigash:9 and Metzora:7).

[16] Pesachim 68a; *Shemot Rabba* 30:2. See also *Midrash Tehilim* 145:1.

[17] *Eliyahu Rabba* ch. 4.

[18] See also Isaiah 49:23 and 60:10-12.

[19] Shabbat 30b; Ketuvot 111b.

[20] Cf. Leviticus 26:5; and Joel 4:18, and see Vayikra Rabba 17:4, and Pesikta deR. Kahana, ch. VII, p. 65bf., and the notes there. See also Hosea 2:23f.Note that Amos 9:13 is one of the few Scriptural verses that contain all the letters of the aleph-bet. On the significance of this, see Hadar Zekeinim, R. Bachaya, and Ba'al Haturim, on Exodus 16:16; and R. Bachaya and Ba'al Haturim on Deuteronomy 4:34. Cf. below, note 99.

[21] *Hilchot Melachim* 12:5. Cf. *Midrash Tehilim* 87:3 ("gold and silver will be like dust").

[22] Jeremiah 23:7-8; Berachot 12bf. Note that in Rambam's view the Messianic era will not see a setting aside of the laws of nature, but "the world will follow its normal course . . . 'The only difference between the present world and the Messianic days is delivery from servitude to foreign powers' (Berachot 34b)." The prophecies of super-natural events and conditions are to be understood figuratively. (*Hilchot Melachim* 12:1-2; and cf. *Hilchot Teshuvah* 9:2) Even so, Rambam himself qualifies this view as a personal opinion and interpretation, allowing for the possibility that everything may be quite literal. (*Ma'amar Techiyat Hametim*, sect. 6. Cf. *Hilchot Melachim* 12:2 that no one is in a position to know the details of the events to occur until they have come to pass etc.) As noted by the commentaries on *Hilchot Melachim*, Rambam's view is fraught with many difficulties, as even he himself enumerates events and conditions (not the least of which would be the resurrection of the dead) which are clearly beyond the normal course of the laws of nature (cf. notes 22, 41, 51 and 68). One resolution to this problem is by distinguishing between two general periods in the Messianic era: a first stage following an essentially natural order, and a later stage marked by supra-natural events and conditions. See R. Yitzchak Abarbanel, *Yeshu'ot Meshicho, Iyun Hashlishi*: ch. 7. For a comprehensive analysis of this subject, see *Likkutei Sichot*, Vol. XXVII, pp. 191–206. Cf. also *Or Hachayim* on Exodus 21:11 and Numbers 24:17!

[23] *Hilchot Melachim* 12:44.

[24] Rambam, *Perush HaMishnah*, Introduction to Sanhedrin, ch. 10.

[25] *Hilchot Teshuvah* 9:26.

[26] Sources cited in notes 24–26.

[27] *Hilchot Melachim* 12:5. Cf. *Netzach Yisrael*, ch. 42.

Mashiach: The Principle of Mashiach and the Messianic Era in Jewish Law and Tradition (Brooklyn, N.Y.: SIE, 2004), ch. 2, pp. 19–33

The Resurrection of the Dead

By the Rebbe, Rabbi Menachem
Mendel Schneerson
Adapted By Rabbi Yanki Tauber

**RABBI MENACHEM MENDEL
SCHNEERSON
1902–1994**

The towering Jewish leader of
the 20th century, known as "the
Lubavitcher Rebbe," or simply
as "the Rebbe." Born in southern
Ukraine, the Rebbe escaped
Nazi-occupied Europe, arriving in
the U.S. in June 1941. The Rebbe
inspired and guided the revival
of traditional Judaism after the
European devastation, impacting
virtually every Jewish community
the world over. The Rebbe often
emphasized that the performance
of just one additional good deed
could usher in the era of Mashiach.
The Rebbe's scholarly talks
and writings have been printed
in more than 200 volumes.

A basic tenet of the Jewish faith is the
belief that those who have died will
again be brought to life. In fact, the
"Resurrection of the Dead" is one of
the thirteen cardinal principles, or
"foundations," of Judaism.[1]

Common wisdom has it that the
idea is more enduring than its incar-
nation, the concept more perfect than
any conceptualization, that spirit is
superior to substance. It would, therefore, follow that the soul is eternal and
invincible, while its physical vessel,
the body, is finite, temporal and destined to dust. This is fairly standard
theological thinking. Yet the principle
of the Resurrection runs contrary to
such reasoning. For, if the body is but
a temporary and deficient container
for the soul, why recompose and
revive it?

The Lame and the Blind

On the most basic level, the future
reunion of body and soul is crucial
to the realization of another of the
Thirteen Foundations, the principle
of "Reward and Punishment." In the
words of our sages, "G-d does not
deprive any creature of its due."[2]
There are no loose strings in G-d's
creation: ultimately, all good must
be rewarded, all negative must be
corrected.[3] So because life is a joint
enterprise of the body and the soul,
they will be rejoined in order to experience the results of their failings and
attainments.

An analogy from the Talmud illustrates this point:

Once there was a king who
appointed two handicapped watch-
men to guard his orchard. One was
blind and the second was lame. The
two conspired to rob their master:
the lame man rode on the blind
man's shoulders and steered him to
the fruit. When the king confronted
them, the blind man said, "How can
I steal what I cannot see?" while the
lame guard argued, "How can I take
when I cannot reach the fruit?" So
the king had the lame man set on the
blind man's shoulders and judged
them as one.[4]

This is the story of man's mission
in life. In this material world, man's
physical body is able-bodied but
blind. It possesses all the necessary
tools to fulfill the purpose of its creation—all except the vision to apply
these tools in the appropriate manner.
The body's selfish, animalistic drives
distort its priorities and cloud its perception of the truth.

The vision to discern right from
wrong must come from the soul, the
spark of divinity within man that
never loses sight of its Creator and
purpose. Yet the soul is helpless on
its own. To realize its mission on
earth, it needs a physical mind, heart,
hands and feet to deal with the physical reality.

Only when body and soul com-
bine and integrate to form the entity
called "man," can they safeguard and
develop the "orchard"[5] that has been
entrusted to them in accordance with
its Master's plans.

In this dark and imperfect world, we cannot yet behold and enjoy the fruits of our labor.[6] But in the Era of Moshiach, the accumulated attainments of all generations of history will reach their ultimate perfection. And since "G-d does not deprive any creature of its due," all elements that have been involved in realizing His purpose in creation will be reunited to perceive and experience the perfect world that their combined effort has achieved.

Three Worlds

All this, however, only explains why the Resurrection must take place at some future time. Yet why is it a cardinal principle of the Jewish faith? The Torah includes thousands of beliefs, practices and ideas; of these, only thirteen merit the designation of "foundation," implying that it is upon them that the entire body of Judaism rests—that without any one of them, there would be something lacking in everything a Jew believes in and does.

To understand the centrality of the Resurrection to the whole of Judaism we must first examine the views of two great Jewish thinkers, Maimonides (Rabbi Moshe ben Maimon, 1135–1204) and Nachmanides (Rabbi Moshe ben Nachman, 1194–1270), on what constitutes the ultimate realization of G-d's purpose in creation.

Generally speaking, the entirety of existence is divided into three periods:

A.   Our present reality (*Olam Hazeh*).

B.   The Era of Moshiach (*Y'mos HaMoshiach*).

C.   The World to Come (*Olam Habah*).

In our present world is the scene of a daily struggle between good and evil. As in every struggle, there are ups and downs—times when the animal in man gets the better of him and times when his inherent goodness triumphs. So ours is a world that allows for the existence of greed, hate and suffering. Although G-d created the world to reflect His infinite goodness and perfection, He also shrouded it in a veil of corporeality—a veil that conceals and distorts its true nature, giving man the freedom to choose between good and evil. So man can either labor to bring to light the good inherent in himself and the world about him, or he can act to intensify the illusion of evil.

Ultimately, however, our every moral victory, because they reflects the quintessential nature of reality, is eternal and cumulative, while our negative deeds are but temporary and superficial distortions of the truth. Hence our present-day lives will ultimately result in the second phase of existence, the strife-free Era of Moshiach.

The Era of Moshiach is not a supernatural world; it is the very same world we know today—without the corruptions of human nature. Man will have conquered his selfishness and prejudices; a harmonious world community will devote its energies and resources for the common good and the quest for continued growth in wisdom and perfection. In short, the Era of Moshiach represents man's attainment of the peak of his *natural* potential.

But the laws of nature themselves are finite and confining. So a naturally perfect world cannot be said to truly reflect its Creator's perfection. Death, for example, is a most natural phenomenon, a phenomenon connected with the finite and transitory nature of the physical—and the antithesis of G-d's infinite and eternal reality. Indeed, the world as G-d initially created it was free of death and dissolution, which were caused by man's first sin. So there is much in nature itself that is a subtle form of "evil"—i.e., part of the veil which obscures the Divine truth.

Thus, the Era of Moshiach is also a period of human labor and achievement, although its challenges differ greatly from our present-day struggles.

Today, our lives are completely taken up with combating the negative: feeding the hungry, enlightening the ignorant, bringing peace to warring factions. Then, the more blatant aspects of evil having been overcome, we will strive for the attainment of ever greater heights within the realm of good itself—struggling to overreach the limitations that define our natural existence.

The Era of Moshiach will be followed by the ultimate realization of G-d's vision of His creation—a world that expresses His quintessential perfection. Such a world, by definition, is beyond the confines of nature as we know it. This is the World to Come, the world of eternal life.

Two Definitions of Perfection

Is there a place for physicality in such a world?

This is the substance of the debate between Maimonides and Nachmanides. Maimonides is of the opinion that the ultimate utopia is a world of utter spirituality. "In the World to Come," he writes, "there are no physical forms or bodies—only souls. . . . So there is no eating or drinking, or any of the things that bodies need in the present world. Nor will there happen any of the events that befall bodies in the present world . . . [the souls] will enjoy the radiance of the Divine Presence—they will know and comprehend the Divine truth, which cannot be known while in the dark and lowly body. . . . This is a life without death, for death is only an occurrence of the body. . . . This is the reward of which there is no higher reward, and the good of which there is no greater good. . . ."[7]

Where and how does the Resurrection figure in all this? As Maimonides explains in his *Letter on the Resurrection of the Dead*, the reuniting of the bodies and souls of all who have lived throughout the generations of our present world is an important part of the Messianic Era, when all of the natural creation, including its physical elements, will achieve their ultimate perfection. But this will only be *their* ultimate—not *the* ultimate. The dead will be revived to a perfect life—as perfect as a finitely physical reality can be. But this life will also be subject to the dissolutive nature of all physical matter. This life, too, will come to an end, to be followed by the spiritual perfection of the World to Come.

Nachmanides disagrees. The ultimate realization of G-d's creation is not a spiritual world of souls, but a world in which spirit and matter together express the perfection of their Creator—a perfection that is both all-transcendent and all-embracing. According to Nachmanides, the resurrection of the dead will lead to eternal physical life, and usher in the World to Come—a world populated by souls enclothed within physical bodies.[8]

The teachings of Kabbalah and Chassidism concur with Nachmanides' definition of perfection.[9] Citing the axiom that "the higher something is, the lower it can descend," chassidic teaching explains that the ultimate expression of the Divine truth is that there is no aspect of reality in which it cannot be found. To consider the physical too finite and too lowly a place for the perfection of G-d to be realized, is to say that He can extend this far and no further. But the essence of G-d transcends all labels and definitions. To categorize Him as "spiritual" is no less a definition than to attribute physical properties to Him, G-d forbid. He is neither one nor the other (having created them both), and both serve Him equally.

In our present-day reality, the material nature of our world is perhaps the cause of a greater concealment of G-dliness than the spirituality of the soul; but, in the World to Come, nature itself will prove the most potent statement of G-d's all-pervading truth. The intensity of a lamp is measured by the farthest point its light reaches. The true mark of genius is the ability to explain the most profound idea to the simplest mind. In the same way, a physical world that conveys the Divine truth is the most powerful indicator of the infinite perfection of G-d.

Indeed, this is the purpose of the entirety of G-d's creation: that man, leading a physical existence, should overcome the imperfections of the material and bring to light its true nature and function—to express the goodness and perfection of its Creator.[10]

ENDNOTES

[1] As enumerated by Maimonides in his introduction to the eleventh chapter of the talmudic tractate *Sanhedrin*.

[2] Rashi's commentary on *Exodus 22:30*.

[3] For a broader discussion of the nature of "punishment," see Y. Tauber, *Beyond the Letter of the Law* (Brooklyn, N.Y.: Meaningful Life Center, 2012), "Crime Repays," p. 191.

[4] *Talmud, Sanhedrin* 91a.

[5] "And G-d took man, and He placed Him in the Garden of Eden to work it and to safeguard it"—*Genesis 2:15*.

[6] See *Beyond the Letter of the Law* (op. cit.), "Essence and Expression" on pg. 196.

[7] *Mishneh Torah, Laws of Repentance* 8:2–3.

[8] Nachmanides' *Shaar Hagmul*. Such is also the view of R. Saadia Gaon (882–942) in his *Emunot V'deyot*, chs. 47 and 49.

[9] See *Zohar*, part I, 114a; *Avodat Hakodesh*, 2:41; *Shaloh*, introduction to *Beit Dovid*; *Likkutei Torah, Tzav*, pg. 30, and *Shabbat Shuvah*, pg. 130; *Derech Mitzvotecho*, pgs. 28–30.

[10] Based on two responsa by the Rebbe, on the subject of the Resurrection, written in 5704 and 5705 (1944 and 1945).

Beyond the Letter of the Law: A Chassidic Companion to the Talmud's Ethics of the Fathers (Brooklyn, N.Y.: Meaningful Life Center, 2012), pp. 207–216.

Reprinted with permission of the Meaningful Life Center: meaningfullife.com

Acknowledgments

We are grateful to the following individuals who helped shape this innovative course:

Rabbis Mordechai Dinerman and **Naftali Silberberg,** codirectors of the JLI Curriculum Department and the Flagship editorial team; **Rabbi Dr. Shmuel Klatzkin,** JLI's senior editor; and **Rabbi Shmuel Karp,** director of JLI's Flagship division.

Rabbis Baruch Shalom Davidson, Mordechai Dinerman, Ahrele Loschak, Ari Sollish, Naftali Silberberg, and **Yanki Tauber** assisted in the development of the curriculum. **Rabbi Yakov Gershon**—of JLI's Machon Shmuel: The Sami Rohr Research Institute—provided extensive research. **Rabbis Mendel Glazman, Zalman Margolin,** and **Yakov Paley,** and **Mushka Grossbaum** provided editorial assistance.

Rabbis Yishaya Benjaminson, Dovid Flinkenstein, Meir Hecht, Meir Moscowitz, and **Yochanan Posner,** the Instructor Advisory Board for this course, spent many hours reviewing the course materials with the JLI team and provided many invaluable suggestions that have enhanced the course and ensured its suitability for a wide range of students.

Rivki Mockin streamlined and ensured the smoothness and timeliness of the content production. **Naomi Heber,** JLI Flagship's administrator, capably oversaw the entire project. **Rachel Musicante, Mimi Palace, Ya'akovah Weber,** and **Moshe Wolff** enhanced the quality and accuracy of the writing with their proofreading.

Avi Webb led the vision for the marketing of this course, and **Rabbi Levi Weingarten** created and designed the course marketing materials. The textbooks were designed with taste and expertise by **Chaya Mushka Kanner** together with **Rivky Fieldsteel, Shayna Grosh** and **Rabbi Zalman Korf.** The textbook images were researched and selected by **Rabbi Zalman Abraham.** Permissions for all imagery and texts was systematically obtained by **Shulamis Nadler.** The entire design and layout department is skillfully coordinated by **Rochel Karp. Rabbi Mendel Sirota** coordinated the book's printing and distribution.

Mushka Druk, Rivka Rapoport, Estie Ravnoy, and **Mashie Vogel** designed the aesthetically pleasing PowerPoint presentations, and **Moshe Raskin** and **Getzy Raskin** produced the lesson videos. **Rabbi Yaakov Paley** penned the video scripts. **Rabbi Motti Klein** created the Key Points videos.

We are immensely grateful for the encouragement of JLI's visionary chairman, and vice-chairman of *Merkos L'Inyonei Chinuch*—Lubavitch World Headquarters, **Rabbi Moshe Kotlarsky**. Rabbi Kotlarsky has been highly instrumental in building the infrastructure for the expansion of Chabad's international network and is also the architect of scores of initiatives and services to help Chabad representatives across the globe succeed in their mission. We are blessed to have the unwavering support of JLI's principal benefactor, **Mr. George Rohr,** who is fully invested in our work, continues to be instrumental in JLI's monumental growth and expansion, and is largely responsible for the Jewish renaissance that is being spearheaded by JLI and its affiliates across the globe.

The commitment and sage direction of JLI's dedicated Executive Board—**Rabbis Chaim Block**, **Hesh Epstein**, **Ronnie Fine**, **Yosef Gansburg**, **Shmuel Kaplan**, **Yisrael Rice**, and **Avrohom Sternberg**—and the countless hours they devote to the development of JLI are what drive the vision, growth, and tremendous success of the organization.

Finally, JLI represents an incredible partnership of more than 2,000 *shluchim* and *shluchot* in more than 1,700 locations across the globe who contribute their time and talent to further Jewish adult education. We thank them for generously sharing feedback and making suggestions that steer JLI's development and growth. They are our most valuable critics and our most cherished contributors.

Inspired by the call of the **Lubavitcher Rebbe**, of righteous memory, it is the mandate of the Rohr Jewish Learning Institute to provide a community of learning for all Jews throughout the world where they can participate in their precious heritage of Torah learning and experience its rewards. May this course succeed in fulfilling this sacred charge!

On behalf of the Rohr Jewish Learning Institute,

RABBI EFRAIM MINTZ
Executive Director

RABBI YISRAEL RICE
Chairman, Editorial Board

11 Nisan, 5781

CURRICULUM DEVELOPMENT

Rabbi Mordechai Dinerman
Rabbi Naftali Silberberg
EDITORS IN CHIEF

Rabbi Shmuel Klatzkin, PhD
ACADEMIC CONSULTANT

Rabbi Yanki Tauber
COURSE DESIGNER

Rabbi Baruch Shalom Davidson
Rabbi Chaim Fieldsteel
Rabbi Eliezer Gurkow
Rabbi Berry Piekarski
Rabbi Shmuel Super
CURRICULUM AUTHORS

Rabbi Yaakov Paley
Rabbi Boruch Werdiger
WRITERS

Rabbi Ahrele Loschak
EDITOR, TORAH STUDIES

Rabbi Mendel Glazman
Mrs. Mushka Grossbaum
EDITORIAL SUPPORT

Rabbi Yakov Gershon
Rabbi Shmuel Gomes
RESEARCH

Rabbi Michoel Lipskier
Rabbi Mendel Rubin
EXPERIENTIAL LEARNING

Mrs. Rivki Mockin
CONTENT COORDINATOR

MARKETING AND BRANDING

Rabbi Zalman Abraham
DIRECTOR

Mrs. Mashie Vogel
ADMINISTRATOR

Avi Webb
BRAND COPYWRITER

Ms. Rochel Karp
DESIGN ADMINISTRATOR

Mrs. Chaya Mushka Kanner
Ms. Estie Ravnoy
Mrs. Mussi Sharfstein
Mrs. Shifra Tauber
Rabbi Levi Weingarten
GRAPHIC DESIGN

Mrs. Rivky Fieldsteel
Mrs. Shayna Grosh
Rabbi Motti Klein
Rabbi Zalman Korf
Rabbi Moshe Wolff
PUBLICATION DESIGN

Lazer Cohen
Yosef Feigelstock
Ms. Basya Hans
Menachem Klein
SOCIAL MEDIA

Rabbi Yaakov Paley
WRITER

Rabbi Yossi Grossbaum
Rabbi Mendel Lifshitz
Rabbi Shraga Sherman
Rabbi Ari Sollish
Rabbi Mendel Teldon
MARKETING COMMITTEE

MARKETING CONSULTANTS

Alan Rosenspan
ALAN ROSENSPAN & ASSOCIATES
Sharon, MA

Gary Wexler
PASSION MARKETING
Los Angeles, CA

JLI CENTRAL

Rabbi Isaac Abelsky
Rabbi Mendel Abelsky
Ms. Rochel Karp
Mrs. Adina Lerman
Mrs. Aliza Scheinfeld
ADMINISTRATION

Rabbi Motti Klein
Rabbi Shlomie Tenenbaum
PROJECT MANAGER

Mrs. Mindy Wallach
AFFILIATE ORIENTATION

Mrs. Bunia Chazan
Mrs. Mushka Druk
Mrs. Baila Goldstein
Mrs. Mushka Grossbaum
Rabbi Motti Klein
Getzy Raskin
Moshe Raskin
Estie Ravnoy
Mrs. Mashie Vogel
MULTIMEDIA DEVELOPMENT

Rabbi Mendel Ashkenazi
Yoni Ben-Oni
Rabbi Mendy Elishevitz
Mendel Grossbaum
Rabbi Aron Liberow
Mrs. Chana Weinbaum
ONLINE DIVISION

Mrs. Ya'akovah Weber
LEAD PROOFREADER

Mrs. Rachel Musicante
Dr. Rakefet Orobona
Ms. Mimi Palace
PROOFREADERS

Levi Goldshmid
Rabbi Mendel Sirota
PRINTING AND DISTRIBUTION

Mrs. Musie Liberow
Mrs. Shaina B. Mintz
Mrs. Shulamis Nadler
ACCOUNTING

Rabbi Zalman Abraham
Mrs. Chana Dechter
Mrs. Shulamis Nadler
Mrs. Mindy Wallach
Mr. Yehuda Wengrofsky
DEVELOPMENT

Mrs Shulamis Nadler
Mrs. Mindy Wallach
CONTINUING EDUCATION

JLI FLAGSHIP

Rabbi Yisrael Rice
CHAIRMAN

Rabbi Shmuly Karp
DIRECTOR

Mrs. Naomi Heber
PROJECT MANAGER

Rabbi Yisroel Altein
Rabbi Hesh Epstein
Rabbi Sholom Raichik
Mrs. Michla Schanowitz
Rabbi Shraga Sherman
Mrs. Rivkah Slonim
Rabbi Ari Sollish
Rabbi Avraham Steinmetz
Rabbi Avrohom Sternberg
EDITORIAL BOARD

PAST FLAGSHIP AUTHORS

Rabbi Yitschak M. Kagan
of blessed memory

Rabbi Zalman Abraham
Brooklyn, NY

Rabbi Berel Bell
Montreal, QC

Rabbi Nissan D. Dubov
London, UK

Rabbi Tzvi Freeman
Toronto, ON

Rabbi Eliezer Gurkow
London, ON

Rabbi Aaron Herman
Pittsburgh, PA

Rabbi Simon Jacobson
New York, NY

Rabbi Chaim D. Kagan, PhD
Monsey, NY

Rabbi Shmuel Klatzkin, PhD
Dayton, OH

Rabbi Nochum Mangel
Dayton, OH

Rabbi Moshe Miller
Chicago, IL

Rabbi Yosef Paltiel
Brooklyn, NY

Rabbi Yehuda Pink
Solihull, UK

Rabbi Yisrael Rice
S. Rafael, CA

Rabbi Eli Silberstein
Ithaca, NY

Mrs. Rivkah Slonim
Binghamton, NY

Rabbi Avrohom Sternberg
New London, CT

Rabbi Shais Taub
Cedarhurst, NY

Rabbi Shlomo Yaffe
Longmeadow, MA

ROSH CHODESH SOCIETY

Rabbi Shmuel Kaplan
CHAIRMAN

Mrs. Shaindy Jacobson
DIRECTOR

Mrs Chana Dechter
ADMINISTRATOR

Mrs. Malky Bitton
Mrs. Shula Bryski
Mrs. Chanie Wilhelm
EDITORIAL BOARD

Mrs. Devorah Kornfeld
Mrs. Chana Lipskar
Mrs. Chana Alte Mangel
Mrs. Ahuva New
Mrs. Dinie Rapoport
Mrs. Sorah Shemtov
Mrs. Binie Tenenbaum
Mrs. Yehudis Wolvovsky
STEERING COMMITTEE

JLI TEENS

*In Partnership with CTeen:
Chabad Teen Network*

Rabbi Chaim Block
CHAIRMAN

Rabbi Shlomie Tenenbaum
DIRECTOR

TORAH STUDIES

Rabbi Yosef Gansburg
CHAIRMAN

Rabbi Shlomie Tenenbaum
PROJECT MANAGER

Rabbi Ahrele Loschak
EDITOR

Rabbi Levi Fogelman
Rabbi Yaacov Halperin
Rabbi Nechemia Schusterman
Rabbi Ari Sollish
STEERING COMMITTEE

SINAI SCHOLARS SOCIETY

In Partnership with Chabad on Campus

Rabbi Menachem Schmidt
CHAIRMAN

Rabbi Dubi Rabinowitz
DIRECTOR

Ms. Basya Hans
Ms. Chaya Mintz
Ms. Mussi Rabinowitz
Mrs. Manya Sperlin
COORDINATOR

Mrs. Devorah Zlatopolsky
ADMINISTRATOR

Rabbi Shlomie Chein
VICE PRESIDENT STUDENT ENGAGEMENT,
CHABAD ON CAMPUS INTL.

Rabbi Yossy Gordon
Rabbi Efraim Mintz
Rabbi Menachem Schmidt
Rabbi Avi Weinstein
EXECUTIVE COMMITTEE

Rabbi Levi Friedman
Rabbi Chaim Leib Hilel
Rabbi Yossi Lazaroff
Rabbi Levi Raichik
Rabbi Shmuel Tiechtel
Rabbi Shmuly Weiss
STEERING COMMITTEE

THE WELLNESS INSTITUTE

Adina Lerman
ADMINISTRATOR

Rabbi Zalman Abraham
VISION AND STRATEGIC PLANNING

Pamela Dubin
IMPACT ANALYSIS

Jeffrey Wengrofsky
ACADEMIC LIAISON

Mindy Wallach
ADMINISTRATIVE SPECIALIST

Mushky Lipskier
PROJECT MANAGER

Dina Zarchi
NETWORKING AND DEVELOPMENT

Shayna Horvath
PROJECT L'CHAIM COORDINATOR

CLINICAL ADVISORY BOARD

Sigrid Frandsen-Pechenik, PSY.D
CLINICAL DIRECTOR

Thomas Joiner, PhD
Kammarauche Asuzu
M.D., M.H.S.
Casey Skvorc, PhD, JD
David A. Brent, M.D.
Bella Schanzer, M.D.
Madelyn S. Gould, PhD, M.P.H.
Jonathan Singer, PhD, LCSW
Darcy Wallen, LCSW, PC
Gittel Francis, LMSW
Ryan G. Beale, MA, TLLP
Lisa Jacobs, M.D., MBA
Jill Harkavy-Friedman, PhD
E. David Klonsky, PhD

JLI INTERNATIONAL

Rabbi Avrohom Sternberg
CHAIRMAN

Rabbi Dubi Rabinowitz
DIRECTOR

Rabbi Berry Piekarski
ADMINISTRATOR

Rabbi Eli Wolf
ADMINISTRATOR, JLI IN THE CIS

*In Partnership with the Federation
of Jewish Communities of the CIS*

Rabbi Shevach Zlatopolsky
EDITOR, JLI IN THE CIS

Rabbi Nochum Schapiro
REGIONAL REPRESENTATIVE, AUSTRALIA

Rabbi Avraham Golovacheov
REGIONAL REPRESENTATIVE, GERMANY

Rabbi Shmuel Katzman
REGIONAL REPRESENTATIVE, NETHERLANDS

Rabbi Avrohom Steinmetz
REGIONAL REPRESENTATIVE, BRAZIL

Rabbi Bentzi Sudak
REGIONAL REPRESENTATIVE,
UNITED KINGDOM

Rabbi Shlomo Cohen
FRENCH COORDINATOR,
REGIONAL REPRESENTATIVE

NATIONAL JEWISH RETREAT

Rabbi Hesh Epstein
CHAIRMAN

Mrs. Shaina B. Mintz
DIRECTOR

Bruce Backman
HOTEL LIAISON

Rabbi Menachem Klein
PROGRAM COORDINATOR

Rabbi Shmuly Karp
SHLUCHIM LIAISON

Rabbi Mendel Rosenfeld
LOGISTICS COORDINATOR

Ms. Rochel Karp
Mrs. Aliza Scheinfeld
SERVICE AND SUPPORT

JLI LAND & SPIRIT
Israel Experience

Rabbi Shmuly Karp
DIRECTOR

Mrs. Shaina B. Mintz
ADMINISTRATOR

Rabbi Yechiel Baitelman
Rabbi Dovid Flinkenstein
Rabbi Chanoch Kaplan
Rabbi Levi Klein
Rabbi Mendy Mangel
Rabbi Sholom Raichik
STEERING COMMITTEE

SHABBAT IN THE HEIGHTS

Rabbi Shmuly Karp
DIRECTOR

Mrs. Shulamis Nadler
SERVICE AND SUPPORT

Rabbi Chaim Hanoka
CHAIRMAN

Rabbi Mordechai Dinerman
Rabbi Zalman Marcus
STEERING COMMITTEE

MYSHIUR
Advanced Learning Initiative

Rabbi Shmuel Kaplan
CHAIRMAN

Rabbi Shlomie Tenenbaum
ADMINISTRATOR

TORAHCAFE.COM
ONLINE LEARNING

Rabbi Mendy Elishevitz
WEBSITE DEVELOPMENT

Moshe Levin
CONTENT MANAGER

Mendel Laine
FILMING

MACHON SHMUEL
The Sami Rohr Research Institute

Rabbi Zalman Korf
ADMINISTRATOR

Rabbi Gedalya Oberlander
Rabbi Chaim Rapoport
Rabbi Levi Yitzchak Raskin
Rabbi Chaim Schapiro
Rabbi Moshe Miller
RABBINIC ADVISORY BOARD

Rabbi Yakov Gershon
RESEARCH FELLOW

FOUNDING DEPARTMENT HEADS

Rabbi Mendel Bell
Rabbi Zalman Charytan
Rabbi Mendel Druk
Rabbi Menachem Gansburg
Rabbi Meir Hecht
Rabbi Levi Kaplan
Rabbi Yoni Katz
Rabbi Chaim Zalman Levy
Rabbi Benny Rapoport
Dr. Chana Silberstein
Rabbi Elchonon Tenenbaum
Rabbi Mendy Weg

Faculty Directory

ALABAMA

BIRMINGHAM
Rabbi Yossi Friedman 205.970.0100

MOBILE
Rabbi Yosef Goldwasser 251.265.1213

ALASKA

ANCHORAGE
Rabbi Yosef Greenberg
Rabbi Mendy Greenberg 907.357.8770

ARIZONA

CHANDLER
Rabbi Mendy Deitsch 480.855.4333

FLAGSTAFF
Rabbi Dovie Shapiro 928.255.5756

FOUNTAIN HILLS
Rabbi Mendy Lipskier 480.776.4763

PHOENIX
Rabbi Zalman Levertov
Rabbi Yossi Friedman 602.944.2753

SCOTTSDALE
Rabbi Yossi Levertov 480.998.1410

TUCSON
Rabbi Yehuda Ceitlin 520.881.7956

CALIFORNIA

ALAMEDA
Rabbi Meir Shmotkin 510.640.2590

BEL AIR
Rabbi Chaim Mentz 310.475.5311

BURBANK
Rabbi Shmuly Kornfeld 818.954.0070

CARLSBAD
Rabbi Yeruchem Eilfort
Mrs. Nechama Eilfort 760.943.8891

CONTRA COSTA
Rabbi Dovber Berkowitz 925.937.4101

DANVILLE
Rabbi Shmuli Raitman 213.447.6694

ENCINO
Rabbi Aryeh Herzog 818.784.9986
Chapter founded by Rabbi Joshua Gordon, OBM

FOLSOM
Rabbi Yossi Grossbaum 916.608.9811

FREMONT
Rabbi Moshe Fuss 510.300.4090

GLENDALE
Rabbi Simcha Backman 818.240.2750

HUNTINGTON BEACH
Rabbi Aron David Berkowitz 714.846.2285

LA JOLLA
Rabbi Baruch Shalom Ezagui 858.455.5433

LOMITA
Rabbi Eli Hecht
Rabbi Sholom Pinson 310.326.8234

LOS ANGELES
Rabbi Leibel Korf 323.660.5177

MALIBU
Rabbi Levi Cunin 310.456.6588

MARINA DEL REY
Rabbi Danny Yiftach-Hashem
Rabbi Dovid Yiftach 310.859.0770

MARVISTA
Rabbi Shimon Simpson 646.401.2354

NEWHALL
Rabbi Choni Marosov 661.254.3434

NORTHRIDGE
Rabbi Eli Rivkin 818.368.3937

OJAI
Rabbi Mordechai Nemtzov 805.613.7181

PACIFIC PALISADES
Rabbi Zushe Cunin 310.454.7783

PALO ALTO
Rabbi Menachem Landa 415.418.4768
Rabbi Yosef Levin
Rabbi Ber Rosenblatt 650.424.9800

PASADENA
Rabbi Chaim Hanoka
Rabbi Sholom Stiefel 626.539.4578

PLEASANTON
Rabbi Josh Zebberman 925.846.0700

POWAY
Rabbi Mendel Goldstein 858.208.6613

RANCHO MIRAGE
Rabbi Shimon H. Posner 760.770.7785

RANCHO PALOS VERDES
Rabbi Yitzchok Magalnic 310.544.5544

RANCHO S. FE
Rabbi Levi Raskin 858.756.7571

REDONDO BEACH
Rabbi Yossi Mintz
Rabbi Zalman Gordon 310.214.4999

RIVERSIDE
Rabbi Shmuel Fuss 951.329.2747

S. CLEMENTE
Rabbi Menachem M. Slavin 949.489.0723

S. CRUZ
Rabbi Yochanan Friedman 831.454.0101

S. FRANCISCO
Rebbetzin Mattie Pil 415.933.4310
Rabbi Gedalia Potash 415.648.8000
Rabbi Shlomo Zarchi 415.752.2866

S. MATEO
Rabbi Yossi Marcus 650.341.4510

S. RAFAEL
Rabbi Yisrael Rice 415.492.1666

SUNNYVALE
Rabbi Yisroel Hecht 408.720.0553

TEMECULA
Rabbi Yonason Abrams 951.234.4196

TUSTIN
Rabbi Yehoshua Eliezrie 714.508.2150

VACAVILLE
Rabbi Chaim Zaklos 707.592.5300

WEST LOS ANGELES
Rabbi Mordechai Zaetz 424.652.8742

YORBA LINDA
Rabbi Dovid Eliezrie 714.693.0770

COLORADO

ASPEN
Rabbi Mendel Mintz 970.544.3770

DENVER
Rabbi Yossi Serebryanski 303.744.9699
Rabbi Mendy Sirota 720.940.3716

FORT COLLINS
Rabbi Yerachmiel Gorelik 970.407.1613

HIGHLANDS RANCH
Rabbi Avraham Mintz 303.694.9119

VAIL
Rabbi Dovid Mintz 970.476.7887

WESTMINSTER
Rabbi Benjy Brackman 303.429.5177

CONNECTICUT

GREENWICH
Rabbi Yossi Deren
Rabbi Menachem Feldman 203.629.9059

HAMDEN
Rabbi Moshe Hecht 203.635.7268

MILFORD
Rabbi Schneur Wilhelm 203.887.7603

NEW HAVEN
Rabbi Mendy Hecht 203.589.5375

NEW LONDON
Rabbi Avrohom Sternberg 860.437.8000

STAMFORD
Rabbi Yisrael Deren
Rabbi Levi Mendelow 203.3.CHABAD

WEST HARTFORD
Rabbi Shaya Gopin 860.232.1116

DELAWARE

WILMINGTON
Rabbi Chuni Vogel 302.529.9900

DISTRICT OF COLUMBIA

WASHINGTON
Rabbi Levi Shemtov
Rabbi Yitzy Ceitlin 202.332.5600

FLORIDA

ALTAMONTE SPRINGS
Rabbi Mendy Bronstein 407.280.0535

BAL HARBOUR
Rabbi Dov Schochet 305.868.1411

BOCA RATON
Rabbi Zalman Bukiet
Rabbi Arele Gopin 561.994.6257
Rabbi Moishe Denburg 561.526.5760
Rabbi Ruvi New 561.394.9770

BOYNTON BEACH
Rabbi Yosef Yitzchok Raichik 561.732.4633

BRADENTON
Rabbi Menachem Bukiet 941.388.9656

CAPE CORAL
Rabbi Yossi Labkowski 239.963.4770

CORAL GABLES
Rabbi Avrohom Stolik 305.490.7572

CORAL SPRINGS
Rabbi Yankie Denburg 954.471.8646

CUTLER BAY
Rabbi Yossi Wolff 305.975.6680

DAVIE
Rabbi Aryeh Schwartz 954.376.9973

DELRAY BEACH
Rabbi Sholom Ber Korf 561.496.6228

FISHER ISLAND
Rabbi Efraim Brody 347.325.1913

FLEMING ISLAND
Rabbi Shmuly Feldman 904.290.1017

FORT LAUDERDALE
Rabbi Yitzchok Naparstek 954.568.1190

HALLANDALE BEACH
Rabbi Mordy Feiner 954.458.1877

HOLLYWOOD
Rabbi Leibel Kudan 954.801.3367

JUPITER
Rabbi Berel Barash 561.317.0968

KENDALL
Rabbi Yossi Harlig 305.234.5654

LAUDERHILL
Rabbi Shmuel Heidingsfeld 323.877.7703

LONGWOOD
Rabbi Yanky Majesky 407.636.5994

MAITLAND
Rabbi Sholom Dubov
Rabbi Levik Dubov 470.644.2500

MIAMI
Rabbi Mendy Cheruty 305.219.3353
Rabbi Yakov Fellig 305.445.5444

MIAMI BEACH
Rabbi Yisroel Frankforter 305.534.3895

N. MIAMI BEACH
Rabbi Eli Laufer 305.770.4412

ORLANDO
Rabbi Yosef Konikov 407.354.3660

ORMOND BEACH
Rabbi Asher Farkash 386.672.9300

PALM BEACH
Rabbi Zalman Levitin 561.659.3884

PALM BEACH GARDENS
Rabbi Dovid Vigler 561.624.2223

PALM HARBOR
Rabbi Pinchas Adler 727.789.0408

PEMBROKE PINES
Rabbi Mordechai Andrusier 954.874.2280

PLANTATION
Rabbi Pinchas Taylor 954.644.9177

PONTE VEDRA BEACH
Rabbi Nochum Kurinsky 904.543.9301

S. AUGUSTINE
Rabbi Levi Vogel 904.521.8664

S. JOHNS
Rabbi Mendel Sharfstein 347.461.3765

SARASOTA
Rabbi Chaim Shaul Steinmetz 941.925.0770

SATELLITE BEACH
Rabbi Zvi Konikov 321.777.2770

SINGER ISLAND
Rabbi Berel Namdar 347.276.6985

SOUTH PALM BEACH
Rabbi Leibel Stolik 561.889.3499

SOUTH TAMPA
Rabbi Mendy Dubrowski 813.922.1723

SOUTHWEST BROWARD COUNTY
Rabbi Aryeh Schwartz 954.252.1770

SUNNY ISLES BEACH
Rabbi Alexander Kaller 305.803.5315

TAMARAC
Rabbi Kopel Silberberg 954.882.7434

WESLEY CHAPEL
Rabbi Mendy Yarmush
Rabbi Mendel Friedman 813.731.2977

WEST PALM BEACH
Rabbi Yoel Gancz 561.659.7770

WESTON
Rabbi Yisroel Spalter 954.349.6565

GEORGIA

ALPHARETTA
Rabbi Hirshy Minkowicz 770.410.9000

ATLANTA
Rabbi Yossi New
Rabbi Isser New 404.843.2464
Rabbi Alexander Piekarski 678.267.6418

ATLANTA: INTOWN
Rabbi Eliyahu Schusterman
Rabbi Ari Sollish 404.898.0434

CUMMING
Rabbi Levi Mentz 310.666.2218

GWINNETT
Rabbi Yossi Lerman 678.595.0196

MARIETTA
Rabbi Ephraim Silverman 770.565.4412

HAWAII

KAPA'A
Rabbi Michoel Goldman 808.647.4293

IDAHO

BOISE
Rabbi Mendel Lifshitz 208.853.9200

ILLINOIS

CHAMPAIGN
Rabbi Dovid Tiechtel 217.355.8672

CHICAGO
Rabbi Meir Hecht 312.714.4655
Rabbi Dovid Kotlarsky 773.495.7127
Rabbi Mordechai Gershon 773.412.5189
Rabbi Yosef Moscowitz 773.772.3770
Rabbi Levi Notik 773.274.5123

DES PLAINES
Rabbi Lazer Hershkovich 224.392.4442

ELGIN
Rabbi Mendel Shemtov 847.440.4486

GLENVIEW
Rabbi Yishaya Benjaminson 847.910.1738

HIGHLAND PARK
Mrs. Michla Schanowitz 847.266.0770

NORTHBROOK
Rabbi Meir Moscowitz 847.564.8770

OAK PARK
Rabbi Yitzchok Bergstein 708.524.1530

SKOKIE
Rabbi Yochanan Posner 847.677.1770

WILMETTE
Rabbi Dovid Flinkenstein 847.251.7707

INDIANA

INDIANAPOLIS
Rabbi Avraham Grossbaum
Rabbi Dr. Shmuel Klatzkin 317.251.5573

IOWA

BETTENDORF
Rabbi Shneur Cadaner 563.355.1065

KANSAS

OVERLAND PARK
Rabbi Mendy Wineberg 913.649.4852

KENTUCKY

LOUISVILLE
Rabbi Avrohom Litvin 502.459.1770

LOUISIANA

BATON ROUGE
Rabbi Peretz Kazen 225.267.7047

METAIRIE
Rabbi Yossie Nemes
Rabbi Mendel Ceitlin 504.454.2910

NEW ORLEANS
Rabbi Mendel Rivkin 504.302.1830

MAINE

PORTLAND
Rabbi Levi Wilansky 207.650.1783

MARYLAND

BALTIMORE
Rabbi Velvel Belinsky 410.764.5000
Classes in Russian

BEL AIR
Rabbi Kushi Schusterman 443.353.9718

BETHESDA
Rabbi Sender Geisinsky 301.913.9777

CHEVY CHASE
Rabbi Zalman Minkowitz 301.260.5000

COLUMBIA
Rabbi Hillel Baron
Rabbi Yosef Chaim Sufrin 410.740.2424

FREDERICK
Rabbi Boruch Labkowski 301.996.3659

GAITHERSBURG
Rabbi Sholom Raichik 301.926.3632

OLNEY
Rabbi Bentzy Stolik 301.660.6770

POTOMAC
Rabbi Mendel Bluming 301.983.4200
Rabbi Mendel Kaplan 301.983.1485

ROCKVILLE
Rabbi Shlomo Beitsh 646.773.2675
Rabbi Moishe Kavka 301.836.1242

MASSACHUSETTS

ANDOVER
Rabbi Asher Bronstein 978.470.2288

BOSTON
Rabbi Yosef Zaklos 617.297.7282

BRIGHTON
Rabbi Dan Rodkin 617.787.2200

CAPE COD
Rabbi Yekusiel Alperowitz 508.775.2324

LONGMEADOW
Rabbi Yakov Wolff 413.567.8665

NEWTON
Rabbi Shalom Ber Prus 617.244.1200

SUDBURY
Rabbi Yisroel Freeman 978.443.0110

SWAMPSCOTT
Rabbi Yossi Lipsker 781.581.3833

MICHIGAN

ANN ARBOR
Rabbi Aharon Goldstein 734.995.3276

BLOOMFIELD HILLS
Rabbi Levi Dubov 248.949.6210

GRAND RAPIDS
Rabbi Mordechai Haller 616.957.0770

WEST BLOOMFIELD
Rabbi Elimelech Silberberg 248.855.6170

MINNESOTA

MINNETONKA
Rabbi Mordechai Grossbaum
Rabbi Shmuel Silberstein 952.929.9922

S. PAUL
Rabbi Shneur Zalman Bendet 651.998.9298

MISSOURI

S. LOUIS
Rabbi Yosef Landa 314.725.0400

NEVADA

LAS VEGAS
Rabbi Yosef Rivkin 702.217.2170

SUMMERLIN
Rabbi Yisroel Schanowitz
Rabbi Tzvi Bronchtain 702.855.0770

NEW JERSEY

BASKING RIDGE
Rabbi Mendy Herson
Rabbi Mendel Shemtov 908.604.8844

CHERRY HILL
Rabbi Mendel Mangel 856.874.1500

CLINTON
Rabbi Eli Kornfeld 908.623.7000

ENGLEWOOD
Rabbi Shmuel Konikov 201.519.7343

GREATER MERCER COUNTY
Rabbi Dovid Dubov
Rabbi Yaakov Chaiton 609.213.4136

HASKELL
Rabbi Mendy Gurkov 201.696.7609

HOLMDEL
Rabbi Shmaya Galperin 732.772.1998

MANALAPAN
Rabbi Boruch Chazanow
Rabbi Levi Wolosow 732.972.3687

MEDFORD
Rabbi Yitzchok Kahan 609.451.3522

MOUNTAIN LAKES
Rabbi Levi Dubinsky 973.551.1898

MULLICA HILL
Rabbi Avrohom Richler 856.733.0770

OLD TAPPAN
Rabbi Mendy Lewis 201.767.4008

RED BANK
Rabbi Dovid Harrison 718.915.8748

ROCKAWAY
Rabbi Asher Herson
Rabbi Mordechai Baumgarten 973.625.1525

RUTHERFORD
Rabbi Yitzchok Lerman 347.834.7500

SCOTCH PLAINS
Rabbi Avrohom Blesofsky 908.790.0008

SHORT HILLS
Rabbi Mendel Solomon
Rabbi Avrohom Levin 973.725.7008

SOUTH BRUNSWICK
Rabbi Levi Azimov 732.398.9492

TOMS RIVER
Rabbi Moshe Gourarie 732.349.4199

WEST ORANGE
Rabbi Mendy Kasowitz 973.325.6311

WOODCLIFF LAKE
Rabbi Dov Drizin 201.476.0157

NEW MEXICO

LAS CRUCES
Rabbi Bery Schmukler 575.524.1330

NEW YORK

BAY SHORE
Rabbi Shimon Stillerman................................631.913.8770

BEDFORD
Rabbi Arik Wolf................................914.666.6065

BINGHAMTON
Mrs. Rivkah Slonim................................607.797.0015

BRIGHTON BEACH
Rabbi Moshe Winner................................718.946.9833

BRONXVILLE
Rabbi Sruli Deitsch................................917.755.0078

BROOKLYN
Rabbi Nissi Eber................................347.677.2276
Rabbi Dovid Okonov................................917.754.6942

BROOKVILLE
Rabbi Mendy Heber................................516.626.0600

CEDARHURST
Rabbi Zalman Wolowik................................516.295.2478

COMMACK
Rabbi Mendel Teldon................................631.543.3343

DOBBS FERRY
Rabbi Benjy Silverman................................914.693.6100

EAST HAMPTON
Rabbi Leibel Baumgarten
Rabbi Mendy Goldberg................................631.329.5800

FOREST HILLS
Rabbi Yossi Mendelson................................917.861.9726

GLEN OAKS
Rabbi Shmuel Nadler................................347.388.7064

GREAT NECK
Rabbi Yoseph Geisinsky................................516.487.4554

KINGSTON
Rabbi Yitzchok Hecht................................845.334.9044

LARCHMONT
Rabbi Mendel Silberstein................................914.834.4321

LITTLE NECK
Rabbi Eli Shifrin................................718.423.1235

LONG BEACH
Rabbi Eli Goodman................................516.897.2473

MONTEBELLO
Rabbi Shmuel Gancz................................845.746.1927

NEW YORK
Rabbi Mendy Weitman................................917.232.7577

NYC TRIBECA
Rabbi Zalman Paris................................212.566.6764

NYC UPPER EAST SIDE
Rabbi Uriel Vigler................................212.369.7310

OCEANSIDE
Rabbi Levi Gurkow................................516.764.7385

OSSINING
Rabbi Dovid Labkowski................................914.923.2522

OYSTER BAY
Rabbi Shmuel Lipszyc
Rabbi Shalom Lipszyc................................347.853.9992

PARK SLOPE
Rabbi Menashe Wolf................................347.957.1291

PORT WASHINGTON
Rabbi Shalom Paltiel................................516.767.8672

PROSPECT HEIGHTS
Rabbi Mendy Hecht................................347.622.3599

ROCHESTER
Rabbi Nechemia Vogel................................585.271.0330

SOUTHAMPTON
Rabbi Chaim Pape................................917.627.4865

STATEN ISLAND
Rabbi Mendy Katzman................................718.370.8953

STONY BROOK
Rabbi Shalom Ber Cohen................................631.585.0521

SUFFERN
Rabbi Shmuel Gancz................................845.368.1889

NORTH CAROLINA

CARY
Rabbi Yisroel Cotlar................................919.651.9710

CHARLOTTE
Rabbi Yossi Groner
Rabbi Shlomo Cohen................................704.366.3984

GREENSBORO
Rabbi Yosef Plotkin................................336.617.8120

RALEIGH
Rabbi Pinchas Herman
Rabbi Lev Cotlar..919.637.6950

OHIO

BEACHWOOD
Rabbi Shmuli Friedman...216.282.0112

CINCINNATI
Rabbi Yisroel Mangel..513.793.5200

COLUMBUS
Rabbi Yitzi Kaltmann..614.294.3296

DAYTON
Rabbi Nochum Mangel
Rabbi Shmuel Klatzkin...937.643.0770

OKLAHOMA

OKLAHOMA CITY
Rabbi Ovadia Goldman...405.524.4800

TULSA
Rabbi Yehuda Weg..918.492.4499

OREGON

PORTLAND
Rabbi Mordechai Wilhelm..503.977.9947

SALEM
Rabbi Avrohom Yitzchok Perlstein..............................503.383.9569

PENNSYLVANIA

AMBLER
Rabbi Shaya Deitsch...215.591.9310

BALA CYNWYD
Rabbi Shraga Sherman...610.660.9192

LAFAYETTE HILL
Rabbi Yisroel Kotlarsky...484.533.7009

MONROEVILLE
Rabbi Mendy Schapiro...412.372.1000

NEWTOWN
Rabbi Aryeh Weinstein..215.497.9925

PHILADELPHIA: CENTER CITY
Rabbi Yochonon Goldman...215.238.2100

PITTSBURGH
Rabbi Yisroel Altein...............................412.422.7300 EXT. 269

PITTSBURGH: SOUTH HILLS
Rabbi Mendy Rosenblum..412.278.3693

RYDAL
Rabbi Zushe Gurevitz...267.536.5757

WYNNEWOOD
Rabbi Moishe Brennan...610.529.9011

PUERTO RICO

CAROLINA
Rabbi Mendel Zarchi..787.253.0894

RHODE ISLAND

WARWICK
Rabbi Yossi Laufer...401.884.7888

SOUTH CAROLINA

COLUMBIA
Rabbi Hesh Epstein
Rabbi Levi Marrus..803.782.1831

TENNESSEE

KNOXVILLE
Rabbi Yossi Wilhelm..865.588.8584

MEMPHIS
Rabbi Levi Klein...901.754.0404

TEXAS

AUSTIN
Rabbi Mendy Levertov...512.905.2778

BELLAIRE
Rabbi Yossi Zaklikofsky..713.839.8887

DALLAS
Rabbi Mendel Dubrawsky
Rabbi Moshe Naparstek..972.818.0770

EL PASO
Levi Greenberg...347.678.9762

FORT WORTH
Rabbi Dov Mandel...817.263.7701

HOUSTON
Rabbi Dovid Goldstein
Rabbi Zally Lazarus 281.589.7188
Rabbi Moishe Traxler 713.774.0300

HOUSTON: RICE UNIVERSITY AREA
Rabbi Eliezer Lazaroff 713.522.2004

LEAGUE CITY
Rabbi Yitzchok Schmukler 281.724.1554

PLANO
Rabbi Mendel Block
Rabbi Yehudah Horowitz 972.596.8270

S. ANTONIO
Rabbi Chaim Block
Rabbi Levi Teldon 210.492.1085
Rabbi Tal Shaul 210.877.4218

SOUTHLAKE
Rabbi Levi Gurevitch 817.451.1171

UTAH

SALT LAKE CITY
Rabbi Benny Zippel 801.467.7777

VERMONT

BURLINGTON
Rabbi Yitzchok Raskin 802.658.5770

VIRGINIA

ALEXANDRIA/ARLINGTON
Rabbi Mordechai Newman 703.370.2774

FAIRFAX
Rabbi Leibel Fajnland 703.426.1980

GAINESVILLE
Rabbi Shmuel Perlstein 571.445.0342

LOUDOUN COUNTY
Rabbi Chaim Cohen 248.298.9279

NORFOLK
Rabbi Aaron Margolin
Rabbi Levi Brashevitzky 757.616.0770

RICHMOND
Rabbi Shlomo Pereira 804.740.2000

WASHINGTON

BELLINGHAM
Rabbi Yosef Truxton 360.224.9919

MERCER ISLAND
Rabbi Elazar Bogomilsky 206.527.1411
Rabbi Nissan Kornfeld 206.851.2324

OLYMPIA
Rabbi Yosef Schtroks 360.867.8804

SEATTLE
Rabbi Yoni Levitin 206.851.9831
Rabbi Shnai Levitin 347.342.2259

SPOKANE COUNTY
Rabbi Yisroel Hahn 509.443.0770

WISCONSIN

BAYSIDE
Rabbi Cheski Edelman 414.439.5041

MEQUON
Rabbi Menachem Rapoport 262.242.2235

MILWAUKEE
Rabbi Levi Emmer 414.277.8839
Rabbi Mendel Shmotkin 414.961.6100

ARGENTINA

BUENOS AIRES
Mrs. Chani Gorowitz 54.11.4865.0445
Rabbi Menachem M. Grunblatt 54.911.3574.0037
Rabbi Mendi Mizrahi 54.11.4963.1221
Rabbi Mendy Gurevitch 55.11.4545.7771
Rabbi Pinhas Sudry 54.1.4822.2285
Rabbi Shloimi Setton 54.11.4982.8637
Rabbi Shiele Plotka 54.11.4634.3111
Rabbi Yosef Levy 54.11.4504.1908

CORDOBA
Rabbi Menajem Turk 54.351.233.8250

SALTA
Rabbi Rafael Tawil 54.387.421.4947

S. MIGUEL DE TUCUMÁN
Rabbi Ariel Levy 54.381.473.6944

AUSTRALIA

NEW SOUTH WALES

DOUBLE BAY
Rabbi Yanky Berger 612.9327.1644

DOVER HEIGHTS
Rabbi Motti Feldman 614.0400.8572

NORTH SHORE
Rabbi Nochum Schapiro
Rebbetzin Fruma Schapiro 612.9488.9548

QUEENSLAND

BRISBANE
Rabbi Levi Jaffe 617.3843.6770

VICTORIA

MOORABBIN
Rabbi Elisha Greenbaum 614.0349.0434

WESTERN AUSTRALIA

PERTH
Rabbi Shalom White 618.9275.2106

AZERBAIJAN

BAKU
Mrs. Chavi Segal 994.12.597.91.90

BELARUS

BOBRUISK
Mrs. Mina Hababo 375.29.104.3230

MINSK
Rabbi Shneur Deitsch
Mrs. Bassie Deitsch 375.29.330.6675

BELGIUM

BRUSSELS
Rabbi Shmuel Pinson 375.29.330.6675

BRAZIL

CURITIBA
Rabbi Mendy Labkowski 55.41.3079.1338

S. PAULO
Rabbi Avraham Steinmetz 55.11.3081.3081

CANADA

ALBERTA

CALGARY
Rabbi Mordechai Groner 403.281.3770

EDMONTON
Rabbi Ari Drelich
Rabbi Mendy Blachman 780.200.5770

BRITISH COLUMBIA

RICHMOND
Rabbi Yechiel Baitelman 604.277.6427

VANCOUVER
Rabbi Dovid Rosenfeld 604.266.1313

VICTORIA
Rabbi Meir Kaplan 250.595.7656

MANITOBA

WINNIPEG
Rabbi Shmuel Altein 204.339.8737

ONTARIO

MAPLE
Rabbi Yechezkel Deren 647.883.6372

MISSISSAUGA
Rabbi Yitzchok Slavin 905.820.4432

OTTAWA
Rabbi Menachem M. Blum 613.843.7770

THORNHILL
Rabbi Yisroel Landa 416.897.3338

GREATER TORONTO REGIONAL OFFICE & THORNHILL
Rabbi Yossi Gansburg 905.731.7000

WATERLOO
Rabbi Moshe Goldman 226.338.7770

QUEBEC

CÔTE S.-LUC
Rabbi Levi Naparstek 438.409.6770

DOLLARD-DES ORMEAUX
Rabbi Leibel Fine 514.777.4675

HAMPSTEAD
Rabbi Moshe New
Rabbi Berel Bell 514.739.0770

MONTREAL
Rabbi Ronnie Fine
Pesach Nussbaum 514.738.3434

OLD MONTREAL/GRIFFINTOWN
Rabbi Nissan Gansbourg
Rabbi Berel Bell 514.800.6966

S. LAZARE
Rabbi Nochum Labkowski 514.436.7426

TOWN OF MOUNT ROYAL
Rabbi Moshe Krasnanski
Rabbi Shneur Zalman Rader 514.342.1770

SASKATCHEWAN

SASKATOON
Rabbi Raphael Kats 306.384.4370

COLOMBIA

BOGOTA
Rabbi Chanoch Piekarski 57.1.635.8251

COSTA RICA

S. JOSÉ
Rabbi Hershel Spalter
Rabbi Moshe Bitton 506.4010.1515

CROATIA

ZAGREB
Rabbi Pinchas Zaklas 385.1.4812227

DENMARK

COPENHAGEN
Rabbi Yitzchok Loewenthal 45.3316.1850

DOMINICAN REPUBLIC

S. DOMINGO
Rabbi Shimon Pelman 829.341.2770

ESTONIA

TALLINN
Rabbi Shmuel Kot 372.662.30.50

FRANCE

BOULOGNE
Rabbi Michael Sojcher 33.1.46.99.87.85

DIJON
Rabbi Chaim Slonim 33.6.52.05.26.65

LA VARENNE-S.-HILAIRE
Rabbi Mena'hem Mendel Benelbaz 33.6.17.81.57.47

MARSEILLE
Rabbi Eliahou Altabe 33.6.11.60.03.05
Rabbi Mena'hem Mendel Assouline 33.6.64.88.25.04
Rabbi Emmanuel Taubenblatt 33.4.88.00.94.85

PARIS
Rabbi Yona Hasky 33.1.53.75.36.01
Rabbi Acher Marciano 33.6.15.15.01.02
Rabbi Avraham Barou'h Pevzner 33.6.99.64.07.70

PONTAULT-COMBAULT
Rabbi Yossi Amar 33.6.61.36.07.70

VILLIERS-SUR-MARNE
Rabbi Mena'hem Mendel Mergui 33.1.49.30.89.66

GEORGIA

TBILISI
Rabbi Meir Kozlovsky 995.32.2429770

GERMANY

BERLIN
Rabbi Yehuda Tiechtel 49.30.2128.0830

DUSSELDORF
Rabbi Chaim Barkahn 49.173.2871.770

HAMBURG
Rabbi Shlomo Bistritzky 49.40.4142.4190

HANNOVER 49.511.811.2822
Chapter founded by Rabbi Binyamin Wolff, OBM

GREECE

ATHENS
Rabbi Mendel Hendel 30.210.323.3825

GUATEMALA

GUATEMALA CITY
Rabbi Shalom Pelman 502.2485.0770

ISRAEL

ASHKELON
Rabbi Shneor Lieberman 054.977.0512

BALFURYA
Rabbi Noam Bar-Tov 054.580.4770

CAESAREA
Rabbi Chaim Meir Lieberman 054.621.2586

EVEN YEHUDA
Rabbi Menachem Noyman 054.777.0707

GANEI TIKVA
Rabbi Gershon Shnur 054.524.2358

GIV'ATAYIM
Rabbi Pinchus Bitton 052.643.8770

JERUSALEM
Rabbi Levi Diamond 055.665.7702
Rabbi Avraham Hendel 054.830.5799

KARMIEL
Rabbi Mendy Elishevitz 054.521.3073

KFAR SABA
Rabbi Yossi Baitch 054.445.5020

KIRYAT BIALIK
Rabbi Pinny Marton 050.661.1768

KIRYAT MOTZKIN
Rabbi Shimon Eizenbach 050.902.0770

KOCHAV YAIR
Rabbi Dovi Greenberg 054.332.6244

MACCABIM-RE'UT
Rabbi Yosef Yitzchak Noiman 054.977.0549

NES ZIYONA
Rabbi Menachem Feldman 054.497.7092

NETANYA
Rabbi Schneur Brod 054.579.7572

RAMAT GAN-KRINITZI
Rabbi Yisroel Gurevitz 052.743.2814

RAMAT GAN-MAROM NAVE
Rabbi Binyamin Meir Kali 050.476.0770

RAMAT YISHAI
Rabbi Shneor Zalman Wolosow 052.324.5475

RISHON LEZION
Rabbi Uri Keshet 050.722.4593

ROSH PINA
Rabbi Sholom Ber Hertzel 052.458.7600

TEL AVIV
Rabbi Shneur Piekarski 054.971.5568

JAPAN

TOKYO
Rabbi Mendi Sudakevich 81.3.5789.2846

KAZAKHSTAN

ALMATY
Rabbi Shevach Zlatopolsky 7.7272.77.59.49

KYRGYZSTAN

BISHKEK
Rabbi Arye Raichman 996.312.68.19.66

LATVIA

RIGA
Rabbi Shneur Zalman Kot
Mrs. Rivka Glazman 371.6720.40.22

LITHUANIA

VILNIUS
Rabb Sholom Ber Krinsky 370.6817.1367

LUXEMBOURG

LUXEMBOURG
Rabbi Mendel Edelman 352.2877.7079

NETHERLANDS

ALMERE
Rabbi Moshe Stiefel 31.36.744.0509

AMSTERDAM
Rabbi Yanki Jacobs 31.644.988.627
Rabbi Jaacov Zwi Spiero 31.652.328.065

EINDHOVEN
Rabbi Simcha Steinberg 31.63.635.7593

HAGUE
Rabbi Shmuel Katzman 31.70.347.0222

HEEMSTEDE-HAARLEM
Rabbi Shmuel Spiero 31.23.532.0707

MAASTRICHT
Rabbi Avrohom Cohen 32.48.549.6766

NIJMEGEN
Rabbi Menachem Mendel Levine 31.621.586.575

ROTTERDAM
Rabbi Yehuda Vorst 31.10.265.5530

PANAMA

PANAMA CITY
Rabbi Ari Laine
Rabbi Gabriel Benayon 507.223.3383

RUSSIA

ASTRAKHAN
Rabbi Yisroel Melamed 7.851.239.28.24

BRYANSK
Rabbi Menachem Mendel Zaklas 7.483.264.55.15

CHELYABINSK
Rabbi Meir Kirsh 7.351.263.24.68

MOSCOW
Rabbi Aizik Rosenfeld 7.906.762.88.81
Rabbi Mordechai Weisberg 7.495.645.50.00

NIZHNY NOVGOROD
Rabbi Shimon Bergman 7.920.253.47.70

NOVOSIBIRSK
Rabbi Shneur Zalmen Zaklos 7.903.900.43.22

OMSK
Rabbi Osher Krichevsky 7.381.231.33.07

PERM
Rabbi Zalman Deutch 7.342.212.47.32

ROSTOV
Rabbi Chaim Danzinger 7.8632.99.02.68

S. PETERSBURG
Rabbi Shalom Pewzner 7.911.726.21.19
Rabbi Zvi Pinsky 7.812.713.62.09

SAMARA
Rabbi Shlomo Deutch 7.846.333.40.64

SARATOV
Rabbi Yaakov Kubitshek 7.8452.21.58.00

TOGLIATTI
Rabbi Meier Fischer 7.848.273.02.84

UFA
Rabbi Dan Krichevsky 7.347.244.55.33

VORONEZH
Rabbi Levi Stiefel 7.473.252.96.99

SINGAPORE

SINGAPORE
Rabbi Mordechai Abergel 656.337.2189
Rabbi Netanel Rivni 656.336.2127
Classes in Hebrew

SOUTH AFRICA

JOHANNESBURG
Rabbi Dovid Masinter
Rabbi Ari Kievman 27.11.440.6600

SWITZERLAND

LUZERN
Rabbi Chaim Drukman 41.41.361.1770

THAILAND

BANGKOK
Rabbi Yosef C. Kantor 6681.837.7618

UKRAINE

BERDITCHEV
Mrs. Chana Thaler 380.637.70.37.70

DNEPROPETROVSK
Rabbi Dan Makagon 380.504.51.13.18

NIKOLAYEV
Rabbi Sholom Gotlieb 380.512.37.37.71

ODESSA
Rabbi Avraham Wolf
Rabbi Yaakov Neiman .... 38.048.728.0770 EXT. 280

ZAPOROZHYE
Mrs. Nechama Dina Ehrentreu 380.957.19.96.08

ZHITOMIR
Rabbi Shlomo Wilhelm 380.504.63.01.32

UNITED KINGDOM

BOURNEMOUTH
Rabbi Bentzion Alperowitz 44.749.456.7177

CHEADLE
Rabbi Peretz Chein 44.161.428.1818

LEEDS
Rabbi Eli Pink 44.113.266.3311

LONDON
Rabbi Moshe Adler 44.771.052.4460
Rabbi Mendel Cohen 44.777.261.2661
Rabbi Shneor Glitzenstein 44.792.585.7050
Rabbi Hillel Gruber 44.208.202.1600
Rabbi Chaim Hoch 44.753.879.9524
Rabbi Dovid Katz 44.207.624.2770
Rabbi Eli Levin 44.7540.461.568
Rabbi Yisroel Lew 44.207.060.9770
Rabbi Yossi Simon 44.208.458.0416

MANCHESTER
Rabbi Levi Cohen 44.161.792.6335
Rabbi Shmuli Jaffe 44.161.766.1812

RADLETT, HERTFORDSHIRE
Rabbi Alexander Sender Dubrawsky 44.79.4380.8965

The Jewish Learning Multiplex

Brought to you by the Rohr Jewish Learning Institute

In fulfillment of the mandate of the Lubavitcher Rebbe, of blessed memory, whose leadership guides every step of our work, the mission of the Rohr Jewish Learning Institute is to transform Jewish life and the greater community through the study of Torah, connecting each Jew to our shared heritage of Jewish learning.

While our flagship program remains the cornerstone of our organization, JLI is proud to feature additional divisions catering to specific populations, in order to meet a wide array of educational needs.

THE ROHR JEWISH LEARNING INSTITUTE

A subsidiary of Merkos L'Inyonei Chinuch,
the adult educational arm of the Chabad-Lubavitch movement

Torah Studies

Torah Studies provides a rich and nuanced encounter with the weekly Torah reading.

MyShiur
TALMUD LEARNING INITIATIVE

MyShiur courses are designed to assist students in developing the skills needed to study Talmud independently.

SINAI SCHOLARS SOCIETY

This rigorous fellowship program invites select college students to explore the fundamentals of Judaism.

JLI TEENS

Jewish teens forge their identity as they engage in Torah study, social interaction, and serious fun.

ROSHCHODESH society

The Rosh Chodesh Society gathers Jewish women together once a month for intensive textual study.

TORAHCafé

TorahCafe.com provides an exclusive selection of top-rated Jewish educational videos.

NATIONAL JEWISH RETREAT

This yearly event rejuvenates mind, body, and spirit with a powerful synthesis of Jewish learning and community.

THE LAND & THE SPIRIT
JLI ISRAEL EXPERIENCE

Participants delve into our nation's past while exploring the Holy Land's relevance and meaning today.

JLI ACADEMY

Select affiliates are invited to partner with peers and noted professionals, as leaders of innovation and excellence.

מכון שמואל
THE SAMI ROHR RESEARCH INSTITUTE

Machon Shmuel is an institute providing Torah research in the service of educators worldwide.

NOTES